MAR 0 1 1996

D1321338

George Washington Cable Revisited

Twayne's United States Authors Series

Nancy A. Walker, Editor

Vanderbilt University

TUSAS 258

GEORGE WASHINGTON CABLE.
Photograph courtesy of the Huntington Library, San Marino, California.

George Washington Cable Revisited

John Cleman

California State University, Los Angeles

Twayne Publishers
An Imprint of Simon & Schuster Macmillan
New York

Prentice Hall International
London   Mexico City   New Delhi   Singapore   Sydney   Toronto

Twayne's United States Authors Series No. 655

George Washington Cable Revisited
John Cleman

Twayne Publishers
An Imprint of Simon & Schuster Macmillan
866 Third Ave.
New York, NY 10022

Library of Congress Cataloging-in-Publication Data

Cleman, John.
    George Washington Cable revisited / John Cleman.
        p.   cm. — (Twayne's United States authors series ; TUSAS 655)
    Includes bibliographical references (p.) and index.
    ISBN 0-8057-3991-2 (alk. paper)
    1. Cable, George Washington, 1844–1925—Criticism and interpretation.
2. Louisiana—In literature.   I. Title.   II. Series.
PS1246.C54 1995
813'.4 — dc20
                                                                                                95-6128
                                                                                                CIP

10 9 8 7 6 5 4 3 2 1

Printed in the United States of America

For my Father and Mother

Contents

Preface

After being celebrated as one of the major writers of his age, then largely forgotten, then rediscovered as a courageous pioneer of Southern literature and a heroic civil rights activist, George Washington Cable has
settled into a relatively stable critical niche as an interesting minor writer
whose early promise was never realized. The promise seems inevitably to
be connected to his critique of Southern society and particularly his
attacks on racism and caste, and the importance of his views is enhanced
by the loneliness of his position at the time and the fact that he was a
morally conservative white Southerner. In his day Cable was often
attacked for his racial views and pressured to keep them out of his fiction, but their presence has also limited his current reputation, for social
attitudes toward racial equality have caught up with and gone beyond
Cable, making him seem less progressive and less satisfying than other
writers on the same subject. More important, as many critics early and
late have recognized, Cable's social criticism, to whatever degree relevant, is not alone the most compelling aspect of his best work. In *The
Grandissimes,* some of the *Old Creole Days* stories, and other works Cable
writes with fascinating subtlety and complexity, alluring beyond subject
matter and theme, inviting and baffling explanation. Cable was a social
critic and public figure, but he was also a considerable artist.

The aim of this study is to provide a critical introduction to Cable's
life and work with particular emphasis on the terms of his artistic
achievement. Although the series considers this treatment a "revisit" to
Cable, the first visit was not mine but Philip Butcher's; this is more a
new study with a different focus. As with previous treatments of Cable's
life, I have relied heavily on Arlin Turner's masterful biography for facts,
but in several instances I have interpreted them differently. I have purposely reduced discussion of certain aspects of Cable's life, however, particularly his reading tour with Mark Twain and his involvement with the
Home Culture Clubs, to focus more attention on his fiction and political
writing and because those aspects have been so thoroughly described by
others. I have provided lengthy analyses of *Old Creole Days, Madame
Delphine,* and especially *The Grandissimes* because these are the works on
which Cable's reputation largely rests. With his lesser known or less successful books I have tried to expose the interest they might have, at least

for students of Cable's work and particularly for what their weaknesses suggest about the unique quality of his achievement. It is the uniqueness of that achievement—the complex allure and power of his best work—that has driven me in this study and that I hope to have conveyed.

Acknowledgments

I am grateful for the help of many people, some who encouraged my studies of Cable over many years and others who contributed specifically and significantly to this book. I have a long-standing debt to Professor Robert McClean of Washington State University, who introduced me to *The Grandissimes* and guided my initial study of Cable's work, and to the late Professor William T. Lenehan of the University of Wisconsin, Madison, who ably directed my doctoral dissertation on Cable. I thank my colleagues professors Sidney Richman and Alfred Bendixen for reading all or part of the manuscript and offering valuable suggestions for revision, Marilyn Elkins for tips about New Orleans and the literary representation of race, and Paul Zall for helping me solve numerous research problems. Series editor Nancy A. Walker has been extremely patient, encouraging, and helpful at nearly every stage of my writing. I have appreciated also the cooperative support of the editors at Twayne and especially the sharp eye and good sense of copy editor Barbara Sutton in helping guide the manuscript to print.

I am grateful to the staffs of the Howard-Tilton Memorial Library at Tulane University, the Huntington Library in San Marino, and the John F. Kennedy Memorial Library at California State University, Los Angeles, for their cooperation and kindness in making their collections available to me and helping me locate necessary research materials. My research in New Orleans was enabled by a Travel to Collections Grant from the National Endowment for the Humanities. Through the whole of this project I have been helped in many ways by my wife, Donna, who has been understanding and supportive, a patient listener, and (because she knows better than I how to get things done) a valuable advisor.

Chronology

1881   *Madame Delphine.* Becomes full-time man of letters. Meets William Dean Howells and Mark Twain. Begins prison reform work following grand jury term.

1882   Twain visits Cable in New Orleans. Gives first public lecture at University of Mississippi.

1883   Lectures and reads from own work at Johns Hopkins University. U.S. Supreme Court declares 1875 Civil Rights Act unconstitutional. Daughter Isabel is born.

1884   *The Creoles of Louisiana, Dr. Sevier,* and "The Convict Lease System in the Southern States" published. Begins joint reading tour with Mark Twain.

1885   Publication of "The Freedman's Case in Equity" generates furor in South. *The Silent South.* Moves to Northampton, Massachusetts. Son William is born.

1886   Home Culture Clubs begun. "The Dance in Place Congo" and "Creole Slave Songs" published.

1887   Belief in "Silent South" is encouraged by visit to region. Meets Adelene Moffat. Teaches Bible study in Northampton and Boston.

1888   With W. M. Baskervill organizes Open Letter Club. *Bonaventure.*

1889   *Strange True Stories of Louisiana.* Controversy is stirred by Cable's dining with a black lawyer, J. C. Napier. Mother dies. Daughter Dorothea is born.

1890   Abandons Open Letter Club. *The Negro Question.*

1891   *The Busy Man's Bible.*

1892   Ends civil rights crusade. Relies on public readings for income and tours West Coast. Friend and supporter Roswell Smith dies. Moves residence to "Tarryawhile."

1895   *John March, Southerner.* Is editor for Home Culture Clubs *Letter.*

1896   Edits *Symposium.* Publishes several articles of literary theory. *Plessy* v. *Ferguson* decision establishes segregation as law of the land.

1897   Is editor for *Current Literature* in New York.

1898   Makes first trip to England and Scotland on invitation from British novelist J. M. Barrie. Establishes warm relationship with Andrew Carnegie.

1899   First annual Carnegie Garden Competition in Northampton. *Strong Hearts.*

1901   *The Cavalier* becomes best-seller. "Angel of the Lord" appears anonymously in the anthology *A House Party.*

1902   *The Cavalier* produced as play. *Bylow Hill.* Cable tries hand at playwriting.

1904   Wife, Louise, dies.

1905   Carnegie House dedicated in Northampton.

1906   Marries Eva Stevenson.

1907   Adelene Moffat's dismissal as secretary of Home Culture Clubs creates controversy.

1908   *Kincaid's Battery.* Son William dies.

1909   Visits New Orleans. *"Posson Jone'"* and *Père Raphaël.*

1914   *Gideon's Band* and *The Amateur Garden.*

1915   Lectures at Louisiana State Historical Society meeting in New Orleans.

1918   *The Flower of the Chapdelaines* and *Lovers of Louisiana.*

1923   Second wife, Eva, dies. Marries Hanna Cowing.

1925   Dies in St. Petersburg, Florida, on 31 January.

Chapter One
Backgrounds

Unique New Orleans

George Washington Cable is credited with "discovering" New Orleans as a literary subject in the 1870s, and he is indeed largely responsible for shaping the image of the city and its inhabitants that appears in fiction through much of the twentieth century. In doing so, he drew on features of New Orleans and the region that had appealed to the imagination of visitors from its earliest days as an American city. The most captivating quality was the sense of New Orleans's uniqueness, its exotic difference from other American cities. To understand Cable's art it is necessary to understand some of the factors that contribute to this sense of difference.

One factor, certainly, was that New Orleans had been developed as the capital of a French colony and had remained predominantly French in culture. To be sure, there were traces of Choctaw and other Native American influences in language and food, and while the Spanish rule from 1763 to 1801 was largely an administrative shell, the many buildings rebuilt after fires during this period left an obvious Spanish imprint on the city's architecture. Large numbers of German, Irish, and Italian immigrants also left their mark, as did the even greater number of Africans, both slaves and *gens de couleurs libres* (free persons of color), and thus, in 1844, *Norman's New Orleans and Environs* described the city's society as "made up of a heterogeneous mixture of almost all nations."[1] Nevertheless, at the time of the American purchase in 1803 the French-speaking Creoles were the dominant class in Louisiana, and to the essentially Anglo consciousness prevailing in the other states, this fact made New Orleans more remote and foreign than other U.S. cities.

Consequently, Louisiana's history, legends, and major figures—Iberville, Bienville, Vaudreuil, Ulloa, Lafrénière, O'Reilly—were largely unknown outside the region and reflected a different sense of relationship to the European past than that of Boston, Philadelphia or New York. Colonial Louisianans were often noted for their independence; indeed, the distinguished nineteenth-century Louisiana historian Charles

Gayarré could justly claim "for Louisiana the merit of having been the first European colony that entertained the design of proclaiming her independence."[2] But the background of this design was less republican principle than a good deal of anger over the cession of Louisiana to Spain in 1763. When the American governor William Claiborne arrived in New Orleans to assume control in 1803, he found a French-speaking population aligned with their Old World heritage out of resistance to the usurpation of the New. Also, under both French and Spanish rule Louisiana was predominantly Catholic (a provision of the 1724 Code Noir ["Black Code"] established Catholicism as the state faith), which meant, at least to many Protestants in and out of New England, more worldly customs, festivals, and morality. To the Presbyterian Cable family (mother and author-son especially), New Orleanians were aggressively, devoutly non-Sabbatarian, using Sunday for all kinds of entertainments—from picnics, balls, opera, and theater to horse races, circuses, and cock-fights.

Perhaps the most significant feature of New Orleans's French origins was the emergence of a distinct, genuine ruling class: the Creoles. The root of the term is generally recognized as the Spanish *criollo* from the verb *criar,* meaning to raise or breed. Hence, in general, a Creole is a descendant of an immigrant, someone born and "bred" in the new place, regardless of national or racial parentage. In Louisiana, Creoles were usually (although not exclusively) persons of French or Spanish ancestry (regardless of surname or other ancestral mixtures), and in the early nineteenth century the term was often used by this group to distinguish themselves from the more recently arrived *Américains* and from the peasantlike Acadians ("Cajuns"), descendants of the French settlers driven by the British from Nova Scotia (then Acadia) in 1755 and relocated in the bayou, swamp, and prairie regions south and west of New Orleans. In short, Creole became a status label, not only marking a difference between language and national-origin groups but also implying historical priority and cultural superiority.[3]

Many visitors to antebellum New Orleans, struck by the oddity of an aristocratic society so remotely located, commented on the Creoles' manners and mores. From 1743 to 1752 the Marquis de Vaudreuil as colonial governor imported a sense of social life and style imitative of the Court of Versailles and thus helped establish the city's reputation for gaiety and pleasure. New Orleans became famous for its elaborate, almost nightly balls, its French opera and theater, and the Creoles' passion for card games and gambling. Creole manners were defined by elegant courtesy and reserve, especially among the women, although the Creole men were also known for their fierce pride and volatile tempers, which led to many duels. Perhaps the most striking Creole trait, especially after the U.S. purchase, was their rigid exclusiveness, which made them both interesting and irritating to outsiders and which, because it isolated them from the dynamics of economic and social growth, made them seem relics within a few decades. Ironically, insofar as their exclusiveness and distinction was expressed in the label they applied to themselves, they found that for many the word *Creole* had come to mean a person of racially "mixed blood." As much as the white Creoles wished to distinguish themselves from the detested Anglo-Americans, as the nineteenth century progressed and particularly after the Civil War, they insisted even more on distinction from persons of African ancestry.

One source of this confusion lay in the history of race relations in Louisiana—that is, in the fact that many of the people with French and Spanish ancestry who were "bred" in the New World also had ancestors of other races. Sexual unions, including marriages, with neighboring Native-American women were relatively common for the first colonizers of Louisiana, the soldiers and adventurers of Iberville and Bienville, and the introduction of African slaves in 1719 complicated the picture further. Sexual relations between master and slave, or more generally between whites and persons of African descent, were, if anything, more common and widespread, more openly tolerated in Louisiana than in the other slave states. Therefore, as John Blassingame observes, "By the time Reconstruction began, miscegenation had been going on for so long that more people of both the 'white' and 'Negro' populations in New Orleans and Louisiana had ancestors in the other race than did the residents of any other city or state in America. In fact, the population was so mixed that it was virtually impossible in many cases to assign individuals to either group."[4] Yet regardless of the difficulty (or, more likely, *because* of it) whites developed elaborate schemes and an extensive lexicon to identify various racial categories based on blood proportions: mulatto, griffe, sacatro, marabon, tierceron, quadroon, octoroon, and so forth. It might be argued that the combined phenomena of the white Creoles' exclusiveness and the widespread sexual contact between whites and blacks produced in Louisiana the country's greatest preoccupation with racial identity and its most complex caste system based on race.

A distinguishing feature of Louisiana's caste system was the size and importance of the population of persons designated *gens de couleurs libres*, free persons of color. Although augmented by freed slaves and refugees from the West Indies, the size of the population bore further evidence to the amount of sexual contact between blacks and whites in Louisiana. Some were the offspring of master-slave relationships, but many more were the children of white and free women of color and were, therefore, by law born with their mother's free status. Although distinctly relegated to second-class citizenship in a three-tiered system, free persons of color in colonial and antebellum Louisiana could own property, marry each other (but not either whites or blacks), and form other contracts that would be recognized by the courts. Many were artisans, professionals, and landlords in New Orleans, and many, too, were planters, owning large plantations and hundreds of slaves. As a result of their measure of wealth and privilege, free persons of color were frequently well-educated—sometimes at universities in Paris and elsewhere abroad—and they formed their own highly exclusive social organizations. They organized theaters and a Philharmonic Society and published *L'Album Litteraire* (1843), a literary journal, and *Les Cenelles* (1845), an anthology of poetry "by seventeen Louisiana Creoles of color."[5] A militia of free men of color fought with Andrew Jackson at the battle of New Orleans in 1815 and also briefly on the side of the Confederacy in the early stages of the Civil War. As persons of social standing (between whites and slaves), having French or Spanish ancestry and "bred" in the New World, the *gens de couleurs libres* also claimed the status label Creole to describe themselves. In editions up to 1869 the *Larousse* standard French dictionary seemed to justify this usage, making no distinction as to race in defining Creole (Dominguez, 14).

The best known feature of the city's race relations—both highly romanticized and notorious—was the system of semi-official concubinage that centered in the quadroon balls and the custom of *plaçage*. In this system the more attractive and fair-skinned daughters of free women of color would be groomed for a long-term relationship with a white Creole or American gentleman—generally someone both wealthy and respectable—whom they would meet at an elaborate ball held specifically for the purpose of facilitating these relationships (only white males and women of color could attend). These quadroon balls were famous in and out of antebellum New Orleans, celebrated both for the exotic beauty of the women and for the more tasteful splendor and greater decorum of the events as compared with other Creole balls. Mothers would act as agents for their daughters in making the arrangements or *plaçage,* which might involve a separate house in the woman's name, wardrobe, income, education for male children, and similar amenities. While these relationships might begin as a preliminary to the white man's marrying another (white) woman, some became a substitute for or lasted beyond marriage and involved feelings of love, respect, and commitment from both parties.

Despite the potential material benefits, the situation of the quadroon women was hardly enviable. As Mrs. Trollope reports in her famous account of her visit to Jacksonian America, the

> Quadroon girls, the acknowledged daughters of wealthy American or Creole fathers, educated with all the style and accomplishments which money can procure at New Orleans, and with all the decorum that care and affection can give . . . are not admitted, nay, are not on any terms admissible, into the society of the Creole families of Louisiana. They cannot marry . . . yet such is the powerful effect of their peculiar grace, beauty, and sweetness of manner, that unfortunately they perpetually become the objects of choice and affection.[6]

Such, of course, is the stuff of romance, and indeed the "tragic mulatto" (quadroon or octoroon) was a conventional literary figure, often appearing in a Louisiana setting as in the case of Longfellow's "The Quadroon Girl" (1842), Stowe's *Uncle Tom's Cabin* (1852), and Beaucicault's *The Octoroon* (1859), well before the time of Cable's New Orleans fiction. She was also, however, the product and hence powerful living symbol of racial and sexual injustice, of the painful illogic and devastating effects of caste, of the tortured psychology of desire and fear in the attitude of many white Americans toward blacks, of the hypocrisy and absurdity of white supremacists' claims of their own "racial purity" or the existence of a "natural race antagonism."

Indeed, for all the glamour associated with the quadroon women and the appearance of some racial equality in the relatively advantaged situation of free persons of color, Louisiana and New Orleans were also specifically identified with some of the worst evils of slavery. In 1724, in part to protect whites from rebellion, Governor Bienville issued the infamous Code Noir, which established strict laws governing the rights and treatment of slaves, including precise provisions for punishment. In addition, the cane and cotton plantations of Louisiana were notorious for debilitating and frequently fatal working conditions for slaves, so that, as readers of Mark Twain's *The Adventures of Huckleberry Finn* will recall, to be "sold down the river" was a particularly ominous fate for slaves in the Mississippi valley. Harriet Beecher Stowe was no doubt aware of this image when, in *Uncle Tom's Cabin,* she located in Louisiana the plantation of the man whose name became a synonym for the cruel overseer—

Simon Legree. Certainly, while race relations in Louisiana and New Orleans offered some of the stuff of romance, and even hope for amelioration, they also offered plenty of targets for social commentary, condemnation, and reform.

New Orleans was also characterized by a number of features linked to its location. The striking flatness of the region, the mixture of salt and freshwater marshes, of sluggish rivers and bayous, cypress swamps, dense forests, open prairies, seemingly endless cane and rice plantations, the tropical fauna (egrets, herons, pelicans, and alligators) and flora (palmetto, magnolia, and Spanish moss) created an exotic, picturesque landscape, both luxuriantly enticing and mysteriously forbidding. Governor Bienville chose to build his colonial capital on a "Crescent" of the Mississippi, 107 miles upriver from its mouth, to assure French control of the river, but the advantage was at first dubious. The low, poorly drained land was subject to violent storms and frequent flooding, which necessitated the city's celebrated above-ground cemeteries and, with the stifling heat and humidity of tropical summers, contributed to frequent epidemics of smallpox, cholera, and yellow fever. Add a number of devastating fires, and for a time the survival of the small French colonial city was uncertain.

Nevertheless, from colonial days through at least the Civil War years New Orleans's location near the mouth of the Mississippi was viewed as the city's promise of a prosperous future. With the economic expansion in the Ohio, Mississippi, and other river valleys of the trans-Appalachian West during the 1830s and 1840s, New Orleans developed into one of the nation's major ports. The Americans who began to flood into Louisiana soon after its purchase were the major participants in New Orleans's population growth and economic boom. Despised by the Creoles for their singular, unrelenting orientation to trade, the American newcomers nevertheless prospered, settling in and building magnificent new homes in the *faubourgs* (or suburbs) of St. Marie and Lafayette west of Canal Street, which marked the upper (i.e., upriver) boundary of the French Quarter. Between 1836 and 1852 New Orleans had separate, nearly autonomous municipal governments for its French and American sectors, but the Americans soon outnumbered and outcompeted the Creoles both commercially and politically and were the dominant population by mid-century in all but social standing. In the 1840s, when Cable was born, New Orleans was the fourth largest city in the nation (after Boston, New York, and Philadelphia), with a population of 102,192.

The robust commercial life of New Orleans especially along the river-front also had appeal for tourists, although with a decidedly different tone. In addition to the ornate, gaily decorated riverboats and large oceangoing vessels, the human scene offered a fascinating spectacle, a picturesque mix of costumes and manners among planters, cotton merchants, sailors, pilots, foreign immigrants, Indians, Kentucky riflemen, Acadian pothunters and fishermen, riverboatmen, and black "roustabouts." In fact, the sense of New Orleans mentioned earlier as a uniquely diverse, polyglot city was largely the result of its role as a port and commercial center, a magnet for both the "tired and homeless" from overseas and the fortune-seeking, the adventurous, the rough-and-tumble restless from the still unfirmly settled regions upriver.

Given this cast of characters, New Orleans predictably acquired a celebrity for entertainments other than the refined and picturesque. Grog shops, card rooms, and brothels were common in the wharf areas, along with high levels of violence and crime. Also, restrictive trade and tariff laws in Louisiana under both the French and Spanish administrations had made smuggling, pirating, and other forms of disregard for authority both a condition of survival and an accepted custom, even patriotic practice, evidenced most notably by the social standing of the Creole pirate Jean Lafitte. New Orleans's reputation as the "Big Easy," a wide-open sin city, was longstanding and multifaceted, going well beyond the refined exotica of the quadroon balls and river/port-city debaucheries to include various forms of governmental corruption and the mysterious practices of the African-Caribbean religion known as voodoo.

The recurrent note in nearly every description of New Orleans is striking contrasts—of Old World refinements and frontier coarseness, of rigid exclusiveness and unparalleled openness and tolerance, of languorous decay and vigorous growth and progress, of exotic allure and unmistakable danger. As the narrator in William Gilmore Simms's "A Sketch of the Crescent City" suggests, however, to get much beyond bedazzlement at the incongruous wonders an outsider required someone "able to enlighten [him] on all matters about which [he] was ignorant" and through whom he "obtained access to the society."[7] For thousands of readers of his books and of *Century* and *Scribner's* magazines in the 1870s and 1880s, such a guide was George Washington Cable—a role underscored by Mark Twain on the occasion of his visit to the city described in *Life on the Mississippi* (1883):

The party had the privilege of idling through this ancient quarter of New Orleans with the South's finest literary genius, the author of "The Grandissimes." In him the South has found a masterly delineator of its interior life and its history. In truth, I find by experience, that the untrained eye and vacant mind can inspect it and learn of it and judge of it more clearly and profitably in his books than by personal contact with it.

With Mr. Cable along to see for you, and describe and explain and illuminate, a jog through that old quarter is a vivid pleasure.[8]

Américains

George Washington Cable's parents moved to New Orleans from Indiana in 1837. His father, also George Washington Cable, was a Virginian by birth, of German/Pennsylvania-Dutch ancestry. His family had migrated to Indiana, where he met and married Rebecca Boardman, a descendant of Protestant New Englanders. Cooper, tavernkeeper, and venturesome businessman, George Cable was financially ruined in the panic of 1837, and so, like thousands of others, the Cable family moved to New Orleans to start over in the much ballyhooed city of opportunity near the mouth of the Mississippi. Within a few years George Cable prospered, becoming a partner in a firm that supplied groceries to riverboats and nearby settlements and then invested in property, steamboats, and other enterprises. The family, including four children, eventually settled in a house on Annunciation Square in the expanding *Américain* section known as the Garden District. There, on 12 October 1844, a fifth child and second son, George Washington Cable, was born.

Owing largely to the father's business success, Cable's first five or six years appear to have been spent quite happily in what his daughter and first biographer, Lucy Biklé, describes as "a home of comfort and culture and happy family affection."[9] The family was affluent (owning, by one account, eight slaves),[10] socially active, and, more important, stayed together for a prolonged period. By late 1850, however, George Cable's sources of income had disappeared through a series of business reverses and bad luck. He sold his property at public auction and sent his wife and children to live with her family in Indiana, where they would spend the majority of their time over the next four years. Although he found sporadic work on and off the river and managed to keep his family together in New Orleans after 1855, he was unable either to repeat his earlier successes or again to secure steady employment. When he died in

1859, George Junior, then 15, left school and began work at the New Orleans customhouse in order to help meet family expenses.

Although difficult to measure accurately in their impact on his later life and work, several aspects of Cable's early years are suggestive. The general pattern presented by his daughter and subsequently echoed by Arlin Turner and others stresses the overriding happiness, wholesomeness, and normalcy of the family life and Cable's boyhood, not only during the bountiful late 1840s but also during the leaner, more unsettled 1850s. He apparently attended school regularly (but was not distinguished as a scholar), raised pets, went fishing, explored his environment, joined his father on trips to the market or other excursions, played with friends, and during hard times was clothed, fed, and generally buffered from material hardships through the heroic efforts and resourcefulness of his mother. "It would be a mistake . . . ," Turner argues, "to think of George as a prematurely aged youngster depressed by the family misfortunes" (1956, 19).

The primary evidence for this impression, however, apart from family tradition, is the articles Cable wrote for genteel children's magazines when he was in his fifties.[11] Neither the audience, which expected reminiscence, nor the author's well-established identity with the picturesque and charming aspects of New Orleans, demanded much beyond pleasantry. Such articles would not have emphasized a child's reactions to repeated dislocations and parental absence, or to tensions in the home over money shortages, reduced social standing, and prolonged husband-wife separations. And the mostly positive tone of the parents' correspondence during the periods of their separation may reflect a combination of the father's optimistic temperament and the mother's Christian stoicism.

Suggestive here, apart from any implication of unacknowledged pain, is a family habit of positive thinking, a legacy and strategy of coping. As Turner describes Rebecca's reaction to the death of her elder two children in the year after George's birth, "She was not one to nurture her grief, and the effect seems to have been, ultimately, to intensify her affection for the others, deepen her religious nature, and reinforce the moral intensity . . . most characteristic of her" (1956, 9). Financial struggles (though less severe and less dramatic) and periods of prolonged separation from his family would recur through most of Cable's adult life, met on his part by a similar response of a duty to be cheerful. He, too, would lose a young child and react by writing emotionally restrained accounts to friends "to arrange in order the terrible memories,"[12] one of which concludes, "such is the terrible behavior of this fever in some houses that we are, by comparison, subjects of congratulation, and can, ourselves, sincerely say, 'God has been good to us.' "[13]

Involved in this discussion of coping strategies is a broader question of parental influence in shaping the author's character. The established view, again beginning with Mrs. Biklé's account, is that Cable acquired a kind of doubleness—qualities either conflicting or balancing, from his "Cavalier" father and "Puritan" mother. The father is described as strikingly large (five foot eleven and 194 pounds at age 36, as compared with his son's diminutive five-foot-five-inch, 100-pound adult stature), warm, humorous, sociable, energetic, buoyant, and playful. He was a man with a "commanding presence" (Biklé, 2) in his militia regalia who could also romp on all fours with his children, dance to the music of his own flute, and include bits of doggerel verse in nearly all of his letters to his wife (Turner 1956, 4, 5).

Rebecca Cable is more often characterized in terms of strength of resolve, resourcefulness, devotion to her family and duty, a "heroic spirit," an "intolerance . . . of indolence," and "moral austerity" (these last her son's phrases at the time of her death [Biklé, 4]). For a time at least, Cable's father both smoked and drank, and his wife disapproved. From these contrasting influences Cable is said to have derived his later ambivalence about New Orleans, the Creoles, and the South generally: his attraction to the sensuality of the region and its people and his need to judge them. Cable's later descriptions of trips with his father to the French market, lush with remembered sights, sounds, and aromas, seem to support the link between the father's realm and the author's sensuality.

But, however tempting, such a schema of influence seems a little too neat, and it should be remembered, as Turner observes, that Cable's "recollections could not reach far back of 1850" (1956, 19). The sense of his boyhood was therefore more concretely fixed on the period in which the father's role was considerably diminished. In fact, the more significant feature of Cable's relation to his parents may be less the Cavalier-Puritan contest than the fact that he was raised in and later lived in households with what Anna Elfenbein has called "women without male protectors" and this, along with his wife's "invalidism," "must have worked on Cable and influenced his perception of women and their problems."[14] If so, this is an area of his life and work that has yet to be adequately explored.

A final question to be considered here regarding this formative period is the impact of the Creole-*Américain* conflict on the Cable family and hence on the young author's attitudes toward a subject central to his most significant fiction. Without specific evidence, Turner offers no opinion on whether Cable's father, when he arrived in New Orleans, "thought of himself as one of the intruding *Américains,* or was at once aware of the fight for dominance being waged in the city" (1956, 7). Turner does note that at this time "the rivalry between the Creoles and the hated intruders was openly acknowledged and at its climax." Hence it is difficult to imagine Cable's father not being aware of the conflict, or not sensing that he was of the type Creoles excluded. The portrait of him that emerges from the family descriptions is less that of a Virginia Cavalier than that of a commercially minded go-getter. He was, after all, among those who had amassed a modest fortune in a short period in a "boomtown," and like other newly rich individuals he found means to express that economic rise in some form or evidence of social standing.

Some of George Cable's evidence, apart from signs of visible wealth— house, neighborhood, slaves—was his high office in the First Brigade in the First Division of the Louisiana Militia and his serving on the committee of managers for a ball at nearby Terpsichore Hall. The family also had social standing as active members of their church, and while novel-reading and theatergoing were proscribed, the family was cultivated: they valued reading and learning, enjoyed music, and were stirred by what Cable describes in his mother as "an intellectual ambition" (Biklé, 4). By every account, they seem typical of their class and circumstances, conscious of social status measured in terms of material attainments and position, but even more in terms of moral and intellectual cultivation, none of which—particularly not the latter—would likely lower the walls of Creole exclusiveness. Turner argues that the diversity of New Orleans life was such that after 10 years' residence in the city—that is, at the apex of their economic rise—the Cables were able to feel at home there, to find a niche and feel comfortable even amidst people and practices incompatible with their Northern and Protestant sensibilities. Indeed, there is no record of specific rebuffs or, outside of Cable's writing, particular preoccupation with the Creoles' social attitudes. When Cable later wrote about the Creoles, however, he did so as one whose family had demonstrably gained and demonstrably lost both wealth and status in a city where the Creoles' open disdain for commercial and Protestant people like themselves was a notorious, central feature of social and political life. However keen the insight, however broad the sympathy, his was, inescapably, the perspective of an outsider.

Confederate Soldier with Intellectual Ambition

Louisiana's secession from the Union ended Cable's work at the federal customhouse, and the fall of New Orleans and arrival of General Benjamin F. ("Beast") Butler in early 1862 led to the family's exodus from the city for the duration of the war. Cable would insist later that at the outbreak of the war he shared his neighbors' opinions about the Confederate cause. His parents were slave owners, and he had heard the "peculiar institution" defended vigorously on biblical grounds from the city's pulpits. In New Orleans, however, largely because of the feared effect on river traffic and hence on the city's economy, there was strong Unionist sentiment against secession, especially among those involved in commerce and with Northern origins.[15] Not surprisingly, then, at 16 Cable was "for Union, Slavery, and a White Man's Government!" but "secession, when it came, seemed a dreadful thing and [he] wondered at men and women, even if it was a necessity, rejoicing in it."[16] Nevertheless, he quickly became an ardent Confederate supporter, and his mother and two older sisters, Mary Louise and Antoinette, defied General Butler's order for all former citizens over 18 either to swear allegiance or register as enemies. Declaring themselves enemies of the United States, they "were banished . . . into the starving Confederacy, almost absolutely penniless."

Cable joined the Confederate cavalry on 9 October 1863, three days before his nineteenth birthday but looking more like a schoolboy because of his diminutive stature. He was involved in numerous skirmishes, mostly in Mississippi and later in Alabama, and was twice wounded. Some of his war experiences, including witnessing the fall of New Orleans and his family's flight from the city, would appear in his later fiction, particularly *Dr. Sevier, The Cavalier,* and *Kincaid's Battery,* but the more important outcome of this period may have been the beginning of changes in his moral and political thinking. Soldiering certainly helped mature Cable, and he continued to read and study on his own, even carrying books into battle. As an aide to General Wirt Adams and then to General Nathan Bedford Forrest, he found himself among men of greater accomplishment and involved in a more stimulating exchange of ideas. In letters to his mother, he remained loyal to the Confederate cause and positive in outlook, but he recalled later beginning to recognize flaws in the logic of that cause and gaps between his experience of events and newspaper accounts of them, both in the North and in the South.

At the close of the war Cable returned to New Orleans and began clerking in a cotton firm to make enough money to reunite his family in the city. He found the work relatively light and pleasant, but, signalling his own "intellectual ambition," he wrote to his mother that he could not help "striking higher, & trying for an honorable profession" (quoted in Turner 1956, 37). For a brief period in 1866, engineering offered such a possibility, and he worked with a railroad construction survey crew in the swamp and bayou country along the Atchafalaya River south of its origins near the Red River–Mississippi junction. Although he was an apprentice, he wrote to his mother that he messed and lodged with the engineers "to smooth off the inequality" between him and "the flag, chain & ax-men [who] have a separate tent & table" (Biklé, 35). A severe bout with malaria ended this job and his career as an engineer, but he gained from the experience an interest in the region and in its people, the Acadians, that he would return to later in *Bonaventure*. He also intensified an interest in geography (supposedly begun at age three [Biklé, 8n]), which enters much of his fiction as a surveyor's "map-sense."

Two years later Cable returned to the cotton business as an accountant. Within a year he had gained enough economic security or had bright enough prospects to marry Louise Stewart Bartlett on 7 December 1869. Like Cable she was a native of New Orleans and the decendent of relocated New Englanders. The two had grown up in the same Garden District neighborhood but had not met until adulthood. Louise Bartlett Cable is described as innately poised, dignified, and sober, someone who shared her husband's "seriousness of purpose and became the devoted encourager and assistant in all his work" (Turner 1956, 39). She would bear five children within the first eight years of their marriage, seven children (five girls and two boys) in all, and would suffer chronic ill health for much of their married life. By all accounts theirs was an affectionate, stable, and happy marriage, but it was not without pain: they had to endure the death of their four-year-old son during a yellow-fever epidemic, unrelenting concerns over money, and the predictable strains from periods of separation.

Cable's modest success as an accountant continued but did not quell his desire for a more "honorable profession," and he soon, somewhat by chance, began the first stages of a career in letters. His purported determination to write a book at age nine (Biklé, 8n) seems more boyish bravado than genuine literary ambition, but his early interest and pleasure in writing is apparent from his contributing to and helping edit his high school newspaper and from the turns of style and efforts at evocative description and verse in his early correspondence. Cable's habits of study and reading and his interest in analyzing principles seem also to have stimulated a need for expression, a means to convert his insights and talents to some form of public good. In this regard his Protestant sense of duty and vocation may have made intellectual ambition for Cable both a moral and a social imperative. In any event, when the other members of a literary club he had joined failed to provide copy for the initial article in a planned weekly column in the New Orleans *Picayune,* Cable filled the void, launching his literary career under the name "Drop Shot" on 27 February 1870. The column ran—for the most part weekly—until 9 July 1871 and then reappeared for three Sundays in February 1872.

"Drop Shot"

The mode of the "Drop Shot" columns would be familiar to readers of periodicals and newspapers from Addison and Steele's day down to our own: the commentary of a man-about-town on a variety of topics either of inherent interest, both local and general, or made interesting by the manner of treatment. Especially at first, an original verse was regularly included, but Cable's métier was clearly not poetry. For modern readers most of these "personal essays," as Turner describes them, are too dated, banal, or mannered to retain much value. They are, indeed, apprentice work. Taken together, however, the 90 "Drop Shot" columns provide an interesting reflection of a writer discovering his vocation.

The wide range of subject matter in the columns signals Cable's interest in the affairs of his day and, to some extent, the particulars of his environment. For example, he wrote on such diverse topics as the Franco-Prussian War, the frugality of Queen Victoria, the corruption of Reconstruction government, segregation in the public schools, manners on streetcars, the emptiness of New Orleans in the summer, deadbeats, and the misbehavior of birds. The overall lack of specificity of the columns, however, is at least as noteworthy as the range of subjects. There are numerous local details and topical references, but these are often slight or converted to a generalized discussion. Some of the most detailed, expert, and lyric writing in "Drop Shot" is devoted to nature description, and the focus of later columns is increasingly on literary topics.

One of the more important features of "Drop Shot" is Cable's development—rather early—of a self-aware and remarkably self-assured literary voice, a conscious, confident authorial persona. For all the subject variety and experimentation in these columns, the wholeness in the literary voice or persona, its continuity with that of the novelist to be acclaimed a decade later, is at least equally striking. Cable's indirectness and whimsy—a frequently ironic tone that runs from playful to sarcastic—is characteristic of this voice. His recurring references to Josh Billings, Mark Twain, and Benjamin Franklin's "Poor Richard" suggest not only his literary models and the elements of humor but also the purposefulness of the masking. In his tenth column he introduces a Billings-like vernacular character, Felix Lazarus, complete with heavily ungrammatical dialect, cracker-barrel wisdom, and a penchant for versifying. Felix reappears frequently thereafter (with more readable though still colloquial speech patterns), creating a comic, somewhat naturalized and democratized foil or alter ego for the more urbane Drop Shot, or "Dropie" as he sometimes calls himself. This pairing bears an interesting relation to the comparison Cable makes in one column between Josh Billings and Mark Twain, in which he perceptively recognizes the sharper satiric, social edge of the latter but prefers the gentler humor of the former. It is as if the young writer were exploring modes of satire and in Felix oddly assigning the preferred mode to the lesser character. Felix, though the butt of much humor and a vehicle for social satire, is additionally a poet, and through him and about him Cable explores some of his ideas about art.

The sociopolitical concerns Cable exhibits in "Drop Shot" also suggest certain features of his later writing. Cable's reform impulse is frequently apparent in the columns but is more often directed at universal human foibles—failure to pay debts, bragging, foppish preening, the link between laziness and gambling, and so forth—than specific social injustices. His most recurring social concern seems to be with women's rights and other gender issues. In general, while he does not clearly support these rights, he does not blatantly oppose them, and at his strongest point asserts, "We favor the largest freedom of woman's moral, mental and physical faculties and functions that can result beneficially to herself and society, and to this end are willing to stand almost any amount of experiment."[17]

His more characteristic attitude, however, is to trivialize gender issues, as when he follows the preceding assertion with a list of rights "for which even themselves have not proposed to fight," including "a right to go up stairs alone in the dark, . . . a right *not* to scream at a cat, . . . a right to care more for propriety than for fashion, . . . a right to show by modest but visible acknowledgments that they recognize the graceful privileges accorded to them by men to be *at least* commendable." In another instance he counters the claim that women's participation would improve the moral tone of political life by observing that women's reluctance to admit their ages foretells an opposite moral drift. The point is not the shape or extent of his sexism—which was fairly typical for his era and background—but his inclination to treat the issue of women's rights as ultimately a matter of genteel decorum. He is more concerned with the behavior of the advocates for women's rights than with the rights themselves.

This concern with decorum enters also into some of his treatment of race issues in "Drop Shot." At this time his views on race, as he later acknowledged, were generally those of his fellow Southerners. He attacks the corruptions of the Radical Reconstruction government, imagines a conversation between General Butler and Satan, and composes racist jingles on school desegregation. There is little hint of the courageous positions he would later take on behalf of the freedman, except perhaps in one piece titled "Home Again," where he rides a streetcar with Felix Lazarus. Felix has been away from New Orleans, but he feels himself most "intensely" at home when on the cars: "All is hospitality, cheerful politeness, ease, and even cheapness."[18] Comparing the integrated cars in New Orleans with segregated cars in Richmond and Louisville, Felix seems to affirm the right of segregation but to oppose a mean-spirited inequality of accommodations. Cable's attitude, however, is more subtly shaded in a brief dramatic interchange: "'Nowhere,' at last said Felix, growing enthusiastic, 'but here at home can a man stretch his knees half across the car, as I am doing, and a little African stagger through its whole length with a five gallon can of buttermilk!' A genial laugh and a 'that's so!' from a perfect stranger on the opposite seat did not startle us the least, it being quite the proper thing in a New Orleans street car."

The issue, Cable suggests, is a matter of social freedoms verging on personal violations. Whatever class umbrage is represented in the "little African's" presence on the car (albeit significantly not sitting or even staying), it is blurred by the juxtaposition with the other social affronts: Felix's stretching his legs and the "perfect stranger's" joining their conversation. Like Christopher Newman's leg stretching in Henry James's *The American,* Felix's gesture of relaxation may indicate democratic freedom and expansiveness, but it also violates the space of others, perhaps risking a larger catastrophe should he trip the staggering boy. In a later column Cable refers again to the problem of "the man who sits length-ways in the cars,"[19] suggesting that he might second the stranger's "genial" but ironic intrusion, itself an ironic example of democratic proprieties.

Although such subtle interplay is not common in "Drop Shot," the emphasis on manners in a democratic society, as in his treatment of women's rights, is a recurring feature of the columns and a foreshadowing of what he later says would prompt him to speak out on racial issues. Whether addressing these social issues, the question of keeping the Sabbath, the dangers of the lottery, the writing of poetry, the Christian spirit of Otto Bismarck, or the need for a lecture society in New Orleans, Cable's primary concern seems to be moral, cultural, and intellectual elevation or refinement. Hence in "Drop Shot" Cable not only developed key ingredients of his literary persona and began the exploration of his milieu, but he also signaled the genteel tone of his impulse for reform.

The Mines of Romance

Although Cable began writing "Drop Shot" as a fortuitous avocation, by early 1871 he had left his accounting positions and accepted a post as full-time reporter for the *Picayune*. In addition to his weekly column and several book reviews, he wrote lengthy articles on that year's Mardi Gras celebration, covered a visit to New Orleans by Horace Greeley, and reported meetings of the Teacher's Institute, initially complaining about their not being segregated. Reporting did not suit him, however, and his unwillingness to continue agitating against the integration of the Institute meetings and his refusal for religious reasons to report on a theatrical performance did not suit his employers. He resigned from the paper in July and returned to the counting room of the cotton factor, William C. Black and Company, remaining with the firm until after Black's death in 1879.

Cable's work in the cotton business, although it would drain time and energy away from his writing for nearly a decade, also made him present at the scene of numerous political discussions in Black's offices. The most vital issue was the legitimacy and policies of the Radical (Republican or Reconstruction) government, established by Congress in 1867 and committed to promoting a biracial society through Negro suffrage, integrated public facilities, and other means. White Southern Democrats fiercely resisted these policies, and there were many acts of violence by racist paramilitary groups such as the White League and Knights of the White

Camellia.[20] The men who visited on business the offices of William C. Black and Company and hotly debated the era's politics were among the city's more influential citizens, and as he had with army officers and railroad engineers before, Cable warmed to the opportunity for stimulating discussions of serious issues among men of standing and education. These experiences were crucial to the growth of his political ideas, for as he became dissatisfied by the reasoning he heard and traced the logic of secession and slavery to their putative sources in the Constitution and the Bible, he discovered that the principles for which he and his fellow Southerners had fought the War of Rebellion were wrong.

Cable had resumed clerking to earn a livelihood, but by the early 1870s he was clearly on the road to becoming a professional writer. Shortly after leaving the *Picayune* he sought unsuccessfully to publish a book manuscript, "a story with scenes laid in and about New Orleans" (Turner 1956, 46), apparently composed of materials gleaned from the "Drop Shot" columns. In February 1872 he briefly revived "Drop Shot" and also continued to supply book reviews and other articles for the *Picayune.* To meet the obligations of both the cotton firm and his emerging literary ambitions, Cable established a routine of rising early to write before breakfast and then retiring to his study for more writing and reading in the evenings. When business slackened, he found time to write at his desk during the day.

Two of Cable's writing projects for the *Picayune* in 1872 gave particular impetus and shape to his literary career. In February and March he contributed a series of articles on "The Churches and Charities of New Orleans" and in August wrote two major editorials attacking the powerful and corrupt Louisiana State Lottery Company, which practically owned the state's politics from 1868 to 1892. The latter was Cable's first major effort at serious reform. Although unable to break the power of the Lottery Company, he learned much about real political power from the effort, and he also gained the satisfaction of standing with the city's most highly respected leaders and articulating their position on grounds of seemingly unquestionable moral rectitude.

The earlier series on New Orleans's churches, however, had a greater impact, for writing them required research in the archives of the Cabildo (built to house the Spanish colonial government), the City Hall, and the St. Louis Cathedral. Among these records he discovered the historical materials that formed the basis of his greatest fiction. As he observed in his last "Drop Shot" column, published during the period of this research, to the true poet . . . Louisiana's brief two centuries of history is a rich and profitable mine. Here lie the gems, like those new diamonds in Africa, right on top of the ground. The mines are virgin. Choctaw legends and Spanish adventures may be found overlying each other in profuse abundance. Only one man [Charles Gayarré] . . . in following the annals of colonization, has uncovered the mines of romance. But the half, I am sure, has not been told; and I have sent Felix down . . . to see what he can gather up without digging . . . hoping he may be very successful, even to the drawing forth of a readable book.[21]

Here Cable signals clearly his intention to use his historical research for publication beyond New Orleans and the *Picayune*. By the end of the year he had already begun writing the stories that would appear first in *Scribner's Monthly* and then collected as *Old Creole Days*.

Chapter Two

The Mines of Romance:
Old Creole Days

Local Color

In addition to his talent and the strength of his literary ambition, timing was also a key factor in Cable's initial success as a fiction writer. His efforts to mine the unique features of New Orleans and its history for romance coincided with a boom in regional writing in general and Southern literature in particular among Northern readers during the 1870s and 1880s.

As illustrated by the work of its best known practitioners—Bret Harte, Joel Chandler Harris, Thomas Nelson Page, Mary Noailles Murfree, Sarah Orne Jewett, Hamlin Garland, and others—most of the regional writing qualifies as "local color," the phrase implying an emphasis on the unique, picturesque aspects of specific locales. With its "uniform tendency," as one critic put it, "a gift of the scientific spirit, to lay stress on the background, the milieu, the atmosphere, the environment, the setting,"[1] characters in local color fiction are often flat or stereotyped and the plots weakly sentimental, usually romantic love stories. In order to characterize the uniqueness of a locale, however, writers found it necessary to observe carefully and record accurately the specific details (landscape, manners, costume, architecture, and especially speech or dialect) that made the locale different, and in so doing they contributed to the development of literary realism.

The vogue for such writing in post–Civil War America developed from specific social and political conditions. One of these is suggested in Eric Sundquist's observation that "as a literature of memory, local color often has elements of the historical novel; yet it strives to delineate not history's great figures or movements but the scant record of time's passage left when a simpler way of life succumbs to one more complex."[2] Insofar as local color fiction usually depicts rural or small-town life, it centers on a world threatened by the rapid industrialization, urbanization, and centralization of America stimulated by the Civil War and by the victory of the North. Hence the nostalgic tone and pastoral design of much local-color writing, especially in the South, reflect in part a desire to retreat in space and time from a contemporaneous scene of unsettling changes. In addition, the editors of such literary magazines as *Harper's, Lippincott's, Appleton's Journal, Scribner's Monthly, Atlantic Monthly,* and *Century,* where most of the local-color stories appeared, sought to use regional writing to reconcile sectional differences, to help heal the recently divided nation. Local-color fiction, therefore, involves a paradox or twofold project: to celebrate regional diversity while reassuring the reading public "that this need not mean division," that the differences were contained in a unified whole.[3]

The image of the South that served these purposes was consistent with a "New South" ideology in which the wrong of slavery and secession were accepted but white supremacy and the essential nobility of the white Southerner were imperatives, and the revival of the South was based on industrial expansion with the help of Northern capital. Romanticized versions of the "Old South"—plantations, belles, dashing "colonels," loyal and contented "darkies"—were acceptable because they offered no real alternative to the Northern industrial order. As Wayne Mixon observes, "Now that Southern differences no longer threatened the union, Yankees found them quaint and picturesque."[4] Furthermore, to be published in magazines aimed primarily for readers in middle-class homes, all novels and stories had to conform to the standards of genteel taste in the Gilded Age—specifically to avoid any direct, unpleasant references to sexual passion, social disadvantage, economic hardship, and religion, and to be agreeable and uplifting. Because of these strictures, Louis Rubin has argued that "the public taste for local color provided . . . both a signal opportunity and a potentially severe liability for George W. Cable in his drive to become a successful writer":[5] the taste made the literary materials available to him marketable but pressured him to shape those materials to a limiting literary standard, one to which, in part, his own tastes inclined him.

Cable attributed his "discovery" to Edward King, who visited New Orleans in 1873 along with the illustrator J. Wells Champney in order to gather materials for a series of articles entitled "The Great South" that would appear in *Scribner's Monthly* during the following year and later was published as the two-volume *The Southern States of North America.* Consistent with the political aims just described, King presented the recently defeated region, still under Northern-imposed Reconstruction governments, in images and terms that would, as Arlin Turner put it, "recommend the South to the sympathy and generosity of his Northern readers, and to their sense of justice" (1956, 53). At the time of their meeting Cable was involved in research for his second *Picayune* article on the Mistick Krewe of Comus, and he readily shared with King his knowledge and views of the region. He also entertained King and Champney in his home and there read to them the stories he had been fashioning out of his archival research.

King was so impressed by Cable and by these stories that he carried some of them back to New York and urged them on the associate editor at *Scribner's Monthly,* Richard Watson Gilder. Despite King's efforts, Gilder rejected the first of the stories, a powerful melodrama called "Bibi," probably on the grounds that the story of a proud African prince who refuses to accept the terms of his American enslavement was too "distressful."[6] Gilder accepted, however, the second story King promoted, " 'Sieur George," for the October 1873 *Scribner's Monthly.* Although he would remain in the cotton business for another eight years, with the publication of " 'Sieur George" and six more stories (all but one appearing in *Scribner's*) over the next two and a half years, Cable's literary career was essentially launched.

In many ways Cable's first stories exhibit the characteristics and weaknesses of local-color writing during the period. Although not all are love stories, many of the plots are highly sentimental or melodramatic and frequently less interesting than the setting and atmosphere. The characters, especially the various Creoles, quadroons and other well-known New Orleans personae, are also the sort of stereotyped regional oddities that abound in local-color fiction, some of the "folk" that Merrill Skaggs argues were among the most important contributions of the local-color movement.[7] Cable's use of dialect is a signature feature of the genre and contributed enormously to the initial appeal and lasting popularity of his stories for editors and readers, for fellow writers like Twain and Howells, and for more than a decade of lecture audiences. This appeal was based not on the linguistic accuracy of Cable's dialect renditions (now generally acknowledged) but on the flavoring or picturesque charm they added to the stories. The same applies to his descriptions of the physical environment, both the landscape and the Vieux Carré. In most of the stories the former surveyor's helper provides readers with a carefully drawn mental map of the setting, including street and geographical names, distances, and, most notably, accurate descriptions of actual, usually still-standing buildings that serve as authenticating landmarks within the narratives and that became—and remain—tourist attractions in New Orleans because of the popularity of these stories.[8]

These stories also exhibit, however, an artistry and a social and historical exploration well beyond the usual limits of the local-color genre. Despite the family's suspicion of novels, Cable's reading certainly influenced his early literary practice, and critics have suggested a number of sources.[9] Alice Hall Petry, who has studied Cable's artistry in greatest depth, argues that the four most prominent are Dickens, Shakespeare, Poe, and Hawthorne.[10] Cable early drew comparisons to Hawthorne, and indeed he seems to offer the closest parallels in technique—the hinting indirection, play of narrative angle, ironic tone, suggestions of allegory—and in the use of history as a moral template by which to understand and critique the present.

Cable places each of the stories in a specific historical context, but the myth of an agrarian, nobly aristocratic, antebellum paradise that dominated so much of the Southern local color of this period does not appear. The settings are generally urban or urban-frontier, not pastoral, and the emphasis is on decay and the seeds of that decline in the social and cultural history he examines. This inclination to criticize or judge the sensuous Creole world he was otherwise drawn to—a tendency usually attributed to the maternal, Presbyterian, reforming side of his nature—meant that Cable's local color only partially served the project of reconciliation. The picturesque quality of the stories may have made the South attractive and sympathetic to contemporary Northern readers, but Cable found other elements in the "rich and profitable mine" of Louisiana history—moral corruption, social injustice, violence—and these he wove into the fabric of his tales as well.

" 'Sieur George"

Although it was the first of Cable's stories to be published nationally, " 'Sieur George" illustrates what would become the signature features of his art. Opening and setting his story "in the heart of New Orleans," he clearly embarks on the project of mining Louisiana romance that he announced in his last "Drop Shot" article. Even more than in most local-color fiction, the setting, although sparingly detailed, is richly evocative and predominates over action. The main plot, revealed indirectly and somewhat confusingly through a series of hints, allusions, partial revelations and observations, seems safely sentimental and moral, basically the story of a man who wastes his life through gambling. The evocations of the background are not, however, limited to the exotic and picturesque, and the moral failings of the central character go deeper than playing the lottery.

Typical of many of his New Orleans stories, Cable establishes tone and introduces themes with an opening description of a building or locale. The tone in "'Sieur George" mixes a bit of the charm of Old World antiquities ("immense batten doors with gratings over the lintels, barred and bolted with masses of cobwebbed iron, like the door of a don-jon")[11] and exotic French tropicality (a scattering of French phrases and occasional snippets of Creole dialect) with heavier doses of decay and squalor ("many lines of wet clothes," "rotten staircases that seem vainly trying to clamber out of the rubbish," "fifth-rate shops," "innumerable children [who] swarm about, and . . . obstruct the sidewalks playing their clamorous games"). The focus on the "large four-story brick build-ing"[12] that is to be the scene of all the story's main action is particularly subtle and shaded with social and moral implications. When he observes that it "has a solemn look of gentility in rags, and stands, or, as it were, hangs, about the corner of two ancient streets, like a faded fop who pre-tends to be looking for employment," he suggests something of the atti-tudes of the Creole neighbors and renters ("a class of persons occupying them [the rooms] simply for lack of activity to find better and cheaper quarters elsewhere"). In words like *hangs* and *pretends* he also hints at and critically judges causes for the area's decline, and thus the picturesque qualities of the description are infused with a sense of social reality.

The social and economic decline emphasized in the opening descrip-tion of the building and neighborhood are echoed in the "symptoms of a decay" (*OCD,* 4), the evidences of moral decline in George's life. He may have killed a man in a duel, he drinks, he gambles, and he offers mar-riage to his foster daughter—all except the last presented indirectly. The final emphasis on the useless lottery tickets and George's still believing he "knows a combination which would repair all the past" suggest a rather blatant Sunday-school sermon against the evils of gambling, con-sistent with Cable's earlier attack against the Louisiana Lottery Company. Largely because of the narrative indirection, however, it is not clear whether gambling is a symptom or the cause of his moral weak-ness, but it is apparent that the weakness is part of a pattern of econom-ic and social change hinted in the descriptions of setting in the opening and throughout the story. This pattern is the history of the Americans' ascendency over the Creoles.

Cable represents this history with little mourning for the past and general admiration for the Americans' enterprise. He criticizes especially the Creoles' attitudes and qualities that doomed them to the status of "gentility in rags." For example, he notes that "all spirit of enterprise were gone to Canal Street and beyond" (*OCD*, 9), and in a final panorama of the city and its surroundings, he seems to offer a paean to New South glories and a mocking of Old South follies: "Along its [the Mississippi's] sweeping bends the chimneys of a smoking commerce, the magazines of a surplus wealth, the gardens of the opulent, the steeples of a hundred sanctuaries and thousands on thousands of mansions and hovels covered the fertile birthright arpents which 'Sieur George, in his fifty years' stay, had seen tricked away from dull colonial Esaus by their blue-eyed brethren of the North" (*OCD*, 23). While the only important Creole character in the story is George's déclassé landlord, Kookoo, the saga of Creole-American conflict is presented as a contest of culture and values in which industry and enterprise triumph over pride, languor, exclusiveness, and the naive dream of an eternal plantation order. The winners succeed by their virtues; the losers fail by their vices.

'Sieur George's moral decay is not a direct reflection of the larger social decline, for the Creoles are not shown to be drinkers or gamblers, and George is, after all, an *Américain,* his name supplied by his Creole neighbors perhaps in a mildly mocking reference to George Washington. Still, his reclusiveness mirrors the Creoles' exclusiveness, and he seems infected with some measure of the Creoles' pride and sense of honor. In this vein his aspirations to fortune and a restored social standing based on winning the lottery rather than finding gainful employment can be seen to reflect a larger pattern of Creole illusions in the face of economic realities. Furthermore, as Alice Hall Petry has argued, that George is an American and that his corruptions include a fair measure of sensuality suggest that Cable's theme is similar to that in Conrad's *Heart of Darkness.* Like Kurtz, 'Sieur George is an example of the Anglo-American seduced by the greater luxury or sophistication of the culture in which he is alien, "going native" at the cost of his soul or integrity of being. Even more than the "dull colonial" Creoles, it is 'Sieur George who has forsaken his "birthright" of prosperity based on American enterprise, industry, and commercialism.[13]

The sense of New Orleans presenting a seductive risk to the outsider is also felt through Cable's narrative technique. In a way characteristic of Cable at his best, the French Quarter is presented as a place of partial visions—of peeps, glimpses, and glances, of closed shutters and doors, walled gardens, and dimly lit interiors—all portending stories to be told. With the most important moments of George's life occurring offstage, the reader's attention is focused on the "events quite queer, if not really strange" (*OCD,* 15) that occur in and around the two rooms he lets some 50 years before the story opens. These events provoke the curiosity of the neighbors and especially that of the Creole landlord, Kookoo, and it is the tracing and satisfying of this curiosity that essentially drives the narrative.

The role of the narrator, therefore, is that of a guide satisfying the curiosity provoked by the milieu, and Cable's style, often aiming at a kind of condescending intimacy with both the reader and his subject, is an appropriate complement to that role. If, however, the narrator is a mediating agent for the reader, so, too, is Kookoo the agent for neighbors, narrator, and reader alike in satisfying the curiosity about 'Sieur George and his strange behavior. Described as "an ancient Creole of doubtful purity of blood," who "smokes cascarilla" and "wears velveteen" (*OCD,* 2, 3), Kookoo is the first of several comic portrayals of Creole character in Cable's fiction and perhaps the most successful creation in this story.[14] He exhibits a good deal of Creole pride and attitude toward work ("in his landlordly old age [he] takes all suggestions of repairs as personal insults"), but the most emphasized feature of his character is his curiosity about what 'Sieur George keeps in the small hair trunk he brings with him to the room when he first appears and which he warns Kookoo not to touch. Because he suspects the trunk to contain treasure, Kookoo's desire to look inside it is driven less by curiosity alone than by greed and ultimately ancestral pride: "He felt a Creole's anger . . . that a tenant should be the holder of wealth while his landlord should suffer poverty" (*OCD,* 21). Ultimately, he resorts to eavesdropping beneath the stairways and then at George's keyhole, where finally he becomes a clandestine witness to a partial unraveling of George's secret in the story's climactic scene.

The key point is that the narrator's role as guide to the secrets of the French Quarter has been projected into the story in the form of Kookoo's keyhole peeking, and the scene he witnesses is a voyeur's delight. The orphaned daughter of the "youngish lady in black" (*OCD,* 6), who mysteriously occupies George's rooms during his absence, has become a young woman. Although he has raised her from infancy, George recognizes the impropriety of their continuing to share quarters, and, as Kookoo listens, he tries to rescue her honor by suggesting marriage as the only solution. Shocked, the orphan utters "a low, distressful cry, and gliding swiftly into her room, for the first time in her young life turn[s] the key between them" (*OCD,* 20).

At this, a scene of sentiment and pathos becomes suddenly, disturbingly sexual, even more so upon reflection. Before his proposal, the "very beautiful" (*OCD,* 17) 16-year-old girl was sitting at his feet "with her interlocked hands upon his knee, and her face, full of childish innocence mingled with womanly wisdom." At one point she rose, he opened his arms, "and she sat upon his knee and kissed him," and finally, after lighting the fire, she sat "beside him, laying her head on his knee, and he stroking her brow with his brown palm" (*OCD,* 17). The ambiguous sensuality of these "father-daughter" contacts becomes more lurid when we recognize that intimacy, not propriety, has been George's primary aim, that the 16-year-old he has been holding on his lap, kissing, and caressing has been less a daughter to him than a potential marriage partner.

Louis Rubin (49) and Alice Hall Petry (126–28) seem correct in emphasizing the striking sense of "near depravity" in this scene, including, as Petry argues, more than a hint of incest.[15] The tone seems even more sordid by the presentation of the scene as kind of peep show for Kookoo, which is followed by his sneaking into George's room later that night after the old man has drunk himself to sleep in order to look into the trunk and finally discover its contents. Cable suggests this last act is "a crime" (*OCD,* 22), and thus Kookoo's efforts to satisfy his curiosity involve a moral degeneracy paralleling 'Sieur George's decay and the patterns of decline in the story as a whole. For the reader, however, these efforts are more than an amusing sidelight to the main story of George's decay; they provide the only access to the essential secrets of that story. Hence, when Kookoo's "ear and eye took turns at the keyhole" (*OCD,* 18), the reader is, in essence, eavesdropping with him, made privy to a scene Cable admits was "not intended for outside hearers" and thus ironically implicated in the attainment of guilty knowledge. Here as elsewhere in Cable, while the Sunday School teacher in him might dictate turning away and judging, another part of him could not help looking and recording the allure of what he saw.

In the final analysis, the moral message and social critique in "'Sieur George" remains unclear. Some commentary on the Creoles and the moral implications of their contest with the Americans can be seen, but it is only tentatively delineated; the various strands of social, psychological, and moral insight are left more interestingly paralleled than coherently linked. For this reason critics such as Philip Butcher looking for a strong social message find the story unsatisfying, but its achievement lies elsewhere.[16] With a few carefully selected details and images, and even more with his particular narrative manner—the hints, the whimsy, the ironic intimacy, the suggestive vagueness that seems a constituent element of the locale—Cable artfully established not only the special tone of what would be his literary "province" but also a richly implicit relationship to it. Cable's depiction of old New Orleans, indeed, has local-color charm, but it includes as well the fascination of sin, and the voyeuristic gaze of both author and reader is not altogether innocent.

"Belles Demoiselles Plantation"

The second of his stories to be published (in *Scribner's* in April 1874), "Belles Demoiselles Plantation" remains the most frequently anthologized and, therefore, may be the best known of all Cable's fiction. Its appeal rests on its treatment of social themes—race, caste, ancestral pride, and ancestral guilt—now recognized as central to the Southern literary tradition that became prominent in the twentieth century. This is somewhat apart from what Robert Fulwiler, Donald Ringe, and especially Alice Hall Petry have demonstrated is a strong, orthodox Christian allegory operating in the story, more overt in its message than the muddied moralizing in "'Sieur George." Because this allegory bears also on the story's social issues, however, "Belles Demoiselles Plantation" can be seen as the first formulation of the kind of social and moral critique of the Creoles and the South generally that would characterize Cable's best work.

Editors and readers confused by the elaborate indirections of "'Sieur George" were more pleased by the relatively straightforward plotting of "Belles Demoiselles Plantation." Set around 1820, the central conflict is between Colonel Jean Albert Henri Joseph De Charleau-Marot and De Carlos, known as Injin Charlie, both the aging descendants of Count De Charleau, commissary to the French king during the colonial period. The count, having had two wives—one Choctaw and the other a wealthy, well-born Frenchwoman—began two lines of Creole descent and left two legacies of property: for the pure white descendants, a land grant along the Mississippi below New Orleans, which has been developed into a prosperous cane plantation, and, for the racially mixed descendants, a block of rundown city properties. Urged by his seven beautiful daughters (after whom the plantation is named) to build a fashionable city residence, the widowed Colonel De Charleau tries to buy Injin Charlie's properties. Charlie refuses to sell, however, insisting on maintaining some visible emblem of his "good blood," and offers instead to trade for Belles Demoiselles Plantation. When the colonel discovers that the river has been undermining the bank on which the plantation house is built, he agrees to the trade, but as the two men watch, the bank suddenly collapses, carrying with it the house and the seven daughters. In the dénouement Charlie nurses the devastated De Charleau through a year of madness, and in a brief return to reason before his death, the old Creole redeems his honor by insisting the trade was never completed and rescues his soul by reaffirming his Christianity.

Although the events are presented directly and clearly, Cable's narrative technique contributes considerable subtlety, depth, and dramatic impact to the story. He uses foreshadowing effectively not only to prepare the reader for the melodramatic climax but also to suggest an element of tragic fate in the events. For example, when he describes the river and its action on the count's *pointe* in the fifth paragraph, the details convey an unmistakable sense of ominous natural power, and when he continues with a description of the plantation house and its relation to the river in the succeeding two paragraphs, he adds a vaguer sense of foreboding through the final vista away from the house and garden, past the rice and cane fields, toward "the distant quarters of the slaves" and "on the horizon everywhere a dark belt of cypress forest" (*OCD,* 62). Images such as these permeate the story with a sense of nature as the retributive agent, perhaps more than the God of Christianity.

Cable also makes some use of dialect, more than in " 'Sieur George," but it is not burdensome. As a means of maintaining a certain formal distance between them, De Charleau and Charlie always converse in English rather than their native French, and the resulting use of differing English dialects enables Cable to mark their class differences (De Charleau learned his English from his Scotch wife, while Charlie was taught by "upriver traders") and to signal some of the awkwardness and humor in their relationship. In addition, Cable's narrative tone, as in " 'Sieur George," contributes significantly to the effect and meaning of the story. Still playful at times, the voice is more sharply ironic, sometimes caustic in its treatment of Creole history and De Charleau's character. Much of the sting of the social criticism in the story is generated by this narrative irony, but it is blended with a musical and poetic quality apparent in the descriptions of the natural landscape, the house and garden, and the colonel's daughters. The effect is to both evoke and subtly undermine the luxuriant appeal of the region and its people.

The main outlines of the religious themes in the story are fairly transparent. De Charleau is guilty not only of the youthful sins of the flesh he admits to, but also of pride, failing to love his neighbor (Charlie), and, most of all, worshiping false gods. As Petry has persuasively demonstrated, Cable characterizes the colonel's attitudes toward Belles Demoiselles as a form of pagan worship, with the house, something like Poe's House of Usher, serving as a blurred single icon representing De Charleau's ancestry, his material possessions, and his daughters. Thus, when the man whose daughters "were the seven goddesses of his only worship" sees the action of the river undermining his land and sobs, "My God! . . . My God," Cable pointedly notes that "even while he called, his God answered," a "crevice slowly became a gape, and . . . a ton or more of earth settled into the boiling eddy and disappeared" (*OCD,* 79). The action foreshadows the melodramatic climax, and the language suggests its meaning: De Charleau is punished for his sins by the more powerful true God. He redeems himself in acts of charity and humility—letting Charlie keep his appreciating city properties and calling for a priest and clinging to a crucifix as signs of Christian acceptance.

However important the broad Christian message may have been for Cable, his treatment of the Creoles and issues of race and the plantation South are more likely to interest modern readers. In "Belles Demoiselles Plantation" Cable evokes very little of the color of old New Orleans, but in remarkably complex and subtle ways he develops the main action and central character conflicts to reflect significant aspects of Louisiana history. De Charleau is presented as the type of the white Creole planter-aristocrat, "a hoary-headed patriarch" who disdains the title of colonel because it was bestowed by the first American governor. Cable emphasizes his typicality even more in characterizing his moral nature through a kind of walking tour of New Orleans sin spots: "He had gambled in Royal Street, drank hard in Orleans Street, run his adversary through in the dueling ground at Slaughterhouse Point, and danced and quarreled at the St. Philippe Street Theatre quadroon balls," but he had borne these vices "as his race do, with a serenity of conscience and a cleanness of mouth that left no outward blemish on the surface of the gentleman" (*OCD,* 63). Like so many of his type, his wealth is due to inherited land and the labor of slaves, but even this appearance of value has been undermined by his "luxurious idleness" and "voluptuous ease," mortgaged to his "low-life" relative to pay gambling and other debts.

The contrast between superficial respectability and underlying corruption is the main issue represented in De Charleu's character; it is central to the question of honor in his business dealings with Injin Charlie and, Cable suggests, a recurring element in the region's history. For example, the "lucky accident" of the count's commissariat burning down "with his account books inside" (*OCD*, 60), an accident that allows him to make "excuses" successfully to the French court, suggests the corrupt economic relations between colonial officials and the French government over restrictive duties and trade that led to the region's well-known and widely tolerated smuggling and piracy. That the tract was granted following his successful explaining suggests that the plantation was built on unstable ground from the outset.

Even more clearly, the count's marrying and then conveniently forgetting his Choctaw wife points specifically to Louisiana's history of racial mixing from the days of Iberville's soldiers and to the hypocrisy of the Creole's pride in racial purity. In this regard Charlie's racial identity is significantly blurred, suggesting the broader pattern of race relations. The last of his line "on the Choctaw side," his genealogy includes "injudicious alliances and deaths in the gutters of old New Orleans" (*OCD*, 63). His name, De Carlos, is the result of "Spanish contact," and his designation as "Injin" is an *"alias"* (*OCD*, 64). Given this account of his antecedents and the precision with which many Louisianians used racial labels, Cable's calling Charlie "plainly a dark white man" is subtly oxymoronic and ironic, for his whiteness is no more plain than the significance or origins of his darkness; the whiteness is not possible unless the origins of the darkness are certain. The confident reading of any such externals is belied by the history of tangled relations.

Cable underscores further the ironies in the Creole attitudes toward race by making pride in the same De Charleu blood line the "ancestral nonsense" that keeps Charlie from selling and prevents the colonel "from choosing any other spot for a city home" (*OCD*, 76). Moreover, De Charleau recognizes Charlie's ancestral loyalty as a bond between them, first diminishing his desire to swap properties and then pricking his conscience about the deal when he knows he has been unfair. As Cable notes, the "one thing [he] never knew a Creole to do . . . [is] utterly go back on the ties of blood, no matter what sort of knots those ties may be" (*OCD*, 64).

Cable's pattern of critiquing Creole society in "Belles Demoiselles Plantation" is to undermine and thereby expose the illusions on which the Creoles stake their pride. The plantation itself is a significant symbol of these illusions, representing not only a corrupt past and doomed economic system but also a flawed, fatally egotistic and worldly measure of happiness. The role of women in this representation is interesting, varying between innocent victimization and central culpability. The premature deaths of all the major female characters suggests the victimization, the consequence of which is, ironically, the thinness or sterility and ultimate termination of the De Charleau line. Whatever virility may be implied by the count's and the colonel's "checkered" pasts, Cable compares the De Charleau family to a century plant, foreshadowing the fact that after a sudden, showy display, the line will die.

The daughters' innocence is more problematic, however. Perhaps to avoid an excessive horror for the reader in their deaths, Cable develops the seven "goddesses" more as static, undifferentiated figures in a mythic tapestry—Gallic Southern Belles—than as believable human characters. They seem the very embodiment of the plantation ideal itself, and, at first, the image is positive albeit cloying. As they gather about their father in the garden at dusk, bedecking him with flowers, discussing "some new step in the dance, or the adjustment of some rich adornment," "gaily chatting and jesting with that ripple of laughter that comes so pleasingly from a bevy of girls" (*OCD,* 66, 67), they seem to represent the sort of innocent femininity that Victorian gentlemen such as Cable's soon-to-be friends, Howells and Twain, found charming or "delicious." Yet Cable undercuts their appeal with an emphasis on their shallowness. The considerable beauties and comforts of the plantation are not enough for them, and "for mere vagary, it pleased them not to be pleased" (*OCD,* 67). Then, when they try to stimulate their father into greater efforts to close the deal with Charlie, their charm becomes self-serving and manipulative: "when the native exuberance of a flock of ladies without a want or care burst out in laughter in the father's face, they spread their French eyes, rolled up their little hands, and with rigid wrists and mock vehemence vowed and vowed again that they only laughed at their misery, and should pine to death unless they could move to the sweet city" (*OCD,* 72). Although they later repent such behavior, their social ambition and their taste for frivolous pleasure seem central to the false values—the pride and the materialism—identified with the plantation ideal and that drive the main action.

Thus, if the river's destruction of Belles Demoiselles Plantation is seen as an act of divine judgment, the old man's individual sins, the sins of his caste—the Louisiana Creoles—and of the plantation South generally are figured in the condemnation. In this sense, although the cave-in device and the death-bed dénouement are highly melodramatic and sentimental, the story operates like a good deal of realistic fiction of the day, less detailing the actual than exposing the falsity of illusions. The special appeal and force of the story is not, however, social criticism alone. The exotic allure of the region and its people can be felt, entwined in the narrative voice along with the finely honed critical irony. And, the depiction of the De Charleaus anticipates the archetypes of Southern aristocracy found in twentieth-century fiction, such as Faulkner's Compsons and McCaslins. While an idealized image of the Old South was being earnestly resurrected in the work of Page, Harris, and others, Cable's moral concerns, his reading of history, and his perspective as a fascinated outsider led him to a different version of the Old South, a saga designed to counter fundamentally the other idealization. "Belles Demoiselles Plantation" is the first of several such antimyths Cable would write.

" 'Tite Poulette"

According to Arlin Turner, "'Tite Poulette" was "probably one of the first [stories] Cable wrote and possibly a reworking of the sketch in the *Picayune* entitled 'A Life-Ebbing Monography'" (1956, 59) in which a white man literally mixes his blood with that of his mulatto beloved in order to evade laws against racial intermarriage. By Cable's own account the story was written "in sympathy for the fate of the quadroon caste" (*NQ,* 12–13), feelings engendered by his research in the New Orleans archives. Despite considerable weaknesses in plot and point of view, the story remains interesting principally on the grounds of that sympathy.

"'Tite Poulette" is basically a sentimental love story in which race and caste are the temporary barriers to happiness. Kristian Koppig, a Dutch immigrant to New Orleans, is smitten by a beautiful young girl, known as 'Tite Poulette, whom he discovers to be the daughter of a quadroon woman, Zalli or Madame John. His phlegmatic shyness and the girl's reserve and caste status keep them apart, until Zalli suddenly provides documents proving that the girl is white, which permits Koppig and 'Tite Poulette to marry legally. Cable's handling of plot, character, and point of view in this story is labored and clumsy, perhaps indicative of its

early origins. 'Tite Poulette barely exists except as an object of desire and
pity, and while Zalli is given some complexity, Kristian Koppig is wood-
en and conventional, and both are primarily interesting as typifying
strands in a social and historical fabric. As in "'Sieur George" Cable presents most of the action indirectly, but rather than holding to a single
limited point of view felt as a perspective integral with the milieu, he
shifts the angle of narration repeatedly for no other apparent purpose
than to gain the effect of distancing. There are some effective touches of
irony and reflections of a character's thoughts in the narrative voice, but
these are offset by several instances of intrusive first-person commentary,
the ludicrous use of "thou" to reflect formality and purity in Koppig's
proposal and the painfully clunky deus ex machina conclusion. In sum,
there is simply too much straining after effect, made worse because so
much of it is devoted to creating tension in the insipid love plot, a signal
of what will be a recurrent weakness in Cable's art.

   Nevertheless, the treatment of race and caste in "'Tite Poulette" is
important in establishing the basic terms in which he would develop
these themes in later fiction. As in his best work, Cable establishes a
strong sense of historical and cultural context and presents his main
characters as typifying features of those contextual patterns, most significantly in this case the quadroon caste system represented by Zalli. The
tragic quadroon or octoroon woman, white enough in appearance to be
respectably loved by a white gentleman but forever barred from social
acceptance and marriage by her "taint" of African heritage, was a familiar literary figure in the nineteenth century, but Cable grounds his otherwise conventional plot in a complexly nuanced and realistic depiction of
the social institutions and attitudes, even some of the psychology, producing the tragic figures. The image of the quadroon balls of Zalli's
youth, for example, includes both a surface of exotic but decorous glamour and glimpses of uglier underlying realities, of coarse passions, violence, and racial injustice: Monsieur John had "more times than a few . . .
knocked down some long-haired and long-knifed rowdy . . . for looking
saucily at her" (*OCD,* 30). The patina of respectability gained by the
attendance of "many noble gentleman" fails to obscure the balls' role in
marketing concubines, the system of *plaçage* signalled by the presence of
the mothers and the example of Zalli's relationship with Monsieur John.

   Without directly stating the sexual aspect of this system, Cable clearly suggests it. Zalli's overt statement to her daughter that "Sin made *me*"
(*OCD,* 34) is part of a pervasive sense of impropriety linked to the
quadroon woman's past. When she changes out of her widow's weeds

and puts on makeup to work as a dancer on Sunday (performing the *Danse du Shawl*), there is certainly a hint of prostitution. Even more clearly, both mother and daughter are celebrated for their beauty, and whatever sexual coding may be implicit in their descriptions, especially 'Tite Poulette's "tall, straight, lithe" form and "great black eyes" (*OCD,* 29), the gesticulations of pubescent lads in the street and the references to "a Frenchman's eye for the beautiful" (*OCD,* 37) and "the loose New Orleans morals of over fifty years ago" (*OCD,* 28) in the contexts of appreciating that beauty suggest the women's erotic appeal.

All of this inuendo, moreover, seems continuous with Koppig's constant voyeurism from his dormer window across the street, which has him at one point "see . . . Madame John . . . dressing" (*OCD,* 46) and which is part of what Anna Elfenbein has characterized as a furtive "world of deceptive values" (38). The parallels between Koppig and Cable (Koppig's putative and Cable's actual German ancestry, their employment as accountants, their status as outsiders) may suggest that Koppig's voyeurism, like Miles Coverdale's in *The Blithedale Romance,* figures the author's anxiety about the intrusive role of the artist. It more certainly figures, like the keyhole peeping in "'Sieur George," the potentially corrupting fascination of interior glimpses in this "wicked city."

Cable's treatment of the plight of the quadroon caste, however, is finally less moral than social and economic. The central dilemma for Zalli is her condition of dependence and poverty. The balls provided her Monsieur John, and he provided her social standing and economic security while he was alive and even, for a time, after his death in the title she then assumed, Madame John, and the building he willed her (another of the Cable landmarks now known as Madame John's Legacy). When she sells the building and loses the money received in a bank failure, however, she is left with no capital but the depreciating commodity value of her beauty, no marketable skill other than an ability to please men and, therefore, no recourse but to return to the balls in their more degenerate form, dancing for pay at the Salle de Condé or, even worse, to continue the cycle of dependence by securing an "arrangement" for 'Tite Poulette.

As Elfenbein (41) has pointed out, Cable presents Zalli's plight as a situation affecting both quadroon and aristocratic white women when he observes that "as Madame John had been brought up tenderly, and done what she could to rear her daughter in the same mistaken way, with, of course, no more education than the ladies in society got, they knew nothing beyond music and embroidery" (*OCD,* 31). The bitterness of the quadroons' plight in Cable's presentation is that they suffer not only economic dependence and deprivation but also social exclusion—a marginality that in some ways seems more constricting than slavery. Raised to share tastes and social values of the white upper class, their natural social affinity is to those who scorn them both because of their racial mixture and because of their role as paramours. Further isolated by the protective custody first of their mothers and then of the men who keep them, they may have, as illustrated by the case of Zalli and her daughter, virtually no society but their own. Hence, at one point Zalli laments, "There is no place in this world for us poor women [quadroons]. I wish that we were either white or black" (*OCD*, 34).

The power of Cable's treatment of race and caste issues in " 'Tite Poulette" lies in his emphasis on specific social and economic conditions, for in other respects he exploits conventional "tragic mulatto" sympathy for women who seem white and identify with white social values but are made to suffer the stigma of black identity. For most readers, and for Cable himself, the contrived happy ending is especially weakening because it seems to shift the grounds of sympathy from the quadroon caste to the unfortunate white girl mistakenly trapped in their world. While Kristian Koppig does propose marriage to a girl he believes to be part black, he also expresses a "natural, and . . . [he thinks] proper horror of mixed blood" (*OCD*, 36) in a letter to his mother, which serves as an authorial disclaimer against miscegenation whatever else it may suggest about Koppig's conventionality. The young Dutchman is also, significantly, an outsider, not only to Creole New Orleans but to America as well.

Cable would return to the themes of miscegenation and caste with greater clarity and power in *The Grandsissimes* and *Madame Delphine*. Nevertheless, as a number of critics have argued, despite the sentimental plot and the hedged (or perhaps just uncertain) racial views,[17] " 'Tite Poulette" offers a sincere and powerfully sympathetic exposé of the social and economic plight of the quadroon caste in New Orleans. However safe the racial views and however distanced the exposé by the historical setting, Cable's moral indignation at social injustice and his willingness to present an unflattering view of Southern life are clear—the latter particularly unusual and courageous for a white Southern writer during Reconstruction.

"Jean-ah Poquelin"

Published in May 1875, "Jean-ah Poquelin," has been justly admired as one of Cable's best, most artfully crafted stories. Mark Twain especially enjoyed the dialect, calling it a "treat" to hear Cable read from the story and delighting to read it aloud himself.[18] Modern critics have found greater interest in Cable's use of Gothic elements and his treatment of the Creole-American conflict. The extraordinary power of the story lies in neither of those aspects alone but in the particular fusion of Gothic effects and historically grounded social criticism. A significant achievement in its own right, "Jean-ah Poquelin" also represents Cable's most important initial exploration of the Creole-American conflict that would be central to his masterpiece, *The Grandissimes.*

Like "'Sieur George" and "'Tite Poulette," "Jean-ah Poquelin" is structured as an indigenous mystery leading to a dramatic revelation, but the mystery is more natural and meaningful, less overtly an effect of narrative technique, and the surprise ending, while still somewhat melodramatic and sentimental, is more muted and deeply suggestive in its effect. The story begins in the years immediately after the Louisiana purchase, with Jean Marie Poquelin—formerly an "opulent" (*OCD,* 89) and respected indigo planter and slave trader—living defiantly "aloof from civilization" (*OCD,* 88) in a decaying colonial plantation house on the outskirts of New Orleans, surrounded by "one of the horridest marshes in a circuit of fifty miles." Jean's mysterious isolation had begun five years earlier when he returned from a slaving expedition to Africa without his ship and apparently without his beloved younger half-brother, Jacques. Because of his behavior and his brother's disappearance, foul play is suspected, and Jean becomes "a symbol of witchery, devilish crime, and hideous nursery fictions" (*OCD,* 92).

Eventually the city's expansion into the area known as the Faubourg St. Marie threatens Jean's privacy, leading to confrontations between the old Creole and the new American officials. The board of an American "Building and Improvement Company" send their young secretary, nicknamed Little White, to spy on him, but when he learns the old man's secret, he sympathizes with him and refuses to reveal it. The citizens organize a *charivari* (shivaree) to drive Jean out, but they instead find him dead and thereby, with Little White's help, learn the secret of his isolation: Jean has been hiding and protecting his brother who returned from Africa a leper. In the final scene Jacques and the Poquelins' mute African slave, bearing Jean's coffin on his shoulder, head into the swamp for a leper colony, the Terre aux Lépreux.

The story's obvious Gothic elements—the "haunted mansion," the wild and remote setting, the hints of the supernatural, and the gloomy atmosphere—are conventional, but their use, linked to a specific physical and historical locale, suggests less the psychological and metaphysical

explorations of Poe's "The Fall of the House of Usher," with which
Cable's story has been compared, than the probing at sociopolitical "terrors" in Hawthorne's "My Kinsman, Major Molineux" and Melville's
"Benito Cereno."[19] The evocation of a communal point of view, the clash
of old and new orders, and Jean's ambivalent status in the community's
eyes invite comparison even more obviously with Faulkner's "A Rose for
Emily." One effect of the Gothic elements in all of these stories, including Cable's, is to invest the action and characters with mythic or symbolic values. "Jean-ah Poquelin" has very much the quality of a "primal"
Louisiana legend, embodying fundamental beliefs and values beyond the
simpler superstitions of the Gothic apparatus. Cable's use of the natural
environment, not only to create the atmosphere of mystery and terror
but also to suggest a more profound elemental struggle underlying the
social conflict, contributes a great deal to this legendary quality, adding a
thread of frontier romance to the Gothic fabric.

The social issues of the story center in the Creole-American conflict
Cable establishes in the opening paragraph. Insofar as the Creoles are
represented "still kicking at such vile innovations as trial by jury,
American dances, antismuggling laws, and the printing of the governor's proclamation in English" (*OCD,* 88), they are represented as almost
mindlessly resistant to even the most trivial change, upholding traditions
of dubious value, mostly fearful at losing their "footing" in the coming
"crevasse of immigration." Cable is even more unflattering in characterizing the Creoles as superstitious and, therefore, like "the incoming lower
class of superstitious Germans, Irish, Sicilians, and others" (*OCD,* 103),
given to scapegoating Jean for real or imagined bad fortune. The *charivari,* which Cable suggests is little more than a historical euphemism for
mob, is identified as a Creole custom and led by Creoles—first by the
drunken, ironically named Bienvenu and then by "one huge fellow . . .
who looks capable of any villainy" and in "the Creole *patois*" appeals to
the crowd's sense of honor and "rights" (*OCD,* 120).

Contrasted with this general sense of the Creoles as backward, superstitious, and intolerant, the American flood is associated with progress,
which Cable seems generally to favor, but not without reservations. As a
student of the Constitution, he certainly approved the political changes
lamented by the Creoles, and the conversion of Jean's marshy, "jungly
plain" (*OCD,* 88) into "sweet, dry" (*OCD,* 102) smelling fields and then
"bright new houses" also seems an improvement. There are also generally positive representations of American manners, not only in the heroic
Little White but also in the "patient" and "conciliatory" (*OCD,* 97)

American governor. Even he, however, is insensitive enough to allude to the rumors about Jean's house, and the city official Jean visits next is flippant and smug. Moreover, in the Building and Improvement Company Cable depicts both the speculative economics and dubious ethicality underlying the urban boom.

The Building and Improvement Company, whose name suggests both the fact and idealized rationale of its commercial existence, has "not yet got its charter, 'but was going to,'" and has "not, indeed, any tangible capital yet, 'but was going to have some'" (*OCD,* 104). The proposal to send Little White to spy on Jean is rationalized on the grounds that the board's interest in the project is "not altogether a selfish one," that they "are working in the public interest (the board smiled knowingly)" if they "employ all possible means to oust this old nuisance from among" them. Finally, when the community resorts to violent mob action, it is "certain Américains" (*OCD,* 113) who suggest the idea. That these Americans may be some of the coarser upriver crowd, whose national traditions include tarring and feathering and riding on a rail, suggests that Cable's criticisms are directed more against certain segments of the society than the society as a whole.

The issues of the Creole-American conflict are more complexly figured in the character of Jean Poquelin. The key aspect of his character is the ironically shifting ground of his status in the "public regard." In his prime, "high in the esteem of his small, proud circle of exclusively male acquaintances in the old city," he seems like an early explorer or pioneer, "a bold, frank, impetuous, chivalric adventurer" (*OCD,* 90). By contrast, Jacques is "a gentle, studious, book-loving recluse," and when Jean meets the governor his quality as a man of action is again emphasized, making him seem in his fierce independence and in his resistance to what seems a vulgarized ideal of progress more admirable than his tormentors. Contrasted with the intolerant and violent parochialism of both the latter-day Creoles and the commercial Americans, his devotion to his brother seems saintly.

At the same time, these pioneer qualities bear the seeds of his moral and material decay. Too much of a "roving character" (*OCD,* 91) to manage his father's plantation (while his brother is "too apathetic" to rescue it), Jean adventurously gambles away all but one of his African slaves. Then, like the legendary pirate Jean Lafitte, he boldly turns to smuggling and slave trading without a loss of public standing when the indigo market collapses: "what harm could he see in it? The whole people said it was vitally necessary, and to minister to a vital public necessity—good enough, certainly, and so he laid up many a doubloon, that made him none the worse in the public regard." The wrong signalled in this language, paralleling the self-serving rationalizations of the Building and Improvement Company, is not just the commerce in human flesh, although Cable clearly disapproves of slavery, but the moral evasion of justifying actions on the grounds of social acceptance, the easy accommodation between vice and public necessity.

Jacques's contracting leprosy in Africa, then, seems to symbolize a curse or penalty of sin associated with slavery both for Jean and for the Creole society that condones the practice. Ironically figured in Jacques's "whiteness" and in the smell of death, this is the Hawthornean "imprint of some great grief" recognized by the governor as "an almost imperceptible veil" (*OCD,* 95) over Jean's countenance and borne as a set of ironic misperceptions. Although branded as a "Cain" by the community, he is, as Alice Hall Petry points out, "literally his 'brother's keeper' " (99), and his stubborn isolation, which the Creoles join in condemning as "unneighborly" (*OCD,* 102), mirrors their own exclusiveness and backwardness. Even as he is redeemed, first in Little White's and then in the community's and the reader's eyes, there remains the final ironic symbolism of his being borne to the ultimate isolation of a grave in the Terre aux Lépreux on the shoulder of his last African slave, both "mute" with respect to their "great grief," both veiled before the "public regard."

Cable uses Gothic elements in "Jean-ah Poquelin," then, to expose horrors in Creole society and to some degree in the American community as well. Cable is careful, however, in his treatment of both communities to distinguish between the "charitable few" and the narrow-minded "many," and this is a major function of Little White. Described as "a mild, kind-hearted little man, who, nevertheless, ha[s] no fear of anything, unless it [is] the fear of being unkind" (*OCD,* 106), he seems not only like Kristian Koppig to resemble his author, but also to represent the best of the new American order. In pointed contrast with the Poquelin bachelors, Little White enjoys the support, concern, and counsel of his wife, Patty. Perhaps because of this humanizing influence (a standard role for women in the literature of this era), he is able to be a leader in the party of progress and, at the same time, to understand and sympathize with the old order, even adopt "Creole custom" (*OCD,* 113) as when he and his wife watch the sunset from their doorstep.

Although another of Cable's voyeurs, Little White only agrees to spy on Jean "for reasons of [his] own" (*OCD,* 106), and when he learns Jean's secret he refuses either to persecute him or to permit the knowledge to be used against him. Instead, he tries to ward off Jean's attackers and challenges all suspicions and superstitions with demands for "authority" (*OCD,* 110)—that is, for reason and facts. For this advocacy he suffers the same "disrelish and suspicion" that previously fell on Jean alone, anticipating the ostracism Cable would experience in the 1880s for championing the cause of the freedman. If Jean Poquelin represents for Cable an inherent nobility and strength in the older Creole culture, he also symbolizes its decay, and Little White, a different kind of individualist with a different source of strength, seems to offer greater hope for the future.

Thus, insofar as Cable's message in "Jean-ah Poquelin" finally points beyond the Creole community and the Creole-American conflict to the unreconstructed South generally, he offers a subtle hint about the curse of slavery, a much stronger warning about the dangers of moral and political isolation, and an appeal for persons of reason and goodwill to try to lead or otherwise deflect the unthinking mob. Characterized by Louis Rubin as "perhaps the most somber of all the stories of *Old Creole Days*" (56), it is also one of the most political, focusing not just on social ills but on the dynamics of public opinion and the necessity of moral leadership. Not yet as fully developed as in *The Grandissimes* or as in the civil rights arguments of the next decade, Cable's thinking on the Southern problem in "Jean-ah Poquelin" was already beginning to assume its essential shape.

Other Tales

The last three of Cable's early stories to be published—"Madame Délicieuse" (August 1875), "Café des Exilés" (March 1876), and "Posson Jone'" (April 1876)—have attracted the least critical interest, although the third was enormously popular in the author's day and may be the most artistically satisfying of the entire group. "Madame Délicieuse" and "Café des Exilés" are excessively sentimental, but unlike "'Tite Poulette" they offer little serious social commentary, which accounts a great deal for their critical neglect. None of the three is likely to hold much interest for modern readers, but for students of Cable's work there are features worth more careful examination.

"Madame Délicieuse" was a particular favorite of many of Cable's early readers, including Richard Watson Gilder, H. H. Boyesen, and Edmund Gosse, and Cable himself described it the "best foot" to put forward in a later collection of the stories.[20] The central action concerns a feud between an aristocratic Creole, General Hercule Mossy de Villi-vicencio, and his scientist son, Dr. Mossy, and the efforts of Madame Délicieuse to reconcile them. For the most part, the general presents an unusually positive image of aristocratic Creole masculinity, unqualified by the sorts of ancestral and moral corruptions attached to Colonel De Charleau and Jean Poquelin. When he stands for election, however, Cable clearly uses him to satirize the modes of Creole politics, not only the mindless opposition to "Yankee ideas" (*OCD*, 139) but also the political discussions that seem so much querulous, alcohol-fortified venting. When Madame Délicieuse anonymously attacks the general in an article titled "The Crayfish-Eaters' Ticket," he demands settlement on the field of honor. In short, the Creoles' efforts at political resistance to the American domination are shown to be ridiculously anachronistic and parochial, and except for the threat of violence, mostly pompous strutting.

The most intriguing feature of Cable's political satire in "Madame Délicieuse," however, is the androgynous characterization of both Dr. Mossy and Madame Délicieuse. Whereas his father is characterized by "exterior display" (*OCD*, 125), Dr. Mossy is "small, sedate" (*OCD*, 124), learned, preoccupied with his studies but open to American and other outside influence, and almost saintlike in his concern for the poor and courageous in treating the victims of disease. Because he is opposed to physical combat, he does not measure up to the general's militaristic standard of courage and manhood, and their estrangement deepens when Dr. Mossy refuses to defend his father's honor in a duel. As if to underscore this question of Dr. Mossy's "manhood," Cable repeatedly identifies his "feminine" characteristics, from his smile that is "very sweet and rare on a man's mouth" (124), his kissing his father "like a little wife" (140), to his blushing at the end "for the thousandth" (161) time.

Madame Délicieuse also violates gender stereotype, for while she can certainly play the role of the dark-eyed, bewitching Creole coquette sug-gested by her name, she is also pointedly a strong, independent woman. She is depicted as intelligent, open to the new American ways, interested in politics, and, most important, able to exercise power, not only among the "cluster of Creole beauties" but over "the *whole* city" (*OCD*, 127) and especially over the general. As a woman she cannot vote, but she effec-tively challenges and defeats the Villivicencio ticket with her article. Moreover, where her first marriage was arranged for her, she is the manipulating agent of her second marriage to Dr. Mossy, and thus when the "half-priest, half-woman" (*OCD*, 153) defeats the general in the con-test for the hand of the Creole "queen," his triumph is significantly

qualified by her assistance. In her Cable represents a potential for beneficent female power, superior in force and strategy to the general's
pompous militarism and complementary and bolstering to the doctor's
more feeble virtuousness.

It should also be noted that, like Kristian Koppig and Little White
(and perhaps also Jacques Poquelin), Dr. Mossy seems to reflect aspects
of Cable's own character and circumstances. Diminutive and delicate-
featured, Cable hardly fit the stereotype of the rugged soldier, and he
was certainly conscious of the difference when he fought in the Civil
War. He also shared Dr. Mossy's interest in biological study, and the
political debates in "Madame Délicieuse" may reflect Cable's discussions
in the William C. Black offices. By themselves, these autobiographical
parallels are too general or slight to ground much of an argument about
Cable's attitude toward his father (who also marched proudly in military
parades) or about his sexual security, but they do fit an emerging pattern
of non-Creole characters confronting the bigotry and violence of the old
Creole order, using reason, learning, and moral refinement in lieu of
physical strength. From the outset, Cable's critique of Creole and
Southern society is deeply centered in his own sensibility.

As Arlin Turner has observed (1956, 62), "Café des Exilés" differs
from the other stories in focusing on Spanish rather than French Creole
characters and in using overt first-person narration. The story concerns a
group of refugees from revolutions in Barbados, Martinique, Santo
Domingo, and Cuba who gather in New Orleans at the café of Monsieur
D'Hemecourt in the 1830s to smoke, imbibe nonalcoholic fruit drinks,
reminisce about their homelands, and conspire to smuggle arms to the
Antilles. Two among the group, Major Galahad Shaughnessy and
Manuel Mazarro, vie for the affections of the café owner's daughter,
Pauline, the former winning the courtship and the latter losing his life as
well when he betrays the exiles' conspiracy. Cable solidly grounds the
story's milieu with concrete detail, but he does not directly address the
political or social issues underlying this context. The "double-threaded
plot" (Turner 1956, 62; Petry, 49), labored by narrative indirection and
overuse of various literally transcribed dialects, is difficult to follow and
heavily sentimental. Sensuous descriptions of the café, the garden, and
especially Pauline, figured as both Mary and Eve, drench the atmosphere
with a luxuriant but ultimately cloying tropicality.

Philip Butcher has found "rewards for the student of Cable's work" in
the pattern of "mixed-marriage" as, he argues, represented in the union
between the Celtic Major Shaughnessy and the French-Spanish Creole

Pauline D'Hemecourt,[21] but the most interesting feature of "Café des Exilés" is its narrative technique, which Alice Hall Petry describes as "virtually a tour de force" (49). More than any of the other early tales, "Café des Exilés" focuses attention on both the storyteller and storytelling. In addition to the narrator's frequent references to his own storytelling role, reminiscing—telling and retelling tales of home—is the central social activity in the café. The central plot conflicts also turn on storytelling: Mazarro tells lies to alienate Galahad Shaughnessy from D'Hemecourt and his daughter, and the exiles cover their plot to smuggle guns with the fiction of the Spanish-American "funeral" society meetings, which is exposed by Mazarro's revealing their plans to the police.

The recurring emphasis in this storytelling is the creation of illusion and the corollary repression of unpleasant realities. At the outset, the narrator finds evoking romantic memories of the old café "pleasanter far" (*OCD*, 163) than facing the more mundane reality of a "Shoo-fly Coffeehouse" that may have replaced it, and in the café itself Old D'Hemecourt's injunctions against "strong drink and high words" (*OCD*, 167) squelches heated political debates and replaces them with "draughts" that will make the refugee "see his home among the cocoa palms." That these injunctions are designed to enhance Pauline's social standing and marriageability and that she is turned into a kind of religious icon suggest the sublimation of sexual passion in gentility, spirituality, and marriage.

Part of this emphasis on narrative acts is playful self-reflection, as when the narrator observes that Major Shaughnessy (like Cable) "knows the history of every old house in the French Quarter, or, if he happens not to know a true one, he can make one up as he goes along" (*OCD*, 198). More seriously, just below the surface of nostalgia and dreamy reverie, unredeemable in the cult worship of the feminine ideal, lies the very real violence first of slavery and revolt in the exiles' past, then of the gun-smuggling conspiracy, then of the murder of the traitorous Mazarro. The exiles, like Mazarro, are shown to be victims of the illusions they create, for had they not been "too sly about" their smuggling and "come out flat and said what [they] were doing" (*OCD*, 197) they would have been able to ship their guns unmolested. None of this may make "Café des Exilés" more palatable to contemporary readers, but it does suggest a subtle self-consciousness of Cable's art and the way even the weakest of these early efforts incorporated a form of indirect social critique in the manner of the telling if not in the content of the story told.

"Posson Jone'" was the most difficult of the early stories for Cable to place, rejected first by Gilder for *Scribner's Monthly* and then by three other periodicals before being accepted by *Appleton's Journal.* Both Turner and Louis Rubin point to the irony of this difficulty as suggesting the kind of editorial attitudes Cable had to deal with and their likely effect on his art. What now seems a well-told, relatively innocuous example of frontier humor was rejected for the most part because it portrayed a drunken clergyman and because, as *Harper's* editor H. M. Alden wrote, "the disagreeable aspects of human nature are made prominent, & the story leaves an unpleasant impression on the mind of the reader" (quoted in Turner 1956, 63). Nevertheless, the use of varied dialects and the tightly controlled dramatic action made "Posson Jone'" immediately popular with readers and later with audiences on Cable's reading tours.

The central character is a gigantic backwoods preacher from West Florida, Jimmy Jones, who on his first and only visit to New Orleans with his "body sarvant," Colossus of Rhodes, and with $5,000 of Smyrny Church money under his hat, meets a feckless, opportunistic young Creole, Jules St.-Ange, and in short order finds himself in a gambling house, drunk, missing the money, involved in a riot, and finally locked up in the *calaboza.* As it turns out, Colossus has saved his master by taking the money and returning it as they leave, and Jules is so impressed by the parson's zeal, strength, and integrity that after Jones refuses his offer of using the Creole's gambling winnings to replace the lost church funds, he is moved to repay all his own debts and become henceforth an honest man.

Much of Cable's satire is clearly aimed at both the expedient morality of the "elegant little heathen" (*OCD,* 199) but still professedly Catholic Jules and the uselessly formulaic and naive religiosity of the uneducated and Protestant Parson Jones. Some critics have found it surprising that the supposedly staid Sunday-school teacher should ridicule the views of a Protestant clergyman, including his sabbatarianism, but as a bookish, refined Presbyterian, Cable attacked Protestant fundamentalism as early as the "Drop Shot" articles and had no taste for uneducated evangelicals. As Alice Hall Petry argues, both the Creole and the American are shown to become better, "true" Christians by the action of a genuine Providence operating through their moral influence on each other, and this nondoctrinal religious message is consistent with the practical, applied Christianity Cable formulated later in *The Busy Man's Bible.*

The more interesting feature of the story is the use of "broad comedy" (Turner 1956, 63) that critics have seen as a departure from the earlier tales. Reminiscent of the frontier humor of A. B. Longstreet, Thomas Bangs Thorpe, and Mark Twain, the burlesque tone is appropriate to the story's focus (another departure) on the rowdier portion of Americans and other immigrants pouring into New Orleans a decade after the Louisiana Purchase. New Orleans is depicted as a wicked city, but the onus falls not only on the Creoles but also on the "*Américains, too—* more's the shame—from the upper rivers" who gather on Sunday to watch a bullfight and "who will not keep their seats, who ply the bottle, and who will get home by and by and tell how wicked Sodom is" (*OCD,* 215). In the riot that ensues—clearly a breakdown of social order, a reversion to a state of brutal, violent, elemental passion symbolized by the hurricane of the night before and by the tiger and the buffalo—the Americans are portrayed as boorish *provocateurs.* When Parson Jones begins his drunken preaching, the narrator prays, "Ah, kind Lord, for a special Providence now! The men of his own nation—men from the land of the open English Bible and temperance cup and song are cheering him on to mad disgrace" (*OCD,* 216–17).

Beyond the religious message, Cable undermines a series of stereotypes with an ironic play of "civilized" values and "natural" proclivities. The Congo Plains, for example, where slaves were permitted to congregate and dance and, hence, associated in the Europeans' minds with primitive revels, is where the famed Cayetano's circus performed for civilized New Orleanians "Sunday after Sunday." In the story, a fight between "impotent" beasts serves as an alternative entertainment, but the pious preacher is "wilder, with the cup of the wicked, than any beast" (*OCD,* 218). Similarly, Colossus, who is described as "very black and grotesque" (*OCD,* 204), emerges as the most responsible, "best" man in the cast of characters, the "hero of the moment" (*OCD,* 228) in the final dramatic scene, belying the belief shared by both Parson Jones and Jules St.-Ange that "all niggahs will steal" (*OCD,* 224) and that "a nigger cannot be as good as a white man" (*OCD,* 220). In sum, the beasts are tame, the "civilized" are savage, and the "savage" are moral; the worldly and corrupt Creole learns simple honesty, and the naive, pious man of God becomes a drunken rowdy and from his sins gains wisdom.

In its range of characterizations "Posson Jone'" may be the most richly textured of the early stories, and it remains readable and interesting. Although different from the others in its mode of humor, it, like them, subtly weaves social commentary into the fabric of its materials and manner of presentation.

Book Publication

The gathering of these first seven stories for publication as a book was, of course, an important step in the development of Cable's career as an author. He had received little money from the magazines for his work, and while short-story collections were (as they are still) risky ventures, a published book offered prospects of greater remuneration as well as a wider, more substantial reputation. Although by 1875 Cable had met and established what would be strong and lasting relationships with Gilder, Roswell Smith, Robert Underwood Johnson, and others at Scribners, he was unable to interest them or several other publishing houses in bringing out a collection of his Creole stories until the Norwegian poet, novelist, and Cornell University professor Hjalmar Hjorth Boyesen, without Cable's knowledge, essentially underwrote the publication costs. Boyesen had been impressed by Cable's stories, especially "Madame Délicieuse," and had taught them in his literature classes. In 1877 he began a correspondence with Cable that lasted for many years in which the two explored literary ideas and Cable received much valuable advice and encouragement. *Old Creole Days* appeared in May 1879 and, somewhat to the surprise of both Cable and his publishers, sold remarkably well, the first thousand copies going in only three months.

Initial reviews of *Old Creole Days* both in and out of New Orleans were overwhelmingly favorable. The accuracy of Cable's depictions of Creole character and speech was praised by the New Orleans newspapers, except, most notably *L'Abeille,* the French-language paper, and reviewers generally were enchanted by the new and exotic materials, the engagingly whimsical style, and the apparent eye and ear for realistic detail. As Arlin Turner observes, "The reviewers of *Old Creole Days* did not agree on the merits or the faults singled out, but they all sensed that it was a significant addition to American fiction" (1956, 87).

A recurring theme in some of the early reviews—picked up and expanded by Turner, Louis Rubin, and other more recent critics—is that *Old Creole Days* offered promise of a different, more significantly social fiction to come. Turner's pointing to the experimental quality of the stories—the sense of Cable trying out different ways of managing plot, character, narrative angle, and theme—is consistent with this view, suggesting that whatever their merits the stories represent possibilities not yet fully realized. This is not a charge that Cable's artistic weaknesses undermine his strengths, but that those strengths are not employed to sufficiently serious or significant effect. Rubin, for example, noting that "the art of the stories in *Old Creole Days* is founded upon realistic social observation," specifically identifies what they lack as "any important attempt at social *criticism*" (59).

This sense of the limitations of *Old Creole Days* is certainly defensible, but it also arguably represents an attempt to convert the author's social project to the critic's sense of what that should be. In writing the stories for *Old Creole Days* Cable had a strongly overarching sense of the milieu. That is, an interest in range and coverage is recognizable in the collection, as if the separately published stories were to some degree conceived as parts of a whole ("Bibi" would have admirably rounded out the set of character portraits), producing what Rubin recognizes as "a densely packed social panorama of class and caste" (59) in which "in embryo" most of his later themes are treated.

While *Old Creole Days* does not have the unity of such later short-story collections as *Winesburg, Ohio, In Our Time,* or *Go Down, Moses,* there is a measure of coherency in the whole gained in part from the consistently rendered, inescapable *presence* of the milieu and from the manner or voice of the narrative guide. The special appeal of *Old Creole Days* lies in the reader's engagement with that milieu—the place and the people—mediated by the guide's particular combination of attraction to the sensual and exotic, love of mystery, fascination with history, eye and ear for characterizing detail, moral and intellectual rigor, and rather exquisite—sometimes playful, sometimes savage—sense of irony. Social and political issues are thus addressed in the stories, part of both the milieu and the narrative sensibility, but not on the narrower grounds of reforming zeal or social criticism alone. For all the imperfections of some of the individual stories, the complex engagement suggested earlier represents Cable's most significant literary effect.

Chapter Three
The Grandissimes

While Cable's first stories established his literary reputation and stimulated his ambition, they did not assure his career as a full-time writer. The magazines simply did not pay enough for short fiction to support a family that had grown to include four children by 1875 (five by 1877). The house he began building on Eighth Street in 1876 to accommodate this expansion was a major expense, and the care of his mother and Louise's frequent ill-health added to his concerns. He derived income from Black's cotton house, the New Orleans Cotton Exchange and the National Cotton Exchange, and when he suggested reducing his workload to make time for writing, his salary was raised. Consequently, for three years after the final submission of "Posson Jone'," the little time Cable could carve out for literary effort in the early morning and late evening was devoted primarily to reading and to plans for a novel, *The Grandissimes*.[1]

Cable later credited his family physician, J. Dickson Bruns, with giving him the necessary push to begin work on the novel, but more significant stimulus came from his correspondence with H. H. Boyesen ("After-Thoughts," 17–18). Boyesen's enthusiastic praise certainly helped sustain Cable's confidence, and in commenting on his own literary aims and ideas he stimulated Cable to respond in kind and thus to develop a surer sense of literary purpose. Boyesen shared with Cable a taste for romance and the sense of New Orleans's unique potential for literary treatment, but both were also influenced by the literary realism championed by William Dean Howells. They agreed that fiction should have serious purpose, that, as Cable wrote, "the great problem of a novel should be something beyond and above the mere puzzle of the plot, something great and thought-compelling, that teaches without telling, that brings to view without pointing, that guides without leading and allures without fatiguing."[2] In recommending the Russian novelist Ivan Turgenev to Cable, Boyesen noted that his work would provide "many superb hints of how to manage dramatically a social problem." Cable responded that he had already read *Smoke* (1867), and while he expected further reading of Turgenev would "train" him more, "Smoke did much." Robert O. Stephens has argued that the Russian author's influence is indeed apparent in *The Grandissimes,* most noticeably in the use of a "scenic method" in which "his backgrounds work with his foregrounds" and character rather than plot are used to epitomize social ideas.[3] Clearly the problem of conveying a "moral effect" (that is, a serious or social purpose) without forcing it on the reader (Turner 1951, 359) was a central concern as Cable was writing his first novel.

Cable submitted the initial drafts of *The Grandissimes* to Gilder in the summer of 1878. His progress on the novel had been hampered by bouts of ill-health, concerns over money, and the demands of the counting room. Then, in early October, in the midst of one of New Orleans's most severe yellow-fever epidemics, nearly the whole of the Cable household became ill, and Cable lost his only son, George Junior, to the disease. His sister's husband, James Cox, also died, leaving her and her three children to be supported by Cable's already overstretched resources. When he resumed work on the novel, he faced not only completing it but many more requests for revision than had been made with any of the earlier stories. In response to these requests (primarily from Gilder's assistant editor, Robert Underwood Johnson, and readers Irwin Russell and Mrs. Sophia Bledsoe, both ardent Southerners) Cable generally stuck to his sense of Louisiana history and social nuance but followed advice for greater clarity and for reducing the kind of overt moralizing or "pamphleteering" (Turner 1956, 98), as Johnson put it, that he had described to Boyesen as objectionable. *The Grandissimes* was serialized in *Scribner's Monthly* beginning in November 1879 and appeared as a book in October 1880.

The Creole Moment and Milieu

Boyesen's observation that *The Grandissimes* promised to be "the kind of novel which the Germans call a 'Kulturroman,' a novel in which the struggling forces of opposing civilizations crystalize & in which they find their enduring monument" (Turner 1951, 346) has frequently served as a starting point for critical discussions of the novel, for certainly Cable's choice of historical context and moment is a major strength in the work. The main action is set in 1803–1804, the year in which the Louisiana territory was transferred from French to U.S. authority, and Cable elaborately details the social and historical conditions of early Louisiana, emphasizing historical process and the possibility of social change. Moreover, he uses the conflicts of this transition both for dramatic effect and as a paradigm for the issues of conflict and transition in the South generally after the Civil War. In a sense, *The Grandissimes* offers the kind of "moral history" Michael Colacurcio finds in Hawthorne's early tales, an "explicitly fictional moment of conflict or choice, derived from and referable back to some actuality, but generalized and dramatized in such a way as to stand for the limits of perception or experience at a certain critical moment in the historical past,"[4] limits that bear significantly on the present.

Cable's central device for introducing Louisiana's colonial history and complex social arrangements is to establish a naive German-American immigrant, Joseph Frowenfeld, as the novel's center of consciousness. As a recent arrival whose first days in the city are spent in a feverish delirium, Frowenfeld finds his unfamiliar, exotic milieu, as do most readers, a baffling, heavily masked mystery, "a thick mist of strange names, places and events" over which shines "a light of romance."[5] Frowenfeld's initiation into the mysteries of the region then becomes the reader's initiation as well, and this is important not only in recording the allure of the "mist" but also, as Charles Swann[6] and Tipping Schölin[7] have argued, in exposing the role of tradition and legend, mythmaking and storytelling in the shaping of social and historical consciousness, particularly in the South. A similar effect is produced by the various identity confusions, role-playing, concerns with honor and appearance, coquetry, and other veilings of true feelings that drive the plot: apart from evoking mystery and suspense, the masking centers thematically on the social construction of identity. In short, Cable's habits of narrative indirection are here intricately grounded, felt, as in *Old Creole Days,* to be part of the milieu, but also central to the novel's social and historical themes.

The richness of detail—historical, social, cultural, natural—is also one of the novel's most striking features. Cable's primary sources for the novel were the *Relations* of the early French explorers and especially Charles Gayarré's *History of Louisiana* (1849–66). Nearly all the important names of the colonial and early national period—Iberville, Bienville, the Marquis de Vaudreuil, "Cruel" O'Reilly, Casa Calvo, Boré, Girod, Madame Pontalba, the Lafitte brothers—are mentioned and some portion of their stories told. The new American governor, William Claiborne, is even given a brief cameo role, riding with the novel's hero in the Place d'Armes and then receiving political advice from him. Cable also grounds historically the patterns of racial mixing and the subsequent concerns with racial and ancestral purity in the original shortage of white women for the French soldiers, the taking of Indian and then

African wives and mistresses, the importing of "house of correction" girls and then the more respectable *filles à la cassette.* In addition, specific issues of the American takeover—the use of English in the courts and in public documents, the legality of land titles granted under Spanish authority, the initial prohibition of the slave trade—are made central to the novel's main action.

Cable establishes a tone of authenticity with these details, but he also weaves into them the sentimental love stories and epic conflicts of his fictional characters (with whimsically aristocratic, classical, or allegorical names like Zephyr, Epaminondas, Demosthenes, Achille, Mandarin, Aurora, Agricola, Honoré) in such a way as to construct that history—as does Gayarré—in terms of a romance or saga.[8] But, unlike Gayarré's celebration of Gallic virtues, Cable's Creole civilization is characterized by pride—a perverse and arrogant loyalty to blood lines, however ambiguous, and presumptions of aristocratic status, however dubious.

Cable gains a similar blend of realism and romance through his record of social and cultural detail, for the inherent novelty of the region, as in *Old Creole Days,* generates romantic feeling. Whenever the Creoles are depicted in some gathering, such as in the evening promenade on the Place d'Armes, at the *fête de grandpère,* seeking employment at the apothecary's shop, or talking politics at the Veau-Qui-Tête or Maspero's, Cable records the peculiarities of manners, custom, and appearance with the accuracy of a "sociologist,"[9] as Edmund Wilson describes him, but also with a clear sense of the Creoles' picturesque charm. The use of dialect, including Creole English, Creole French, Black English, and various shadings of these, adds authenticity, differentiates individual characters, and suffuses the whole with the sounds of a foreign land. While many readers have complained of the difficulty of deciphering some of his transcriptions, Cable for the most part avoids the excesses common to much of the dialect writing during this period, and readers such as Howells and Twain were once again enchanted by the exotic phrasing of the Creole ladies. He also includes a number of Creole slave songs, some with accompanying musical scores, that he had gathered with the help of H. E. Krehbiel, music editor of the New York *Tribune,* and which he was known to love to perform. These, along with the descriptions of Sunday dances on the Congo Plain, the numerous references to voodoo practices and lore, and the shadowy status of the quadroons, diversify and color the cultural texture of the work.

Finally, perhaps because New Orleans was yet a small town in 1803, there is less attention to architecture in *The Grandissimes* than in *Old*

Creole Days, but the descriptions of the natural environment make an essential contribution to the sense of the milieu. Cable again gains authenticity by carefully mapping the region, recording the layout of streets, river bends, bayous, marshes, forests, islands and bays and also by scattering meteorological data throughout the text. Landscape descriptions also contribute an atmosphere of "weird," "dream-like" (*G,* 9), and slightly forbidding beauty, such as that the Frowenfelds behold on their journey up the Mississippi, "a land hung in mourning, darkened by gigantic cypresses, submerged; a land of reptiles, silence, shadow, decay." Although there are numerous other scenes of lush but more conventional beauty—tropical verdure and flowers, birds both familiar and exotic—the sense of the primordial in the surrounding swamps and marshes is the predominant note, a recurring reminder that New Orleans was yet on a remote edge of civilization, still something of a frontier town, its society and culture shaped by contact with the wilderness. Taken together, the effect of this thick and subtle detailing of the milieu is to provide something more than the "rococo stage set"[10] that Wallace Stegner found in Cable's work, for in *The Grandissimes,* at least, these elements of background are continuous with the novel's main action and political themes.

Anatomizing Creole Character

As Cable would characterize it later, the main plot of *The Grandissimes* is "little more than the very old and familiar one of a feud between two families, the course of true love fretting its way through, and the titles of hero and heroine open to competition between a man and his friend for the one and a mother and daughter for the other" ("After-Thoughts," 17). The feud begins with two of Iberville's soldiers, Epaminondas Fusilier and Demosthenes De Grapion, competing for the hand of a Natchez-Tchoupitoulas princess, Lufki-Humma, and worsens when Agricola Fusilier, a descendant of the winner, kills the husband of the last of the De Grapion line, Aurora Nancanou, in a duel over charges of cheating after M. Nancanou lost the De Grapion estates in a card game. When the leader of the Fusilier-Grandissime clan, Honoré Grandissime, meets Aurora at a *bal masqué* in the opening chapter, they are mutually smitten, but their love is "fretted" first by confusions of identity and then by the fact that Aurora and her daughter, Clotilde, are impoverished while their former lands are held by the hated Grandissimes under Honoré's management.

Joseph Frowenfeld, after recovering from the yellow fever that destroys the rest of his family, becomes friends with Honoré, establishes himself as an apothecary, and obliquely courts Clotilde, who is admired in turn by Charlie Keene, Frowenfeld's consumptive doctor. That Aurora's landlord is the hero's half-brother, Honoré, f.m.c. (free man of color),[11] adds further complications, as does the vendetta of a freed quadroon and voodoo savant, Palmyre Philosophe, against Agricola Fusilier. Palmyre, who was Aurora's childhood servant and playmate, is hopelessly infatuated with the white Honoré (while the f.m.c. is similarly devoted to her), and she hates Agricola for having separated her from the Grandissime household and forcing her to marry a majestic slave, Bras-Coupé. While the relationship of Palmyre and Honoré, f.m.c., ends tragically with her exile and his suicide in France, Joseph and Clotilde and Honoré and Aurora become happily betrothed.

As with several of the *Old Creole Days* stories, this conventional and complicated love plot is less interesting than Cable's representation of Creole character, and the accuracy and fairness of his depiction has been a frequent concern of critics from the outset.[12] While one Southern writer, Grace King, began her literary career specifically to correct and improve the image of the Creoles Cable created, most critics—including many Creoles of his own day—have defended the general accuracy of his portrayal, however uncomplimentary. His ambivalence about the Creoles and their world—he was sensually attracted but morally disapproving— has been frequently noted, but as Merrill Skaggs points out, so definitive was the image Cable created—however condescending and stereotypical—most subsequent literary representations essentially replicated it, even those of Grace King (Skaggs, 177).

In *The Grandissimes,* as in *Old Creole Days,* Cable frequently calls attention to the Creoles' physical attractiveness, particularly the appeal of the exotic "otherness" of their Gallic-Latin looks for Anglo-Saxon eyes (those of Frowenfeld, Cable, and many *Scribner's* readers). In general the young women, such as those gathered for the Grandissime *fête de grandpère,* seem every bit as mysterious, playful, teasing, and altogether frivolous as De Charleau's daughters in "Belles Demoiselles Plantation," while the older, "courtly matrons" (*G,* 162) are majestic and stately. Similarly, the "Gallant crew" (*G,* 163) of Grandissime men are described as capable of great "splendor of manner" and *politesse,* especially in deferring to the women. The chivalric tone in these depictions suggests on one level that the Creoles exemplify for Cable the best of aristocratic manners vitalized by frontier energies and Latin temperament.

Cable qualifies this image of a Creole Camelot in a number of ways, however. The elaborate shows of courtesy are often insincere, masking real feelings or simply self-centered banality. The attractive, vivacious Raoul Innerarity, who becomes Frowenfeld's loyal assistant and whose "adolescent buoyancy, as much as his delicate, silver-buckled feet and clothes of perfect fit, pronounced him all-pure Creole" (*G,* 113), is essentially a comic figure, appealing and honorable, but also dandyish and trivial. More seriously, Cable alludes frequently enough to signs of Creole immorality—not only drinking, gambling, dueling, and attending the quadroon balls but also the public tolerance of smuggling, bribery, influence-peddling, and other forms of circumventing established laws. Once justified as a defense against the abuses and indifference of the colonial authorities, this behavior has become simply a habit of public corruption.

Such social and political implications of Creole character—both vices and virtues—are clearly among Cable's central interests in *The Grandissimes.* What Cable considers Creole indolence, for example, sometimes noted as an attractive languorousness in speech and manners and perhaps attributable, as Aurora suggests, to "doze climade" (*G,* 143), is also linked to the institution of slavery. The superstition that adds to Aurora's charm and contributes to Palmyre's mystique and power is shown to be part of a general backwardness among the Creoles—a disdain for education, literacy, historical fact, detailed record-keeping, sound business practice, and other forms of "enlightenment"—that not only limits their chances in the new American meritocracy but turns to suspicion and violence against Frowenfeld. As in the attack on Frowenfeld, Cable shows the Creoles' intellectual backwardness to combine with their aristocratic exclusiveness and their "preposterous, apathetic, fantastic, suicidal pride" (*G,* 32) in a self-destructive resistance to all change and to all outsiders. This perverse "'all or nothing' attitude" (*G,* 282) is a crucial point for Cable, for apart from the economic doom it harbors, it also means a refusal to accept the basic democratic ideals embodied in the U.S. Constitution.

Significantly, the Creole women, particularly Aurora and Clotilde Nancanou, are generally exempt from these exposures of Creole weaknesses. As Louis Rubin points out, even the traits of superstition, impracticality, and childishness, presented as faults in the Creole males are, along with physical beauty and musical patois, part of the feminine charm of Aurora (90). Clotilde is portrayed as somewhat more practical and progressive in her social views than her mother, and in making a risqué joke (discreetly in French) on the fertility of the Mississippi, in keeping a note from Honoré *"warm"* in the bodice of her nightgown (a more obvious example of Cable's voyeurism than that found in " 'Sieur George" and " 'Tite Poulette"), and in advising her daughter that "the meanest wickedness a woman can do . . . is to look ugly in bed" (*G,* 288), Aurora is presented as both more voluptuous and more worldly than her daughter. Nevertheless, both Nancanous for the most part fit Rubin's description of them as "heroines in the accepted stereotype of the romance form" (90). In his *Heroines of Fiction* (1901), William Dean Howells found them "easily first among the imaginary ladies with whose sweetness novelists have enriched and enlarged our acquaintance" (Turner 1980, 123).

What makes them more interesting is that, as Anna Elfenbein has argued, they are also depicted as modestly rebellious victims of the Creoles' antiquated social values (25–73). Their penury, originating in Creole vices (gambling and duelling) and in Creole pride, is one of the central plot concerns. Moreover, their inability to alter their condition by earning money is identified as a consequence of the limitations of their role as women in society generally but especially among the chivalrous Creoles. Like their ancestor, however, the Huguenotte *fille à la cassette* who refused to "submit" to the Grand Marquis's request that she either "marry or pray to Mary" (*G,* 26), the Nancanous stubbornly resist their fates. Clotilde, sounding more modern and more easily Americanized than her mother, complains bitterly that "we are compelled not to make a living" (*G,* 255) and enumerates the wide range of occupations—cook, seamstress, accountant, nurse, confectioner, milliner, dressmaker, and so forth—that she has the skills for but is prevented from choosing because "ladies must be ladies."

Aurora is willing to accept such a role as "our first duty," but she goes on to assert that society "does not permit ladies to make a living" because "it makes it *necessary* [for them] to marry," and she admits to contemplating such a step herself in her hungriest moments. This last admission in its despairing pragmatism echoes the situation and psychology of quadroon mothers, such as Madame John in " 'Tite Poulette," and Aurora later specifically compares her struggle to secure her rights with that of Bras-Coupé. Cable links the themes of racial and sexual oppression more fully through the characterizations of Clemence and Palmyre, and the social criticism in his depiction of the Nancanous as victims is considerably softened by his keeping them happily within the romantic formula of rescue by marriage. There is, in short, no radical feminist statement here, but perhaps stirred by the example of the economic struggles of his widowed mother and sister, Cable does depict the Nancanous as suffering the consequences of caste proscriptions based on their identity as white "ladies."

The address to broader social issues through the examination of Creole traits is perhaps best seen in the contrast between Agricola Fusilier and Honoré Grandissime as leaders of the Grandissime clan. In appearance and manner, Agricola is clearly identified with the old order. Frequently characterized as "leonine" (also a "bull," an "orang-outang" and an "eagle"), he is distinctive for his size and vigorous physicality, albeit "adorned with old age" (G, 47). Hence, with his "large, black, and bold" eyes, his dark brow "furrowed partly by time and partly by a persistent ostentatious frown," and his beard sweeping "down over his broad breast like the beard of a prophet," he seems to embody the fierce martial temperament suggested by his surname. He is also distinctive from the outset for his pompous speech and exaggerated manners and for his seizing every opportunity to pontificate on the virtues of all things Louisianan and the evil of all things American. Like Jean Poquelin and like Hawthorne's John Endicott, Agricola is admirable in his strength of will and independence—qualities necessary for establishing a civilization in the wilderness—and in these qualities he is notably the descendant of both a Bienville dragoon and Lufki-Humma. His avuncular friendliness to Frowenfeld, his support of the young immigrant's scientific interest in the region, and his death-bed "blessing" of the union between Honoré and Aurora might also be seen as positive signs reflecting a capacity to grow or change, a fundamental instinct for tolerance and justice.

The overall tone of Cable's portrait of Agricola, however, is closer to ridicule than admiration. In the opening scene, for example, he is introduced in harlequin "mask and domino," alternately complaining about the spuriousness of any treaty that did not mention "the great family of Brahmin Mandarin Fusilier de Grandissime" (G, 2) and then "growling . . . with the teased, half laugh of aged vanity" at Aurora's familiarity. In a later description his dress is "noticeably soiled" and includes hints of "the fashions of three decades" (G, 47), and when he reads Frowenfeld's meteorological journal, his spectacles are "upside down" (G, 138). These suggestions of buffoonery in his manner and appearance, then, characterize his social and political pronouncements as well—for example, in his insistence that "English is not a language, sir; it is a jargon" (G, 48) and that Claiborne "is an American and no American can be honest" (G, 86). In part, Cable seems intent on mocking Agricola's inflated self-importance (as in the several instances of his continuing his speech-making oblivious to the evident disinterest of his audience), which, like the "amateurism" (*G*, 141) of Raoul Innerarity's painting, suggests the Creoles' narrow provincialism.

More pointedly, as Frowenfeld tells him to his face, Agricola is prejudiced, characterized by a habit of mind that defends tribal values and traditions against all appeals to reason. For him "the sacredest prejudices of our fathers" (*G*, 302) are not to be submitted "to the new-fangled measuring-rods of pert, imported theories upon moral and political progress." The "new-fangled measuring-rods," of course, include the democratic values of liberty and equality, so that Agricola, who insists on being called "Citizen," is shown to be not only a narrow-minded, foolish blowhard but also an Old World aristocrat. To whatever degree he espouses "the catch-words of new-fangled reforms[,] they served to spice a breath that was strong with the praise of the 'superior liberties of Europe,'—those old, cast-iron tyrannies to get rid of which America was settled" (*G*, 84).

For Cable, then, Agricola's advocacy of nonparticipation in the new government has more serious implications than petty posturing or jealous resentment at the loss of power and position, and since these issues are not to be reasoned, they must inevitably be defended by force. It may be Cable's most damning brush-stroke that he shows Agricola not only capable of violence himself in killing M. Nancanou in a duel and striking Honoré, f.m.c., but, perhaps worse, in unleashing the mindless violence of the mob that destroys Frowenfeld's shop and finds its ultimate victim in the *marchande des calas,* Clemence. Significantly, in this climactic action, Agricola is set aside as leader, left behind because he waffles, and while he occupies himself with the dream of publishing his *Philippique Générale contre la Conduite du Gouvernement de la Louisiane,* the violence he has set in motion with his bombast is carried out by less principled and more brutal men.

While Agricola is anachronistic and unprogressive, Honoré—"the uttermost flower on the topmost branch of the tallest family tree ever transplanted from France to Louisiana" (*G*, 82)—represents a more positive image of the Creole type. Cable claimed that his Creole hero, like all the other major characters in the novel, was modeled on a real individual, but Honoré is presented in such idealized, romantic terms that he barely exists as a distinctive character. The only sense of his physical appearance is that he is young, tall, and handsome with an "exquisite mould" (*G*, 101), a "compact strength," a "beautiful hand" (*G*, 38), and a "noble countenance" (*G,* 6)—terms so generalized as to make him nearly invisible. Cable's assertion that "his whole appearance was a dazzling contradiction of the notion that a Creole is a person of mixed blood" (*G,* 38) hardly sharpens the image, especially since Charlie Keene speculates (mistakenly, we presume) that some of Honoré's physical qualities derive from "the Indian Queen" (*G,* 101). Similarly, his manner, while marked by a notable formality—signalled, in part, by the " 'my-de-seh' " phrase punctuating his speech—has none of the pompous self-importance of Agricola, and while attractively friendly and humorous, he has none of the exuberant vivacity of Raoul Innerarity. Always polite, "true to his blood" in his ability "at any time to make himself as young as need be" (*G,* 36), Honoré converses easily with Frowenfeld, Agricola, Clemence, Aurora, his mulatto half-brother, and Governor Claiborne.

In presenting Honoré in such vaguely idealized terms, Cable also suggests he is the product of a kind of evolutionary process by which, as Charlie Keene explains to Frowenfeld, the Grandissimes' "greatness began . . . in ponderosity of arm,— of frame, say,—and developed from generation to generation, in a rising scale, first into fineness of sinew, then, we will say, into force of will, then into power of mind, then into subtleties of genius" (*G,* 101). Honoré is "high up on the scale, intellectual and sagacious," but "old Agricola shows the downward grade better," a decline of strength "that was once in the intellect and will . . . going down into the muscles." The importance of this characterization is that it legitimizes Honoré's social and economic views, which are pointedly at variance with those of the majority of Creoles, and characterizes Agricola's majority views as regressive.

Inheriting the hope of his father, Numa Grandissime, that he should "right the wrongs which he [the father] had not quite dared to uproot" (*G,* 109), Honoré has been educated in Paris, and when he returns, "instead of taking office as an ancient Grandissime should have done— to the dismay and mortification of his kindred, established himself in a prosperous commercial business." As a businessman he is much more receptive than the other Creoles to the commercially minded, Anglo-Saxon "invaders," and as the trustee for most of his family's economic interests, rather than defend their prejudices, he cooperates with the new order to secure a place within it.

The most immediate and significant problem for the Grandissime family is that much of their wealth is tied up in land granted under the Spanish colonial administration, and the new American government threatens to nullify many of these titles. By selling dubiously held lands and by participating in the new government, the Grandissimes might lessen the blows and gain some measure of control, but many refuse, scorning any cooperation with the hated *Américains* and deluding themselves into penury with the dream of Casa Calvo's return and the reestablishment of the Spanish grants. Honoré's efforts to establish cordial relationships with Governor Claiborne and to encourage his fellow Creoles' participation in the new government are met with shock and suspicion, undermining his role as the family's financial advisor and trustee. In taking this route, he is like his father, who did not join with the "ill-informed, inflammable, and long ill-governed" French colonists in resisting the earlier transfer of Louisiana to Spain in 1768 but instead "stood by the side of law and government" (*G,* 108) and then "secured valuable recognition of [his fellow Creole's] office-holding capacities" from another feared and maligned but "really good governor," Cruel O'Reilly. Honoré's openness to the Americans, however, signals more than economic and political pragmatism. He also embraces many of the perspectives of the new administration: the importance of "*free* government" (*G,* 94); the transforming, democratizing power of "Religion and Education" (*G,* 95); and, above all, the injustice as well as the social and economic liability of the slave trade.

By shaping Honoré's character in this way, Cable suggests that the capacity for both pragmatic and progressively idealistic thought lies within the Creole character, at least in its most refined and highly evolved form. The Creole trait that enables this enlightenment is that suggested by his name, for the central dilemma with which he struggles throughout the novel is essentially a question of honor. Here again he is pointedly contrasted with Agricola, whose narrowly provincial sense of honor is shaped as a commitment to tribal values regardless of merit and knows no conflict. Honoré knows the views of the Creoles and recognizes that their feelings must be—if not respected—allowed for. He feels both loyalty and responsibility to Creole interests, honor-bound to serve them, but he also recognizes higher values and practical necessities, and so he is shown to be frequently torn as to the most honorable course of action.

His appearing in public with Governor Claiborne, his returning Cannes Brulées to the Nancanous, and his publicly acknowledging his relationship with his half-brother (and, therefore, his father's partially atoned "wrong") are all acts of honor in which Honoré attempts to lead his fellow Creoles in the right course (both morally and practically) against "a common indignation . . . in the breast of that thing dreadful everywhere, but terrible in Louisiana, the majority" (*G,* 81). His vacillation in choosing the course of honor, particularly on the questions of race and slavery and when his own private (romantic) interests are involved, constitutes his most interesting and realistic character dimension, making him something less than a Hamlet or even a Prufrock but more than the amiable Creole statue he otherwise appears.

Old and New South Politics

Cable observed later that he "meant to make *The Grandissimes* as truly a political work as it ever has been called," for "it was impossible that a novel written by me then should escape being a study of the fierce struggle going on around me, regarded in the light of that past history—those beginnings—which had so differentiated the Louisiana civilization from the American scheme of public society" (*NQ,* 14–15). The "fierce struggle" was the resistance of Southern Democrats to imposed Radical government during Reconstruction—debates that dominated election campaigns, newspaper editorials, and office and coffeehouse talk and sometimes ended in violence. Insofar as Cable found himself at odds with his business associates, friends, and neighbors in his views on the "Lost Cause," white rule, and segregation, these issues became increasingly important during the period in which the novel was written, and Cable addressed them through historical analogy. In essence, the Creole-American conflict of 1803 offered an obvious, sometimes explicit comparison with the conflicts between North and South, New South and Old South during and after Reconstruction. With this technique, he anticipates Twain's *The Adventures of Huckleberry Finn* (1885), but Cable's novel is less oblique than Twain's in its social commentary, more specific and detailed in its exposure of ills, and less romantic in positing a solution.

One issue Cable addresses is the economic plight of the Creoles with the arrival of the Americans, which parallels the condition of the war-prostrated South. The signs of illiteracy among the Creoles, their impracticality and indifference to business affairs, their preoccupation with connections, status, good manners, and fine clothes in lieu of more useful qualifications, mark them as doomed economically. Hence, Honoré's characterization as a businessman suggests a New South alternative for economic rebuilding. To survive in the face of imposed change, both the Louisiana Creole of 1803 and the Old Southerner after 1865 had to abandon outdated economic systems rooted in essentially aristocratic values and slave labor and embrace the commercialism of the

North. Also, Cable's concern with the charges of corruption leveled against "carpet-bagger" governments seems apparent in Honoré's warning Governor Claiborne about the danger of the Creoles refusing "all participation in your government" (*G,* 94), thereby forcing him to fill his offices "with men who can face down the contumely of a whole people. . . . One out of a hundred may be a moral hero—the ninety-nine will be scamps; and the moral hero will likely get his brains blown out early in the day."

Throughout much of his political writing Cable would emphasize the need for the best elements in society to accept the responsibility of leadership, even when they were not fully in accord with its principles, for to withdraw was to leave the field to lesser individuals, paving the way for inevitable corruption and violence. Agricola's refusal to cooperate with the Americans, the mob violence he sets in motion and then is unable to control, and even Honoré's hesitation about leading too boldly illustrate the point further, and whether or not Cable had the New Orleans street-car riots of 1867 or the White League insurrection of 1874 specifically in mind in writing these scenes, there were plenty of other incidents of mob and racial violence during and after Reconstruction to spark his concern.

Involved in these questions of economic growth, public morality, and civic responsibility is the obdurate and foolish provincialism of the Creoles, which bears obvious resemblance to the South's suicidal loyalty to the Lost Cause. The issue, however, is not just regional narrowness. When Agricola dies and his last words, "Louisiana forever" (*G,* 329), are inscribed on his tombstone, Cable notes that "even the fair women" who come "to lay coronals upon the old man's tomb" feel "feebly at first, and more and more distinctly as years went by, that Forever was a trifle long for one to confine one's patriotic affection to a small fraction of a great country." As noted earlier, the ex-Confederate soldier Cable was going through his own crisis of loyalty during the 1870s, questioning first the principle of secession for which he had fought and then the justice of slavery. Cable's rethinking of these issues centered in a study of the Bible and of the U.S. Constitution and hence required a refocusing of his own loyalties from the prejudices of his region to the moral and political principles of the reunified "great country." This process is dramatized in the dilemma of loyalty Honoré wrestles with and in the problem of inclusion facing Frowenfeld, becoming "acclimated" without losing his "convictions" (*G,* 37). For the author and for his characters, the problems of slavery, race, and caste are at the center of the drama.

The Issues of Slavery, Caste, and Race

The problem of racial injustice in Louisiana and in the South generally was certainly the most important political issue Cable addressed in *The Grandissimes,* and his treatment of this issue accounts in large part for the novel's continuing interest. Intimations of these concerns appeared in *Old Creole Days* in varying degrees, but in *The Grandissimes* Cable identifies slavery and racial caste as the central problems of Southern life, the guilty burden of the past encumbering the present. Under one of the Congressional Acts by which Louisiana became a U.S. territory the importation of slaves was prohibited. This gave an economic advantage to American immigrants who could bring their slaves with them, but more crucially it seemed to threaten "that institution," as Charles Gayarré described it, "which the South considers as its very life-blood and the indispensable condition of its existence, and also as the very breath and essence of its prosperity."[13] Anticipating Faulkner, Frowenfeld observes that to cling to such convictions is to be under "the shadow of the Ethiopian," and Honoré agrees: "I am *ama-aze* at the length, the blackness of that shadow! . . . It is the *Némésis* w'ich, instead of coming afteh, glides along by the side of this morhal, political, commercial, social mistake! It blanches, my-de'-seh, ow whole civilization! It drhags us a centurhy behind the rhes' of the world! It rhetahds and poisons everhy industrhy we got!—mos' of all our-h immense agrhicultu'e!" (*G,* 156).

Such an analysis, which much of the novel seems designed to illustrate, places the onus of slavery primarily on the master, and, indeed, Cable's attack on slavery in *The Grandissimes* is, for the most part, not based on reiterating the hardships and brutalities of slavery associated with plantation life and familiar to readers of abolitionist literature and slave narratives—not, in other words, based on the slave's experience. "The Story of Bras-Coupé," however, presented in two chapters in the very center of the novel and a revision of the short story "Bibi," which had been rejected earlier as too "distressful," seems to offer an exception to this assertion.[14]

The story of Bras-Coupé is based on actual accounts of a one-armed slave who had struck his master and evaded captivity in the swamps—accounts that had appeared in New Orleans newspapers and were well known to many of Cable's Creole contemporaries. Cable's melodramatic version of the tale centers on the rebellion of an African prince who accepts his captivity as a slave but refuses to work and can only be controlled through his love for the quadroon servant, Palmyre. On his wedding night, he becomes drunk, strikes his master, Don José Martinez, and, after pronouncing a voodoo curse on the land, flees to the swamps, where he remains hidden for several months while the curse takes effect in crop failures and fevers. Efforts to capture him or to induce him to remove the curse are unavailing until he is lured to a dance on the Congo Plain. Lassoed and then punished according to "the old French code, continuing in force by the Spaniards" (*G*, 190), he finally lifts the curse on his death-bed and with his last breath envisions his soul's return "To—Africa" (*G*, 193).

Cable's condemnation of the "peculiar institution" is obvious from the story's outset yet more manifest in the narrator's ironic voice than in the conditions described. For example, of Bras-Coupé's commodification and sale Cable concludes, "In witness whereof, He that made men's skins of different colors, but all blood of one, hath entered the same upon His book, and sealed it to the day of judgment" (*G*, 169). He then generalizes Bras-Coupé's experience of the Middle Passage on the schooner *Egalité* with the observation that "little is recorded—here below; the less the better. Part of the living merchandise failed to keep" and "the captain . . . jettisoned the unmerchantable." Similarly, when the captured prince begins to note the "luxury" (*G*, 171) of his new home compared to what he remembers of Africa, Cable adds, "True, there was more emaciation than unassisted conjecture could explain—a profusion of enlarged joints and diminished muscles." Hence, although Bras-Coupé—a slave owner himself in Africa—objects not to his enslavement but to the demand that he work, Cable makes clear that his name symbolizes "the truth that all Slavery is maiming."

While not centering on the daily hardships of slavery, "The Story of Bras-Coupé" nevertheless powerfully exposes the brutality and violence of the institution. Cable's ostensible purpose in writing the story was to attack the harshness of the specific articles of the Code Noir that called for branding, cutting off the ears of and hamstringing runaways, and capital punishment for any slave who struck his master and "produced a bruise" (*G*, 191). He quotes the language of these articles directly and describes the results of their application with compelling explicitness: "Palmyre burst into tears and sank down, while before her on a soft bed of dry grass, rested the helpless form of the captive giant, a cloth thrown over his galled back, his ears shorn from his head, and the tendons behind his knees severed." Cable notes the injustice of these penalties in that they were prescribed for "the crime he had committed against society by attempting to be a free man." In addition, the overseer speculates that Honoré's sister felt Bras-Coupé "had half a right" (*G*, 188) to his rebellion and curse, and Frowenfeld signals his indignation when he asks Honoré, "And you suffered this thing to take place?" (*G*, 191).

The pathos of Bras-Coupé's treatment under the Black Code is, in part, a function of his development as a stereotypical Noble Savage, a magnificent physical specimen—regal in bearing, fiercely independent, defined by his instinct and an affinity with nature. As such he is instantly admired by all who see him, even Agricola, and the retelling of his story, by the Creoles of the novel as well as by those of Cable's day, owes a great deal to this sentiment over his natural nobility. The Gothicism of a storm on his wedding night and of his flight into the swamp, the melodrama of his casting and releasing the curse, and even the evocation of sentimental love tensions in Palmyre's feelings for Honoré all contribute to this effect, a marshalling of the literary conventions of feeling to generate sympathy for the African's fall from grace.

Still, Bras-Coupé is a more complexly drawn character than this. However noble, Bras-Coupé is nonetheless characterized as a savage—a ferocious, barely tamed animal completely at home in a swamp reminiscent of his own "native wilderness" (*G*, 182) and thoroughly capable of violence. He is the spoils of "a certain war of conquest, to which he had been driven by *ennui*" (*G*, 169), and when it first dawns on him that he is expected to work, he strikes the slave-driver with a hoe—"a sweep as quick as instinct" (*G*, 171)—and then, with more than a hint of cannibalism, lifts "the nearest Congo crosswise" and brings "thirty-two teeth together in his wildly kicking leg and cast him away as a bad morsel' (*G*, 172). He is also shown to become dangerously out of control when he drinks, and the suggestions of sexual power in his passionate attraction to Palmyre (" '*Bras-Coupé oulé so' femme,*' he said, and just then Palmyre would have gone with him to the equator" [*G*, 187]) are more ominously figured in his appearance and capture on the Congo Plain.

Cable's description of the "old barbaric pastimes" (*G*, 189) wherein the slaves were permitted to gather and socialize on Sundays "on a grassy plain under the ramparts" emphasizes the sense of wild abandon—including sensual freedom—in their African-based songs and dances: "They gyrated in couples, a few at a time, throwing their bodies into the most startling attitudes and the wildest contortions, while the whole company of black lookers-on, incited by the tones of the weird music and the violent posturing of the dancers, swayed and writhed in

passionate sympathy, beating their breasts, palms and thighs in time
with the bones and drums." Insofar as these "saturnalian antics" (*G,* 190)
served as a controlled venting, a protection against insurrection, they
project an image of the conditions feared, and Bras-Coupé's joining the
revels "drunk again" and performing so that "all that had gone before
was tame and sluggish" makes him seem an epitome of that image. Even
more ominously threatening, he exacts vengeance on his Creole tormentors with a voodoo curse that until his death he refuses to lift, defying his
master's orders with a smile whose malevolence Cable makes clear: "God
keep thy enemy from such a smile!" (*G,* 192).

In portraying Bras-Coupé in these terms, Cable seems to lend cre-
dence to the Creoles' fear of "insurrection, conflagration and rapine" (*G,*
181) when he strikes Don José (see Ladd, note 14). This is indeed the
significance he has for Palmyre, but Cable blurs the edges of Bras-
Coupé's potential for violence in a number of ways. He identifies the
African's striking his master as "self-defence" (*G,* 180) and in comparing
the Creole response—to "shoot the black devils without mercy!"—to
what "we do to-day whenever some poor swaggering Pompey rolls up
his fist and gets a ball through his body," he suggests that "the whole
Creole treatment of race troubles" (181) is a ludicrous overreaction
extending into his own time. More interestingly, Bras-Coupé's imperious
manner and capacity for violence are qualities Cable also identifies with
the Creoles, especially the Spaniards. Don José, whose "capability to fear
anything in nature or beyond had never been discovered" (*G,* 177),
makes Bras-Coupé his gamekeeper and hunting companion: "Many a
day did these two living magazines of wrath spend together in the dismal swamps . . . , making war upon deer and bear and wildcat . . . when
even a word misplaced would have made either the slayer of the other."
This mirroring is extended further when Bras-Coupé's wedding to
Palmyre is held as a preliminary entertainment to Don José's own marriage to Honoré's sister, suggesting both the Creoles' cruel indifference
to their slaves' feelings and a sacrilegious mockery of the nuptial vows.
Also, as Joseph J. Egan has shown, there are a number of similarities in
the characterizations of Bras-Coupé and Agricola, from the use of animal
imagery to suggest their physicality and naturalness, to their sense of
honor and volatile tempers, and even to the buffoonery noted earlier in
Agricola's costume and echoed in Bras-Coupé's appearing drunk in
"gaudy regimentals" (*G,* 181) before the wedding party.[15]

The effect of this "equality" between Bras-Coupé and the Creoles is to
expose the arbitrariness of the color line, of caste. As a prince and a

member of the fierce, proud Jaloff tribe, Bras-Coupé, like the Creoles, is an aristocrat, and he is, therefore, able to demand and partially receive recognition of the African definition of his circumstances as a prisoner of war rather than a chattel slave. Apart from the sheer brutality of it, punishing him as an "ordinary" slave violates a concept of social order based on refinement. This point is given a further twist, for if Bras-Coupé is shown to be, like his masters, capable of violence and brutality, he is also shown to be amenable to the refining—and therefore civilizing and humanizing—influence of women. Palmyre's influence is complicated by her desire for revenge and her love for Honoré, but this is not the case with Honoré's sister, Bras-Coupé's mistress. Hence, in the final scene, echoing the eighteenth-century sentimental novels of Sterne and Richardson but even more Pearl's becoming human through sorrow in the last scaffold scene of *The Scarlet Letter,* the mutilated and dying Bras-Coupé, while holding his mistress's child and gazing on "its mother's smile," offers up "the first tears of . . . [his] life, the dying testimony of his humanity" (*G,* 193) and lifts the curse. The message of this conversion for the Southerners of Cable's own day seems relatively clear: just as Bras-Coupé has responded to the power of sympathy, so might they if they wish to evolve beyond the savagery of the Code Noir and its modern equivalents in the racial violence and segregation laws that followed in the wake of Reconstruction.

That Cable intended "The Story of Bras-Coupé" to be the thematic and emotional center of *The Grandissimes* is evident not only from its physical location in the text but also from the fact of its early mention and frequent retellings, especially on the occasion of such gatherings of the clan as the *fête de grandpère,* as if it were a favorite fairy tale or primal legend. The sentimentality and melodrama of the tale—at times perhaps more ludicrous than powerful to modern readers—has nevertheless an important function within the novel. Like an early *Uncle Tom's Cabin,* which Cable claimed to have read when he was 10, Bras-Coupé's story engages the sympathy of the novel's two leading "right-minded" characters, Honoré and Frowenfeld, and in the case of the former alters his racial attitudes. As William Bedford Clark aptly observes, "Cable is unquestionably a master of nineteenth-century fictive *pathos,* playing sentiment and social criticism against one another for all they are worth."[16]

Characteristic of his shifting, self-consciously ironic literary method, Cable not only exploits sentimentality to arouse moral fervor against social injustice, but he also mocks it to deny that feeling alone is an adequate response. Thus, for "the fair Grandissimes" who agree that "it was a great pity to have hamstrung Bras-Coupé, who even in his cursing had made an exception in favor of the ladies" (*G*, 194), the sentimental story is just that, a relatively trivial indulgence of emotion. Because "they could suggest no alternative" and think "it was undeniable that he had deserved his fate," they retire "to sleep confirmed in this sentiment"—that "it seemed a pity."

Many of the racial themes in "The Story of Bras-Coupé" also shape the characterization of Clemence, although they are handled with a good deal less sentimentality and melodrama. As the slave of Honoré, f.m.c., and a *marchande des gateaux* (itinerant cake vender), she has considerable freedom of movement in New Orleans, and she is introduced early as one of the familiar, characteristic figures in the picturesque tapestry of the old city—laughing, singing, bantering in both Black English and "gumbo" French dialects. The essential feature of her character, however, demonstrated at some length in a chapter entitled "An Inheritance of Wrong," is that this image is a facade, an artful masquerade of language and manner hiding not only the pain of her experience but the shrewd intelligence and bitterness of her outlook on the Creole world she carefully studies. Through the "cunning aptness of her songs" (*G*, 249) and the "droll wisdom of her sayings," she ironically exposes various lies by which the white masters justify slavery, particularly the paternalistic "old current conviction" that the slaves "were 'the happiest people under the sun.' " The verbal sparring between her and Charlie Keene over this point in which she simultaneously mocks and entertains her white audience suggests more a realistic portrayal of the African oral tradition of signifying than the staged comic debates between Jim and Huck over the wisdom of Solomon and whether Frenchmen are men. Although a comparable character type, she is closer to Charles Chesnutt's Uncle Julius than to Joel Chandler Harris's Uncle Remus.

Through Clemence, Cable launches some of his most pointed and powerful attacks against the treatment of the freedman in his own day. When she is captured in a steel trap, permitted to escape hanging, and then coldly shot as she runs away, there is little of the sentimentality found in Bras-Coupé's death scene, and the sense of the Creoles' brutality may be even greater owing to the apparent benignity of her comic persona. Furthermore, the notions that the slaves were basically happy and benefited from the opportunity to be rescued from their African savagery were among the most popular arguments not only for slavery but for permitting a white-supremacist New South to solve the "race problem" in its own paternalistic way. This is Cable's apparent meaning when he describes those who hold these notions as ones "who will not be decoyed down from the mountain fastnesses of the old Southern doctrines" (*G,* 249).

It was on the basis of such benign, nostalgic versions of plantation life, along with an admission of the wrong of slavery, that Henry W. Grady, editor of the Atlanta *Constitution,* would appeal for Northern sympathy, understanding, and investment capital, just as it was, almost 20 years later, the basis of Booker T. Washington's appeal in his celebrated "Atlanta Exposition Address" for white Southerners to help educate and employ the loyal former slaves in the new industrial order. Cable exposes this "big lie" (*G,* 250) by making clear that Clemence's apparent happiness is a coping strategy, reflecting not contentment with her lot but a loss of hope about the possibility of change. "To Clemence the order of society was nothing. No upheaval could reach the depth to which she had sunk" (*G,* 251), and thus while Honoré and Claiborne discuss political strategy and worry about public demonstrations, "Clemence went up one street and down another, singing her song and laughing her professional merry laugh. How could it be otherwise? Let events take any possible turn, how could it make any difference to Clemence?" (*G,* 252).

This emphasis on Clemence's disinterest in social change, despite her capacity for bitingly acute social satire, is a striking and crucial aspect of Cable's treatment of racial politics in *The Grandissimes* and beyond. While "our [i.e., white] feelings, our sentiments, affections, etc., are fine and keen, delicate and many [,] what we call refined," Clemence is the "heiress" of "feelings handed down to [her] . . . through ages of African savagery" and then slavery, "through fires that do not refine, but that blunt and blast and blacken and char" (*G,* 251). In presenting Clemence in these terms, Cable, to be sure, repeats the familiar and essentially racist European view of Africa, in effect makes her a victim both of slavery and of her racial identity. His aim, however, is not to elicit revulsion or to argue the ultimate and permanent inferiority of either Clemence or the freedman generally.

One consequence of Clemence's having been charred rather than refined by her heritage is that she has been robbed of a sense of social connection: "She had certain affections toward people and places; but they were not of a consuming sort." The emphasis on her lack of refinement is, therefore, an implicit challenge to the responsibility of those with this advantage first to recognize the obvious misery and degradation of others and then to seek its amelioration. In addition to this prod to his fellow Southerners' Christian conscience, Cable also appeals to their genteel reverence for the honor of women, for in recounting Clemence's history as a slave he emphasizes the violations of family and marriage. She remembers only her mother, their early separation, and the mother's auction price, and she has given birth to many children of "assorted colors" who are distributed "here and there . . . some . . . within occasional sight, some dead, some not accounted for" and her "husbands—like the Samaritan woman's"—largely unofficial. To the degree that these experiences have coarsened her, Cable suggests that they are an affront to womanhood.

The mix of sociohistorical realism and Victorian male sentimentality in the characterization of Clemence is even more interestingly at play in the treatment of Palmyre. In her doomed love for Honoré, she seems every bit the conventional "tragic mulatto" figure, the pathos of her situation intensified by the suggestion that she may be Aurora's half-sister. Unlike so many white representations of tragic mulattoes, however, Palmyre does not respond to her fate in passive despair or suicide but in hatred and violence, not in self-destruction but in revenge. She is tall, proud, "royal" (*G,* 175), intelligent, endowed with "concealed cunning and noiseless but visible strength of will"—so strong, in fact, that she is sent away from the De Grapion home to keep her from dominating Aurora. The response she evokes in nearly everyone, but especially in Agricola, is fear, and she gains further power through her "chaste" practice of the "less baleful rites of the voodoos" (*G,* 60). Hence, at Palmyre's first glimpse of Bras-Coupé, "She rejoiced in his stature; she revelled in the contemplation of his untamable spirit; he seemed to her the gigantic embodiment of her own dark, fierce will, the expanded realization of her lifetime longing for terrible strength" (*G,* 175).

Although Palmyre's only direct action is against Agricola, Cable's characterization of her feelings about Bras-Coupé makes clear the political implications of her independence and anger: "She had heard of San Domingo, and for months the fierce heart within her silent bosom had been leaping and shouting and seeing visions of fire and blood. . . . The lesson she would have taught the giant [Bras-Coupé] was Insurrection" (*G,* 184). In short, she has the aspect of a revolutionary, and while this quality is complicated and diminished, as Elfenbein suggests, by her thwarted love for Honoré, it is not effaced (63). She has power to influence others, primarily through fear, and if, like Clemence and like the freedman, she masks her feelings and for a long time is silent, Cable meaningfully observes, "so, sometimes, is fire in the wall" (G, 175).

If Palmyre's fierce, smoldering anger is implicitly political, it is also, in its source and passionate intensity, overtly erotic. With her "jet hair," "large and black eyes," "heavily pencilled eyebrows and long lashes," "yellow skin," "red, voluptuous lips" and "roundness of . . . [a] perfect neck," Palmyre has "even at fourteen, a barbaric and magnetic beauty, that startled the beholder like an unexpected drawing out of a jewelled sword" (G, 59–60). These same qualities of erotic allure and danger appear in subtle counterpoint in one of the novel's most remarkable scenes when Frowenfeld, substituting for the ill Charlie Keene, calls on Palmyre to treat her for a wound she received attacking Agricola. Frowenfeld finds her lying on a bed, wearing "a long, snowy morning-gown, wound loosely about at the waist with a cord and tassel of scarlet silk," "a necklace of red coral heighten[ing] to its utmost her untamable beauty" (G, 134). Her "passionate eyes" fix him in an icy stare, and after balking at any physical contact she allows her "superb shoulder" (G, 135) to be bared for the voyeuristic imagination of the reader as well as for the ministering hands of the apothecary. The implication of sexual liaison in a white man visiting the house of a beautiful quadroon is made clear in the novel, and this is the source of her initially hostile and then wary reaction to him: "So far as Palmyre knew, the entire masculine wing of the mighty and exalted race, three-fourths of whose blood bequeathed her none of its prerogatives, regarded her as legitimate prey." Consequently, "she hated men" (G, 134), and Cable clearly sides with Frowenfeld in understanding her anger—even to the point of attempted murder—as a by-product of miscegenation, a "poisonous blossom of crime growing out of crime."

The center of Palmyre's anger, however, is less racial injustice than the affront to what Cable describes as "that rarest of gifts in one of her tincture, the purity of true womanhood" (G, 60). Frowenfeld is able to gain her confidence and treat her wound because, except "possibly" for Honoré, he is the one man "she had ever encountered whose speech and gesture were clearly keyed to that profound respect which is woman's first, foundation claim on him" (G, 135). Each of his efforts to treat her involves a subtle play of sexual innuendo and decorum challenging not only her sense of honor but his. Insofar as Frowenfeld is able to "tame" Palmyre it is pointedly through giving her the prerogatives, the civility she would enjoy as a white woman—not force or violence—and the result is to convert her image into something still erotically magnetic but comfortably chaste.

It would be many hours before Frowenfeld can "replace with more tranquilizing images the vision of the *philosophe* reclining among her pillows, in the act of making that uneasy movement of her fingers upon the collar button of her robe, which women make when they are uncertain about the perfection of their dishabille, and giving her inaudible adieu with the majesty of an empress" (*G,* 136). The femininity that has been burned out of Clemence remains potential in Palmyre, but it is threatened by her passionate nature, both her anger and her desire for Honoré, making it a "femininity without humanity,—something that made her with all her superbness, a creature that one would want to find chained" (*G,* 71). Thus, when later she begs Frowenfeld to use his sorcery to make Honoré love her, she becomes again startlingly sexual in her "wild posturing," like a spurned lover "with her arms, bared of their drapery," and he revolts from her touch as "poisonous" (*G,* 201).

In her strength of will, sexual energy, and "spirit of righteous wrath,"[17] Palmyre is one of the most powerful and original of Cable's creations. The cycle of response and rejection to her erotic appeal in Frowenfeld may indeed, as Louis Rubin and other critics have suggested, reflect Cable's own ambiguous feelings (the conflict between the mother's and the father's influence), part of a continuum of attraction and repulsion, allure and judgment in his response to New Orleans. The same ambivalence, as Anna Elfenbein has argued, may apply to her identification with violence, the possibility of insurrection, in that Cable refuses "either to sanction or to moralize" her "use of the violent tactics of white society" (64). The only violence in the novel for which no "understanding" is offered, in fact, is white violence. In both her eroticism and capacity for violence, she is linked to deeply held white fears of blacks, and this suggests an even more troubled ambivalence in Cable's racial attitudes.

The Creoles' beliefs in white supremacy, as exemplified by Agricola, is one of Cable's overt targets of social criticism. In one speech, after claiming "how free we people are from prejudice against the Negro" (*G,* 59), the old patriarch goes on to expose his prejudice by explaining that by " 'we people,' we *always* mean we white people" and that "wherever he [the Negro] can be of any service in any strictly menial capacity we kindly and generously tolerate his presence." Cable's ironic strategy here, characteristic of the work as a whole, is to identify a familiar, widely held racial attitude as a part of the Creoles' arrogant exclusiveness and even more as a sign of pompous ignorance, a foolish lack of self-awareness.

While Cable mocks the white supremacist attitudes of the Creoles, however, his own representations of black character reflect some of the same racism. The novel consistently identifies Africa with savagery, however noble (as in the case of Bras-Coupé), or however matched by the savagery of slavery (as in the case of Clemence). The most offensive version of such racial stereotyping is Palmyre's servant, who is described as a "Congo dwarf" (G, 201) and who attacks Frowenfeld "snarling and gnashing like an ape" (G, 201). Involved in this representation is the study of the characteristics of the different African tribes, which Cable knew from his reading M. L. E. Moreau de Saint-Méry's *Description topographique, physique, civile, politique, et historique de la partie française de l'Ile Saint-Dominigue* (Philadelphia, 1797–98). Accounts such as this, which slave owners found useful for plantation management, characterized the warriorlike Jaloffs being admired but less serviceable than the more common and tractable "Congos."

Palmyre, like Bras-Coupé, has Jaloff ancestry, and this is reflected in her ferocity, her willfulness, and her "feline" beauty. Moreover, typical of the tragic mulatto type, her romantic interest in Honoré is implicitly sanctioned or legitimized for white readers by her "white blood" and made impossible by her "black blood." By the same logic, her marriage to a black man, prince or not, would, as her master (father?) warns, "dishonor one who shared the blood of the De Grapions" (G, 176), and Cable essentially rescues her from this fate by having Bras-Coupé flee to the swamps before their union is consummated. That Cable was, as Michael Kreyling puts it, "not entirely free of the pervasive racism of his own age"[18] is hardly surprising, but rather than reflecting an active conflict in his thinking, it seems more an unexamined implication of centering his critique of Creole and Southern society in issues of progress and refinement. For Cable, the barrier to progress—defined in white, Anglo-Saxon, Protestant terms—is not race, but caste. Frowenfeld's soothing influence on Palmyre demonstrates that she is amenable to refinement. In essence, therefore, her potential to develop as a white woman is held captive to her identification—not her identity—as black, and, thus, the strategy of Cable's exposure of the social and moral cost of caste includes an explicit appeal to a white racist sensibility, a call to defend the honor of "true womanhood."

Honoré, f.m.c., offers a parallel example of the penalty of caste, although in something of a reverse of gender roles it is he who attempts

and finally commits suicide in despair over his love for Palmyre. Both
refined and exotic in appearance, his "manners Castilian, with a gravity
almost oriental" (*G,* 42), the "dark" Honoré is presented as "one of those
rare masculine figures which, on the public promenade, men look back
at and ladies inquire about." Although his thick accent marks him as
socially inferior to his white brother, both Honorés were educated in
Paris, and the quadroon is characterized by Frowenfeld as "a man of
intelligence, accomplishments, leisure and wealth" (*G,* 195). Reflecting
his marginalized status, however, he is also shadowy, appearing and disappearing quietly, and languorous, a man without vitality or force. In
part, this is because he is sick with unrequited love for Palmyre, but
there are also political implications to his ineffectuality or "paralysis."

Stirred by hearing the story of Bras-Coupé, Frowenfeld challenges the
f.m.c. to social action: "why do not you give yourself—your time—
wealth—attainments—energies—everything—to the cause of the
down-trodden race with which this community's scorn unjustly compels
you to rank yourself." Honoré's response—that the cause of the slaves
was lost in Africa and that he is not a slave—is both defeatist and elitist,
but Cable also suggests that it is "unmanly," a quality hinted earlier in
the description of a "a woman-like delicacy" (*G,* 41) in his facial features
and confirmed, perhaps, in his ultimately committing suicide. Caste does
not keep Palmyre from him, but the social ostracism of caste and the
cold comforts of property and "sham freedom" (*G,* 196) have apparently
debilitated him, induced a kind of chronic despair, and the result is
again, as with Palmyre, a loss to society. Not only does he fail to attempt
any social reform, but when he dies, he leaves his entire fortune to support Palmyre's reclusive existence in Bordeaux: "But," Cable observes,
"that is only part of the pecuniary loss which this sort of thing costs
Louisiana" (*G,* 331).

The Dilemma of Action

The question of social action is an obvious recurring theme in *The
Grandissimes,* figuring in the representation of each of the major characters, perhaps most importantly in Joseph Frowenfeld. Once he becomes
acquainted with the Creole social and racial attitudes, he becomes a vehicle for social criticism, pontificating to the two Honorés and to the
Nancanous what are recognizably both *Américain* and Northern views.
Because of the somewhat mechanical quality of his narrative role and
even more because of his unrelieved high-mindedness, many critics have

found Frowenfeld to be unrealistically and unappealingly wooden. Cable's editor, Robert Underwood Johnson, urged him to reduce Frowenfeld's "goodness down to digestible portions" by permitting his hero to strike Sylvestre Grandissime after the young Creole insults him at Maspero's, but Cable would only relent to the point of having Frowenfeld raise his fist before another character intercedes (Turner 1956, 98). Indeed, Frowenfeld is not a particularly convincing character, too stiff to be engaging, but with his German-American heritage, his position as an outsider, and his suffering family losses from yellow fever, he is—even more than Kristian Koppig and Little White before him—a version of his creator, and this makes him interesting.

The emphasis placed on Frowenfeld's establishing himself in the Creole world is particularly striking, suggesting the strength of Cable's own feelings of social exclusion. One aspect of this is economic, and Cable certainly could both understand and approve of Frowenfeld's endeavors after the death of his family to combine the benefits of education, intellect, and business sense, just as he might also recognize the difficulty of success in a society that did not seem to value such qualities. There is an element of self-validation if not personal resentment in Frowenfeld's complaints against the Creoles' anti-intellectualism: "When a man's social or civil standing is not dependent on his knowing how to read, he is not likely to become a scholar" (*G*, 143). To find his place, both economically and socially, Frowenfeld must, as Honoré tells him, "get acclimated" (*G*, 37), but therein lies a more serious problem, for the danger is that he will, like 'Sieur George, go too far: "They all do it—," Honoré warns him, "all who come. They hold out a little while—a very little; then they open their stores on Sunday, they import cargoes of Africans, they bribe the officials, they smuggle goods, they have colored housekeepers. My-de'-seh, the water must expect to take the shape of the bucket; eh?" It is the threat of such succumbing to moral corruption that Rubin and others have seen as the crux of Frowenfeld's reaction to Palmyre—the inescapable allure of her sensuality and the shock and repulsion when he recognizes these feelings as sexual. The threat to his social convictions may be more serious, however, but it is less that he will lose them than that he will act on them in the mode of the region—that is, violently.

Negotiating and enabling peaceful transition is at the center of the historical and dramatic issues of the novel. It is the main theme of Honoré's advice to Governor Claiborne, and whether to pass around "this prickly bush" (*G*, 39) of Creole prejudices or "with his naked hands" to "pull it up by the roots" is the problem of honor that vexes the young Creole through much of the novel. Frowenfeld, believing that "a man armed with the truth is far from being bare-handed" and that "there is a peace which is bad" (G, 223), not only urges both Honorés to greater activism but also speaks out himself often and openly enough to become the target of Creole vilification and eventually violent reaction when his shop is destroyed. The more serious moral danger to him, therefore, lies not in seduction by Palmyre (who at that moment, after all, is pleading for an "ounguan" to entrance Honoré) but in efforts he might make to rescue his reputation after he is seen leaving her house wounded by the maid. The real crisis comes when Frowenfeld raises his fist to Sylvestre, for at that point he is on the verge of violence, not in defense of justice but for the sake of his honor, a response to personal insult. For Frowenfeld to become involved in an affair of honor would be to embrace the same flawed social values that gave rise to the Grandissime–De Grapion feud, and it is significant that the attacks on Agricola by both Palmyre and Honoré, f.m.c., are characterized as personal vendettas. The final sequences of the novel—in which the white and black Honorés become business partners and the Creole-American and Grandissime–De Grapion conflicts are symbolically resolved by marriage—suggest that a measure of social progress is possible through conciliation rather than confrontation.

Through Frowenfeld, then, Cable seems clearly to be working out his own attitudes toward social advocacy, of how to be what Honoré calls a peaceful "strifemaker" (G, 223). Frowenfeld's most valuable role, in part prescribed by his status as an outsider, is ultimately to counsel those who have influence as insiders (basically the two Honorés) to act on their principles in efforts at reform. Thus the role Frowenfeld envisions for Honoré, f.m.c., applies to himself and to Cable as well: "I can imagine a man in your place, going about among his people, stirring up their minds to a noble discontent, . . . [and] going, too, among the men of the prouder caste, among such as have a spirit of fairness, and seeking to prevail with them for a public recognition of the rights of all; using all his cunning to show them the double damage of all oppression, both great and petty" (G, 196).

In its political thrust *The Grandissimes* represents for Cable a version of this "going about" and reflects a good deal of such "cunning"—a combination of moral forthrightness and rhetorical subtlety. His attack on slavery—in its emphasis on the brutality of the oppressor, the moral lies used to justify the institution, and the violence it engenders—is as clear and powerful as anything written in the postbellum period. While a violent solution to such injustice is overtly condemned, it is also made vividly possible and understandable, if not fully justified, as a consequence of the brutality of treatment represented by the old Code Noir. This representation in part allows readers to distance themselves from the brutality as a regrettable thing of the past. At the same time, Cable uses the representation to suggest that when the brutality is discovered in the present, it mocks presumptions of progress, and his political focus is unmistakably on the present. In this regard Cable observes, "To-day almost all the savagery that can justly be charged against Louisiana must—strange to say—be laid at the door of the *Américain*" (*G*, 329–30).

Similarly, by emphasizing the problem of caste Cable pointedly updates the political statement to the central problem of his day. As Frowenfeld reminds Aurora, "there is a slavery that no legislation can abolish,—the slavery of caste" (*G*, 143), and clearly for Cable the quadroons epitomize the plight of the freedman after the Civil War; what they need "more than mere free papers can secure them" is "emancipation in the minds and good will of the people . . . , [i.e.] the ruling class" (*G*, 144). To effect this emancipation Cable aims both to elicit sympathy for the oppressed and to make the oppressors recognize and feel their own half of the "double damage." Hence the Creoles' white supremacy is made to seem a somewhat hypocritical extension of their aristocratic and therefore un-American social attitudes. Without directly challenging the racist assumptions underlying segregation, Cable attempts to expose the color line as a barrier to refinement and social progress and a particular affront to the purity of womanhood.

While to twentieth-century readers Cable's approach to the issues of race and violence in *The Grandissimes* might seem ambivalent or temporized, the example of Frowenfeld suggests less uncertainty of conviction than a search for an effective strategy to "show" and to "prevail." The tendency to preach or "pamphleteer" that Cable's editors tried to restrain and that critics have often debated as either a boon or a bane to his art is made one of Frowenfeld's distinguishing characteristics and mildly satirized. More to the point, Cable's narrative voice, unlike Frowenfeld's, is deeply modulated, at times frank, straightforward, and sententious but more often evasive, playful, and ironic. In combination with the recording of social and historical conditions that speak with their own power and the complicated play of issues in the actions and speeches of the characters, this voice makes an extraordinarily complex political statement in *The Grandissimes*. Cable was soon to engage in a more direct public debate over the problem of the freedman, but in all his writing he would never again address the problems of Southern society more fully, more subtly, or more powerfully.

The Critics

The immediate critical reception to *The Grandissimes* was overwhelmingly positive. H. H. Boyesen in *Scribner's Monthly,* William C. Brownell in the *Nation,* and anonymous reviewers in *Harper's Magazine,* the *Atlantic Monthly,* and *Appleton's Journal* all celebrated the unusual effect of the novel's rendering of milieu; the freshness of the materials; the range, depth, and color of the social and historical canvas; the uniqueness and appeal of the characters; and the overall artistry in scenic description and in the embodying of theme in character and action. The reviews noted and praised the novel's striking combination of romantic and realistic elements and, in the North at least, hailed the work and its author as signaling an emerging, universal greatness in Southern literature. Complaints were directed against Cable's use of dialect as a tedious encumbrance to the reader, although some reviewers allowed for the charm of the dialect at least in its overall effect, and while the story of Bras-Coupé was singled out for its power and the Nancanous were found to be "delightful," "charming" or "delicious," Frowenfeld struck many reviewers as either unconvincingly righteous or an underdeveloped mechanical device.

Part of the appeal of *The Grandissimes* to these early reviewers was also its address to serious social issues, particularly slavery. Brownell among others placed the novel in the tradition of Stowe's *Uncle Tom's Cabin,* and while he faulted its wringing "the reader's withers . . . in behalf of a cause already won" (Turner 1980, 19), a reviewer for the *Atlantic Monthly* went beyond this to recognize that the novel offered a "parallel" to "the questions . . . which . . . have perplexed the entire body of thoughtful men in the nation ever since the downfall of the Confederacy" (Turner 1980, 14). With some exceptions, the reviews in the New Orleans papers expressed pride in the accomplishment of a native son and in the truthfulness of his portrait of their region. Cable's most important local defender was Lafcadio Hearn, whose fascination with the exotic and sensual had brought him to New Orleans in 1877 (as it would take him to the West Indies and Japan in later years) and who had befriended Cable and shared his scholarly interest in the Creole songs, the varied dialects, and other peculiarities of the region. In his September 1880 review for the New Orleans *Item,* Hearn described *The Grandissimes* as "the most remarkable work of fiction ever created in the South," characterizing it as producing a "dream which is not all a dream, a tale which is but half a tale, a series of pictures which, although in a certain sense created by the pencil of an Impressionist, wear a terrible resemblance to terrible realities" (in Turner 1980, 8). Hearn also acknowledged what Arlin Turner suggests no one spoke but "everyone knew were the Creoles' objections" (1956, 101) to their unflattering portrayal in the novel, and he attempted to answer these unspoken objections by testifying to the novel's accuracy.

The Creoles' ire did, however, find a voice in a slim pamphlet, *Critical Dialogue between Aboo and Caboo on a New Book; or, A Grandissime Ascension,* published under the pseudonym E. Junius but authored by the primitivist Creole poet-turned-priest, Adrien Rouquette, who knew Cable was a friend of Hearn and had himself suffered censure for sermonizing against slavery before the war. The gist of the attack was that Cable had "slandered" and "ridiculed" the Creoles for Northern favor and profit, but the tone was crudely personal and vicious, mocking Cable's diminutive stature and suggesting that he was guilty of miscegenation with the well-known voodoo queen, Marie Laveau. This ominous sign of the intensity of the Creoles' resentment underlying their public civility ironically parallels Frowenfeld's superficially polite reception by the Grandissime clan after his run-in with Sylvestre, and it frightened Gilder and others at Scribners enough to think that Cable might need to leave New Orleans and move to the North.

The emphasis in the early reviews on the mixture of romance and realism in *The Grandissimes* and its obvious departure from the previous modes of Southern fiction have continued at the center of most subsequent critical discussions of the novel. Boyesen's description of Cable as a literary "pioneer" has been reaffirmed by such critics as Edmund Wilson, Louis Rubin, and most recently Alfred Bendixen,[19] with pointed reference to the flowering of Southern literature that began with Faulkner in the 1920s and continues to this day. What Cable pioneered in *The Grandissimes* is generally recognized as a break from the romantic idealization of the Old South as found in the plantation novels of John Pendleton Kennedy and Thomas Nelson Page—a willingness to examine critically the social and historical traditions of the South, to expose the evils of racism, caste, and violence. For some modern critics, such as Philip Butcher, the social realism is essentially at odds with the romantic elements in the work, and the novel's greatness lies in the degree to which it rises above those elements. For most critics, however, it is not the realism alone, not the political statement or reform impulse, that accounts for the novel's appeal and that places its author in the company of Glasgow, Faulkner, Ransome, Warren, Welty, and McCullers.

Newton Arvin,[20] Louis Rubin, and Thomas Richardson[21] in particular have emphasized the role of Cable's ambivalent feelings toward the South in providing the novel's most interesting tensions—a balance between a nostalgic longing for the past and the desire to redeem it that he shares with other Southern writers attempting to come to terms with the Southern past. Moreover, Richard Chase's characterization of *The Grandissimes* as a "hybrid"[22] blend of literary genres—sentimental, historical and frontier romance, Gothic melodrama, novel of ideas and novel of manners—has special relevance to this ambivalence in that the romance elements are particularly linked to the Old South and are, as literary representations, formulations of feeling about the region. The tensions in Cable's attitudes toward New Orleans and the South are, therefore, significantly centered in the romance elements, providing the novel's deeper psychological explorations of desire, revulsion, terror, violence, and passion, and giving force to his political or ideological messages.

In addition to the indulgence in melodrama and sentimentality, many critics have continued to identify the novel's weaknesses as the inadequate characterization of Frowenfeld, the clumsiness of the apothecary's use as a ideological mouthpiece, and the failure to develop Honoré's moral dilemma. Nevertheless, from the outset, the interplay of diverse elements in *The Grandissimes* has been recognized as the result of considerable artistry. In part, the novel works because its ideas and themes are effectively dramatized and centered in action, character, and milieu. The capacity of *The Grandissimes* to invite and sustain new readings—beyond enlightened reawakenings to its political messages—offers some testimony to this artistry. The precise character of the work has been difficult to define, however, because of another quality variously described as style, manner, atmosphere, mystification, insinuation, or artistic vagueness, which, like the convoluted periodicity of Henry James, creates a *sense* of subtlety and complexity beyond the content of the action, characters, and issues themselves.

The strategy of gaining interest from a blending of manner and matter evident in Cable's apprenticeship as "Drop Shot" is clearly at play in *The Grandissimes* and particularly in the development of his social, historical, and political themes. William Brownell early and astutely noted one aspect of this quality, "that the reader shares his [Cable's] enthusiasm before he suspects its existence, and . . . is led into referring the merit of the book to its material" (in Turner 1980, 17). The result is that a novel once compared favorably to such works as *War and Peace, Fathers and Sons, Middlemarch,* and *The Scarlet Letter*[23] and now relegated to the status of a significant precursor or, at best, a flawed "minor masterpiece" (Chase, 167) continues to compel attention for reasons more often felt than fully understood. The novel's "mélange" of elements may indeed, as Thomas Richardson asserts, indicate "some division in the artist's sensibility" (8), a lack of full artistic control, but it also accounts a great deal for the success of the work, for most of the elements would reappear in Cable's later fiction, but never in the same combination and never again with the same force.

Chapter Four

Literary Profession and Fragmentation

If the promise of *Old Creole Days* was fulfilled in the greater accomplishment of *The Grandissimes,* then this still imperfect first novel would seem to offer Cable even greater hope for future success, or so it seemed, particularly if he might at last devote himself full time to writing. Indeed, the critical success of *The Grandissimes* increased the price Cable could demand for his fiction, generated requests for more literary output, including a second novel, and thus encouraged his becoming a full-time writer. When he finally submitted his resignation from the cotton business in October 1881, he ostensibly ended a time conflict between the accountant's office and his writing desk that he had complained of for a number of years.

The critical consensus is, however, that with the possible exception of *Madame Delphine* (1881), the fiction that follows fails, often dismally, to build on or even repeat the promise of his early work. The question raised by this disappointment is the cause of the failure that is inevitably linked to the way the success of the early work is perceived. The most frequent interpretation is that the strong social realist in Cable succumbed to the weak romanticist under pressure from genteel editors, popular culture, and his own tastes. In this view, novels like *Dr. Sevier* (1884) and *John March, Southerner* (1894), which have elements of social realism, retain some interest for modern readers and demonstrate how the editorial and cultural pressures worked. But in ways not always adequately recognized, the achievement of *Old Creole Days* and especially *The Grandissimes* was the result of a particular combination of factors, a convergence of social, moral, and literary interests and impulses that generated a fruitful tension but by themselves command less interest.

Unfortunately, the apparent opportunity for greater concentration on art that he achieved by leaving the counting room was illusory. Even by then he had begun to enter into the social and public activities of a literary man that would lead to platform readings, which provided income but drew him to the North and made even greater demands on his time.

In addition, his interest in reform activities was re-invigorated, providing outlet for his social conscience and moral concerns beyond his fiction, and this, too, affected not only how much he wrote but the character of his writing as well. In essence, one result of his becoming a professional writer and a public figure was an increasing separation of literary and social interests. As evidenced by the major works he produced in the four years after the publication of *The Grandissimes*—*Madame Delphine, The Creoles of Louisiana* (1884), and especially *Dr. Sevier*—this fragmentation was damaging to his art.

Madame Delphine

The novella *Madame Delphine,* which was serialized in *Scribner's Monthly* from May to July 1881 and published as a book in that same year, clearly derives from the same literary interests and impulses that generated *Old Creole Days* and *The Grandissimes,* and it has been included as the initial story in editions of the former since 1883. While this "placement" of the story has helped keep it in print, it blurs important features of its relationship to the rest of Cable's early fiction. Alice Hall Petry, for example, using an edition of *Old Creole Days* in which both Cable and H. H. Boyesen felt the strongest pieces—*Madame Delphine* and "Madame Délicieuse"—were placed first and last, respectively, describes *Madame Delphine* as "insistently Cablesque" and "an ideal introductory tale" (25) for the collection. Even after 1883, however, the novella was reissued separately or in combination with other stories (for example, with "Carancro," "Au Large," and "Grand Pointe" in an 1887 collection published in Edinburgh), and Cable characterized the story as correcting artistic and moral problems in both "'Tite Poulette" and *The Grandissimes.*

In a Preface to the 1896 edition, Cable explains that he wrote the work to answer a letter he had received from an anonymous quadroon mother asking him to "change the story" of "'Tite Poulette" by telling "the inmost truth of it" that "like many a real quadroon mother . . . Madame John perjured her own soul to win for her child a legal and honorable alliance with the love-mate and life-mate of her choice" (Turner 1980, 104–105). This account places the inception of the story in 1875 and thus provides some merit to Petry's argument that *Madame Delphine* represents a transition from the early stories to *The Grandissimes* (Petry, 141n3). Arlin Turner, however, in suggesting that Cable may have delayed completing and publishing the story out of a reluctance to address the story's racial theme so directly, argues that *Madame Delphine*

can be most valuably read in the order of its publication (1956, 105n1).
In its racial theme and technique the story seems less an introductory or
transitional work than a summation or coda to the Creole romances.

From its initial reception to the present, *Madame Delphine* has generally been acknowledged by critics as Cable's most controlled and artistically finished story. The basic plot is indeed another version of the tragic
mulatto narrative of "'Tite Poulette," in which a quadroon mother,
Delphine Carraze, must eventually deny the parentage of her own
daughter, Olive, so that the beautiful, apparently white octoroon can
legally marry a white man who has fallen hopelessly in love with her.
The white suitor in this case is not a clumsy Anglo-Saxon outsider like
Kristian Koppig but a gallant Creole pirate-turned-banker, Ursin
Lemaitre-Vignevielle. The moral spokesperson is also not a priggish
Américain like Frowenfeld but a humanly fallible Creole priest, Père
Jerome.

In relating this streamlined and somewhat predictable tale, Cable
exhibits most of the signature features of his art—careful evocation of
the picturesque New Orleans setting, use of dialect for both authenticity
and charm, subtle delineation of character, narrative indirection and pervasive sense of mystery, and a strong moral theme—and in all of these
save the last there is evidence of restraint. The transcriptions of Creole
dialect, for example, which would continue to annoy as many of Cable's
contemporaries as it charmed, are pointedly reduced by having the characters speak mostly in French, which is then represented by standard
English. Similarly, while there is some play with confusion of identities,
such as in the conversion of the pirate Lemaitre into the banker
Vignevielle and in his search for the unknown beauty (Olive) who effects
the conversion, these complications are easily deciphered and create little of the "mist" that confounds Frowenfeld in *The Grandissimes*.

The strategy of opening deserves special attention, for as Petry
observes, Cable here and elsewhere was particularly adept at beginnings—that is, at managing exposition, artfully establishing setting and
conflict and engaging the reader's interest (25). More directly than in his
other New Orleans stories the narrator assumes the role of a familiar,
knowledgeable guide, introducing the reader—a visitor, addressed as
"you" and significantly male—to the picturesque oddities of the Vieux
Carré. The perspective begins at the St. Charles Hotel in the modern,
commercial, American section and proceeds as in a walking tour across
Canal Street and along the Rue Royal to "a small, low, brick house of a
story and a half, set out upon the sidewalk, as weatherbeaten and mute

as an aged beggar fallen asleep."[1] The use of a few architectural details and a characterizing metaphor to establish both theme and atmosphere in this and the other descriptions is indeed typical of Cable's best work. The sense of movement is also important both to strike the contrast between the new and old sectors of New Orleans and to suggest a process of curiosity leading to discovery. The impulse to explore the French Quarter, implicitly the reader's, is initially identified as a love of "Creole antiquity," a "fondness for a romantic past" (*MD,* 1), and while the narrator-guide assures the reader that "beauty lingers here" as well as "the picturesque" (*MD,* 2), the predominant notes, as in " 'Sieur George," are poverty, decay, squalor and a sense of the undisclosed.

The subtle effect of the opening, in other words, is to lead the reader away not only from the present and the routes of "the crowd" but also from a superficial interest in the past of Old New Orleans. Behind the obvious signs of social and economic decline and more than the glimpses of "comfort," "opulence," and "rich antiquity" gained through "the unlatched wicket in some *porte-cochère,*" lies a more profound truth figured in the mystery of *Madame Delphine's* house, its shutters "shut with a grip that makes one's knuckles and nails feel lacerated." "The simple key to the whole matter," explains the narrator, is provided by a neighbor's almost casual comment, "Dey's quadroons" (*MD,* 2).

Cable's pointing out that neither the white Creoles nor the quadroons themselves would see anything remarkable in *Madame Delphine's* circumstances suggests that she is typical, representative of a general social and moral pattern. It also invites the history of the free quadroon class in New Orleans that Cable provides to invoke and to explain that interest for the curious outsider-reader. In describing this history Cable's emphasis is less on detailing the beauty of the women—legendary to "old travelers" and to "writers of the day" (*MD,* 8, 9)—than on establishing their social and moral significance. In essence, the *quadroones* (Cable's own spelling "contrived," as he says, "to define the strict limits of the caste as then established") represent a certain ideal of civilization peculiar to the region and, as reflected by the elaborate quadroon balls, supported beyond all other social functions by every aspect of "the white male aristocracy" except the clergy. Cable characterizes their "splendor" as part of a "golden age," suggesting an idealized naturalness and innocence in the era, a prelapsarian world "where it seemed 'always afternoon.' " But in the emphasis on the "beautiful" and the "seductive," reinforced by such terms as "hypernian," "nymphean," and "sirens" to describe the women, he also suggests that the social ideal they represent is pagan: theirs was "a momentary triumph of an Arcadian over a Christian civilization." For the Presbyterian Cable, this last characterization offers judgment enough, ironically undermining the apparent allure. The "pathos" of the quadroons' "charm" is not a foreboding of the inevitable loss of Arcadia but the certainty of their futures as mistresses, the powerlessness and isolation of caste, and thus it has only "a family likeness to innocence." If we were not strangers, the genial narrator confides, *Madame Delphine,* would tell us of the splendors of the era, "though hardly . . . without tears."

Cable also describes the history of the free quadroon class of New Orleans in terms of evolutionary progress. In both beauty and manners the *quadroones* reflect and represent a process of refinement by which the "coarse" and debased features of both their European and their African ancestry are diminished or erased through selection, breeding, and cultivation. On the white side these features come from the "affiliation" of French "merry gallants" with "Spanish-American frontier life" and are visible in "scars of battle or private *rencontre*" (*MD*, 7). On the black side the features include the physical and psychological scars "of servitude on the manumitted [freed] mothers" and the physical characteristics that underlie the initial culling of "comely Ethiopians . . . out of the less Negroidal types of African live goods." The goal of the refinement, as Cable represents it, is not only "the elimination of the black pigment" producing "varied styles of beauty" but also the development of "fascinating manners," "chaste and pretty wit," "grace in the dance," "modest propriety," "taste and elegance in dress." The ideal of civilization represented by the quadroon class in its golden age, then, is not centered in a pleasure principle alone but in a nearly abstract principle of purification that seems the very opposite of sensual pleasure. It is only "in the gentlest and most poetic sense" that the quadroon beauties were "the sirens of this land" (*MD*, 9).

The implications of Cable's representation of the quadroons as products of social and racial refinement are subtle and complex. For one thing, as in the case of the Grandissime family, what evolves can also regress. This seems to be the suggestion of the image of the unprepossessing *gens de couleur* of Cable's own day, sitting in their gardens "with 'Ichabod' legible on their murky foreheads through a vain smearing of toilet powder" (*MD*, 8). Where indeed, Cable seems to ask, is the glory of that earlier era? More important, the erotic appeal of the quadroons for the "male *sang-pur*" derived much of its force from their combination of apparent purity—refinement—and implicit sexual license, a corollary of their overtly white but residually African ancestry. Such tensions are discoverable in the characterization of Olive (whose name suggests racially ambiguous, Mediterranean skin shading), particularly in the scene in which the hero Lemaitre-Vignevielle sees her in her garden.

As most critics agree, Olive is mostly a conventional heroine, a stereotype of the beautiful, virtuous maiden with little more identity, racial or otherwise, than 'Tite Poulette or the Café des Exilé's Pauline Hemecourt. When she confronts Captain Lemaitre on the deck of the ship that he and his pirate crew have boarded and are about to plunder, her quiet courage and simple faith in handing him a small book and asking him to read the Apostle's Creed converts his wonder at her beauty into something like spiritual idolatry. He leaves the ship unmolested, gives up pirating, and later returns to New Orleans where he takes up banking and begins a search for the maiden who converted him. In his voyeuristic peeping through doorways and shutters into shadowy rooms, secluded gardens and interior courtyards, Vignevielle's search echoes the narrator's and the reader's exploration of the French Quarter in the opening chapter, even to the cane both the reader and the Creole are identified as carrying. Thus when Vignevielle finally discovers the mysterious maiden in her mother's garden, the reader too "discovers" something of what he (a cane-carrying reader is implicitly male) was looking for, a glimpse—in the person of Olive—of the remarkable splendor of the bygone quadroon era.

The image Cable creates certainly appears pure and innocent, although, as he suggests later in conventionally Victorian terms, Olive is, at 17, a girl on the threshold of womanhood. Wearing a "snowy" robe and bathed in moonlight, she is almost ghostlike or spiritual in her whiteness—"an outline—a presence—a form—a spirit—a girl!" (*MD*, 66). The tensions in the description, however, begin with the sense that the vision is illicit or forbidden, that it requires a violation, however well-motived on Lemaitre's part, of her interior, private world. He has, after all, been "tempted" (*MD*, 65) into the garden both by a noble "inner vision" of the girl on the ship and by the "ravishing odor" of jasmine, and to gain access he has to force the gate. His voyeuristic gaze—through Cable's description—also involves a subtle focus on her body, which amounts to a genteel but inescapably sensual and erotic disrobing. For example, when Cable describes her as "from throat to instep . . . as white as Cynthia" (*MD*, 66), he exposes parts of her body by naming them.

Similarly, the reader's gaze is directed not only to the sensuality of Olive's "abundant hair rolling in dark, rich waves back from her brows" but also to its caressing fall "in two heavy plaits beyond her round, broadly girt waist and full to her knees, a few escaping locks eddying lightly on her graceful neck and her temples." More overtly, the moment of recognition occurs when she reaches to pluck a jasmine spray, and her arms, which had been "half-hid in a snowy mist of sleeve," are suddenly exposed, "the sleeves falling like a vapor down to the shoulders" (*MD*, 67). When she reaches again, the exposure of both her person and her identity produces in Lemaitre, hidden as "a dark form in the deep shade of the orange," a kind of ecstasy: "That neck and throat! . . . The mockingbird cannot withhold; he bursts into song—she turns—she turns her face—it is she, it is she!"

As discussed earlier, similar scenes of voyeuristic titillation appear in *The Grandissimes* and in such stories as " 'Sieur George" and " 'Tite Poulette," and this scene, like the others, while well within the codes of Victorian propriety, goes beyond a fleeting glimpse of an ankle from beneath floor-length skirts. Compared to a similar scene in "Café des Exilés," the viewing of Olive in her garden is more striking and effective in its epitomizing the general role of quadroon women as objects of overt veneration and covert desire. However pure and chaste the image Vignevielle is seeking and however gentle and restrained the narrator's disrobing hand, the sense of danger accompanying the ex-pirate's clandestine presence (he worries that she might "scream, wheel and vanish" if she saw him, and later both mother and daughter flee and cower when they hear a noise) suggests the particular vulnerability of quadroon women to white-male desire. The reader's specific complicity in the voyeurism, looking over Vignevielle's shoulder and sharing in the illicit, or at least nonconsensual, visual enjoyment of her person, is perhaps the most important aspect of the scene, for Cable's central moral theme in *Madame Delphine* is the shared, social responsibility for the wrongs of racism and caste.

The clarity and the consistency with which Cable develops the theme of shared responsibility is generally recognized as one of the story's strongest features. The history of the quadroon caste as both social ideal and example of moral corruption is paralleled with the history of the Creoles' tolerance for Jean and Pierre Lafitte and the other Baratarian pirates. Ursin Lemaitre-Vignevielle (his name suggesting a combination of "master" and "ancient vine" or "old stock") is "a favored companion and peer" (*MD*, 14) of the brothers Lafitte, and like Jean-ah Poquelin and Agricola Fusilier he is associated with frontier or colonial Creole values. His "rugged old military grandpa of the colonial school" has raised him to be "as savage and ferocious a holder of unimpeachable social rank as it became a pure-blooded French Creole to be who would trace his pedigree back to the god Mars" (*MD,* 13). Lemaitre, then, like the quadroon women, reflects a process of cultivation leading to a social ideal, which in his case, Cable suggests, is the Creoles' aristocratic imperiousness: "Remember, my boy," the grandfather advises, "that none of your family line ever kept the laws of any government or creed," and he is proud that his grandson "is cultivated . . . to that pitch where he scorned to practice any vice, or any virtue, that did not include the principle of self-assertion" (*MD,* 14).

In the colonial period, when "enforcement of the revenue laws" was interpreted by the community as emptying "every man's pocket and dish, into the all-devouring treasury of Spain," "men of capital" who were also "men of action" like the Lafittes became patriots by becoming smugglers: "where," Cable asks with conscious irony, "was the difference?" (*MD,* 14, 15). The social ideal that the Lafittes' represent is criticized by Cable when he points out that as "merchant-blacksmiths" whose social standing placed them "a little higher than the clergy" they "never soiled their hands" with work. Instead they gained their livelihood through the labor of others, both on the open sea and in their famous smithy manned by "African Samsons." Insofar as the Lafittes are reestablished as patriots joining Andrew Jackson to defeat the British at the battle of New Orleans, Cable extends the issue of social responsibility to include the *Américains* as well.

Reinforcing the symmetry of the novella, the theme of moral complicity that is implied in the histories of the *quadroones* and the Lafittes is asserted directly by Père Jerome. In a discussion with Lemaitre-Vignevielle's friends—a Creole doctor, Evariste Varrillat, and a half-American lawyer, Jean Thompson—the little priest "advance[s] the idea" that "there is a community of responsibility attaching to every misdeed" (*MD,* 21), and this becomes the central thesis of his sermon on the stoning of Saint Stephen attended by both the Carrazes and Vignevielle. The "terrible truth" of "the dying saint's prayer for the pardon of his murderers" and of Saint Paul's "I stood by and consented" to the crucifixion of Christ is that "we all have a share in one another's sins" (*MD,* 31). Père Jerome applies this message covertly to the two quadroon women he recognizes sitting among the congregation by charging their sexual sins to the account of a licentious city "to whom society gives the ten commandments of God with all the *nots* rubbed out!" (*MD,* 33). He then overtly, although without naming him, applies the message to

Vignevielle, whose story of conversion from piracy he tells and whose former crimes he asks the congregation to understand and forgive: "God help you, monsieur, and you, madame, sitting here in your *smuggled clothes,* to beat upon the breast with me and cry, 'I, too, Lord—I, too, stood by and consented'" (*MD,* 36). The message of this sermon is then the obvious text for understanding Père Jerome's final words after hearing *Madame Delphine*'s dying confession that she lied about her daughter's parentage and thereby abandoned her in order to assure her happiness: looking up to heaven, he cries "Lord, lay not this sin to her charge" (*MD,* 125).

As Petry has pointed out, Cable develops his moral theme with a recurring emphasis on "charges" and "accounts," as if God were a celestial bookkeeper (38). Such an emphasis, echoed in Vignevielle's "reborn" role as a philanthropic banker, is hardly surprising for a writer who was also both an accountant and a Presbyterian Sunday school teacher, and it is consistent with the fusion of Christian ethics and everyday business sense he would later attempt in *The Busy Man's Bible* (1891). Similar language of "final accounts" appears in "The Story of Bras-Coupé" and elsewhere in *The Grandissimes,* but in *Madame Delphine* it more consistently underscores Cable's effort to awaken social responsibility by exposing the true moral record. Also, as in earlier work, *Madame Delphine*'s moral theme is significantly centered in Victorian attitudes toward women. Cable attempts to arouse indignation against the quadroon caste system as a violation of "all the rights of her womanhood" (*MD,* 42). As Père Jerome observes to *Madame Delphine,* "To you . . . as you are placed, every white man in this country, on land or on water, is a pirate" (*MD,* 46), and the sense of this threat is felt in *Madame Delphine*'s fearing a footstep "merely because it is masculine" (*MD,* 76) and also in her asking Vignevielle, with the ironic implications of *plaçage,* to be a protector for her daughter. Vignevielle, it will be remembered, has been converted from a pirate to "God's own banker" (*MD,* 49) by an image of womanly purity, and in the final melodramatic scenes the pathos of *Madame Delphine*'s perjury is recognizable as a violation of motherhood.

Even more overtly, Cable makes clear that the source of *Madame Delphine*'s original and continuing suffering—the crime chargeable to the account of Creole society—is the law forbidding interracial marriages, a law made, Père Jerome tells her, "to keep the two races separate" (*MD,* 95). *Madame Delphine*'s angry response to this assertion articulates the essential injustice of the law that the story as a whole illustrates: "they made a lie, Père Jerome! Separate! No-o-o! They do not

want to keep us separated; no, no! But they *do* want to keep us despised!
. . . From which race do they want to keep my daughter separate? She is
seven parts white! The law did not stop her from being that; . . . No; I
will tell you what the law is made for. It is made to—punish—my—
child—for—not—choosing—her—father!" (*MD*, 96). By presenting
the racial issues in this way, Cable clearly targets not only the Code Noir
of the 1820s, when the story is set, but also the segregation laws that
were created in the aftermath of Reconstruction, when the story was
written. Much of the novella's appeal to sentiment is based on the sense
that *Madame Delphine* and especially Olive are significantly white and,
therefore, that segregation laws condemn "whiteness" (worse, white
women) to the penalty of "blackness."

Similar arguments appeared in earlier antislavery and civil rights
rhetoric, and 15 years later Mark Twain would make the irony of letting
Roxy's one-sixteenth black blood "outvote" the white central to the
satire in *Puddin'head Wilson and "Those Extraordinary Twins"* (1895).[2] The
crucial point, however, more clearly made in *Madame Delphine* than in
Puddin'head Wilson and other mulatto tragedies of the period, is that the
color line was an arbitrary social fiction. Racial segregation, which would
be established as the law of the land in the *Plessy* v. *Ferguson* decision of
1896, required an absolute determination of whiteness and blackness
and eventually led to the one-drop "blood" theory of black identity. In
the South generally and Louisiana especially, as George Fredrickson, Joel
Williamson, Virginia Dominguez, and others have demonstrated, miscegenation had become such a common part of slavery that drawing a
color line with any ease or certainty was a considerable challenge.[3] Cable
exposes the social fiction of racial purity in *Madame Delphine* not only
through the ambiguous racial appearance of Olive but also through the
general pattern of categories in Creole society in which husband/lover,
wife/mistress, and pirate/patriot are shown to be equally arbitrary blur-
rings of reality. In the dramatic scene in which *Madame Delphine* denies
her maternity to Vignevielle's friends and their wives, a whole series of
these arbitrary boundaries are crossed or blurred.

Normally timid and retiring, Madame Delphine is described in her
approach as walking "like a man" by Madame Varrillat and "like a
woman in a state of high nervous excitement" by the physician—a distinction made comically moot by Thompson's observation (according to
the narrator's translation of his pun) that "she must not forget to walk
like a woman in the State of Louisiana" (*MD*, 110). Thompson is also
disturbed by her wearing a "law-defying bonnet" (*MD*, 112) instead of

the *tignon* required of all free women of color so that they could be so
identified—a law born of Louisiana's blurred racial boundaries. The
social mores become further confused when Dr. Varrillat, apparently in
response to her obviously pained womanhood as she is about to faint,
encourages *Madame Delphine* to sit, which prompts the two white ladies
to rise because, as Cable wryly observes, "somebody had to stand; the
two races could not both sit down at once—at least not in that public
manner" (*MD,* 113). Once inside they all sit, at Madame Thompson's
bidding. Then, the meaninglessness of the racial boundary is demonstrated by the ease with which the Creoles accept *Madame Delphine*'s
proof that Olive is not her daughter. Olive's appearance is shown to be
credibly either white or black depending on who can be established as
her mother, the case for which is supported by the resemblance seen in a
picture of what *Madame Delphine* claims is Olive's real mother but is
actually Vignevielle's sister, underscoring further the fiction of establishing racial identity based on appearance.

Just as Vignevielle's apparent symptoms of insanity at first cast
doubt on his knowing choice of a quadroon bride, *Madame Delphine*'s
signs of apparent mental distraction undermine the "veracity" Père
Jerome attests to, which proves to be unfounded in this instance. That
this group of well-established Creoles recognize her agitation and may,
therefore, as Petry suggests, accept her story knowing it to be false
attests further to the arbitrariness of racial caste (46). They are
Vignevielle's friends and wish his happiness, and Cable has made clear
the pattern in Creole society of obfuscating sins with pretty fictions. All
they ultimately require is *Madame Delphine*'s signed affidavit to be kept
in reserve, and rather than condemn her for having made a white girl
suffer the pains of racial stigma for 17 years, they try to comfort her for
her lost companion.

The most subtle but ultimately most devastating attack on the fiction
of the color line in *Madame Delphine* lies in the fact that the racial intermarriage is left happily intact with no hint of future disclosure. In many
other treatments of this theme in late-nineteenth-century fiction—for
example, in Howells's *An Imperative Duty* (1891) and in Chesnutt's *The
House behind the Cedars* (1900)—the racial intermarriage is clouded or
thwarted by the prospect that "African" traits may later emerge in the
children or in the mixed-blooded spouse or that minor irritations will be
attributed to such traits. Cable suggests no barrier or unhappiness
between the couple other than the arbitrary law they could evade, but
significantly do not, by going to France. Thus, with the early suggestion

that *Madame Delphine*'s situation typifies a broader social pattern ("like many a real quadroon mother"), Cable has written a story of successful "passing" and hence a story of undetected or, at least, erased transmission of the "taint of the tarbrush" across the color line, reversing the transmission pattern of the *quadroones,* undermining at the most fundamental level the fiction that a color line can be meaningfully drawn.

"How many of these Olives," Philip Butcher asks in recognition of the point, "by one deception or another, had brought their taint of Negro blood—imperceptible but legally damning—into some aristocratic Creole family? How many contemporary Creoles, even those adamant in asserting their purity of blood, had, unknowingly, an Olive in one generation or another of their proud ancestry?" (1962, 58–59). Cable's overt point is to awaken the social conscience of his readers— Northern and Southern alike—to their responsibility for the wrongs of caste and segregation, but in Olive's passing he also posits a solution to these problems that is part evasion and part subversion. As James Kinney argues, "Cable seems to have gone beyond his vision in *The Grandissimes* that resolution of miscegenetic problems can come only in violence or in physical escape from the society creating them, to the idea of a third alternative—refusing to accept the rules of that society, not by challenging them but by evading them."[4]

Although critics generally have praised *Madame Delphine* for its thematic unity and artistic control and although Cable himself would later consider it his best story, several modern critics have also acknowledged that the novella lacks the power of *The Grandissimes* and of some of the stories in *Old Creole Days.*[5] For Rubin and Petry the inadequate development of the central characters, Olive and Vignevielle, and the juxtaposition of "a conventionally romantic love plot in a picturesque setting and an urgent social commentary" (Rubin, 103) are major defects. The subtle liminality of Olive's racial and sexual identity and the representation of Vignevielle as a product of cultural conditioning against his moral grain may make them more than "stock characters" (Petry, 42) in their individual relations to the story's social themes, but as lovers the shoe essentially fits. In *The Grandissimes* the historical tensions of the moment of transition to American authority and of the social values reflected in the family feud are essential elements in the "fretted love" between the novel's conventional hero and heroine. In *Madame Delphine,* however, Cable does not dramatize the relationship between Olive and Vignevielle in terms of the social, moral, and historical conflict that shapes their status as individual characters.

For Rubin, all that rescues the story from melodrama is the character-ization of Père Jerome, who as a Creole with human imperfections is justly praised as a more effective moral spokesperson than the excessive-ly upright outsider Joseph Frowenfeld (101).[6] Cable himself, in a letter to Howells, argued this as his intent in shaping the priest's character (in Biklé, 72). Père Jerome's mildly sensual weaknesses—oversleeping and overeating— and his unorthodoxy of making "so much of the Bible and quite so little of the dogmas" (*MD,* 28) interestingly characterize him as a moral spokesperson much as Cable saw himself. Without either a con-vincing love relationship or an effectively dramatized historical conflict, however, the good father's consistent moralizing becomes sententious, heavy-handed, and apparently ineffectual. The more rescuing character-ization, as Elfenbein demonstrates, may be that of Madame Delphine, whose subtly recorded gestures of fear and self-effacement, of stubborn pride and shrewd, albeit self-sacrificing resistance, effectively represents the terms of the quadroon women's victimization (70–72). The scene of her perjury, in its subtly ironic suggestiveness, is one of those passages that justifies the comparisons Turner, Petry, and others have made to the dense fiction of Henry James.

But while Cable could be as nuanced a recorder of social behavior as James, especially through the medium of narrative irony, his sense of dramatic and emotional complexity—the world he imagined or con-structed—was invariably thinner. *Madame Delphine* is a more finished work than any of the individual early stories and a coherent summary— a coda—to the racial themes in "'Tite Poulette" and *The Grandissimes.* For all its clarity of form, however, *Madame Delphine* lacks the rich his-torical, social, political, and environmental texture—the background— that gives *The Grandissimes* and *Old Creole Days,* considered as a whole, their deeper resonance and more enduring power. In this diminishment of elements, it foreshadows the more serious decline in the years ahead.

Man of Letters

Cable's long-contemplated decision to resign from his positions with William C. Black & Company and the New Orleans Cotton Exchange in December 1881 and rely, as he put it, entirely "for offense or defense" on his "grey goose quill"[7] was not without risk. He had received a $500 bonus from Scribners for the success of *The Grandissimes,* and while both it and *Old Creole Days* continued to sell, neither had provided or promised enough income to sustain his family. When he had considered the move two years earlier at the death of his friend Black, his editors E. G. Holland and R. U. Johnson had discouraged him from giving up a source of steady income based on his then likely earning power. At the time of his decision, his most intimate friend in New York, Roswell Smith, warned him that "you cannot live alone by literary production, & there must be a salary somewhere—& somehow" (quoted in Turner 1956, 117). Others, however, were more encouraging, and by the summer of 1881 the demand for his writing from various sources, despite the fact that he was spending little more than one or two hours a day in the counting room, pressured him to resign and gave him grounds for optimism about the future.

One of the stimuli to Cable's launching himself as a full-fledged man of letters came in early 1880 when George E. Waring, Jr., visited New Orleans, sought out Cable, and hired him as a local assistant to supply current information on the region for the Tenth Census of the United States. Cable was paid for the work and commissioned to write the report for both New Orleans and the Acadian country of southwest Louisiana. He revisited the region where he had worked in a surveying crew after the Civil War, and there he gathered abundant social and cultural data about the Acadians that was not included in the census report but that provided the material for the stories he published later as *Bonaventure* (1888). His "Historical Sketch" of New Orleans appeared as a separate report on New Orleans and Austin, Texas, in 1882 (dated 1881) and then was included in the complete Tenth Census in 1887.

Meanwhile, two trips to New York—a week in September 1880 and nearly a month in June 1881—added even greater incentives to quit the counting room. He deepened his friendships with Gilder, Johnson, Smith, and Boyesen, and he met Howells, Charles Dudley Warner, Mark Twain, Harriet Beecher Stowe, and others. During the latter of these trips he completed negotiations for both serial and book rights to his next novel, and he contracted with the Century Company to write a history of New Orleans. These negotiations had been complicated by Waring's securing offers from J. R. Osgood for the serial and book rights to Cable's next novel and by the break-up of Scribners publishing house. In part because of Cable's loyalty to his old friends at Scribners, the newly formed *Century Monthly Magazine* (formerly *Scribner's Monthly*), headed by Roswell Smith, was able to outbid Osgood for the serial rights and to gain commitments for work beyond, but neither Century nor Charles Scribner would meet Osgood's book offer.

This competition for Cable's work augmented not only his earnings but also his confidence in being able to earn a living as a professional writer. In addition to these projects, Cable returned to New Orleans having agreed to write a biography of William Gilmore Simms for the American Men of Letters series, edited by Charles Dudley Warner, and with invitations from the *Century* editors to contribute pieces on the Acadians, on Albion Tourgée's Reconstruction novels, and on issues of prison and asylum reform. There were also generous offers from other magazines—*Critic* and *Our Continent*—for serial novels, an expression of interest in dramatizing *The Grandissimes,* prospects for translations and overseas editions of his works, and an invitation to contribute the New Orleans entry for the *Encyclopaedia Britannica.*

In short, at the point of his leaving the cotton business Cable had a number of writing projects ahead of him that centered in his interests in the region or in reform and that seemed to promise a reasonably steady income. Nevertheless, he set aside the novel that he had begun and for which he had already received a $1,000 advance in order to work on his history of New Orleans because it was nearer to completion and therefore offered more immediate remuneration.

The Creoles of Louisiana

Cable's history of the Creoles has been described by both Turner and Rubin as the result of a long and arduous revision process that begins with the elaborately researched *History and Present Condition of New Orleans* (1881), continues as a trimmed and popularized series of six articles in the January–April and June–July 1883 issues of the *Century Magazine,* and is finally completed in the expanded, more coherent book published by Scribners as *The Creoles of Louisiana* (1884). Reflected in this process is a recurring tension between Cable's inclinations to accuracy and completeness and his editors' desire that he satisfy their and their reader's tastes for picturesque local color. Also, Turner observes that Cable "welcomed this opportunity to chronicle the past of the Creoles so that he could make clear his feelings toward a people he had been accused of maligning in his fiction" and that "the successive revisions show, in fact, a conscious effort not to be unjust or unkind" (1956, 129).

Cable's fondness for his subject and his efforts to praise the Creoles when he can are obvious. The book he produced, however, hardly rescued him from the Creoles' private accusations. In part, this is because the history presented in *The Creoles of Louisiana,* a narrative of the rise and fall of Creole civilization, is essentially the same history—pointedly a moral history—that underlies *Old Creole Days, The Grandissimes,* and *Madame Delphine.* In this sense the book had its origins before the census project in the social, moral, and literary interests that produced the early fiction and thus provides valuable insight into that work.

A recurring theme in Cable's history is the influence of "racial," social, and environmental factors in shaping Creole civilization and determining its fate. Cable carefully locates the Creoles geographically and links their destiny, for both good and ill, with the natural environment, not only the dramatic struggles with storms, plagues, floods, and crevasses but also the city's early promise and later eclipse as a port. The effect of the colonial conditions on Creole character is described as mixed at best. The life of the somewhat coarse and motley first settlers became predictably "idle, thriftless, gallant, bold, rude, free and scornful of labor,"[8] and the children of these settlers—the Creoles—were even more powerfully and fatally stamped. With the introduction of slavery, the fertile soil became "not an incentive to industry, but a promise of unearned plenty"; the "luxurious and enervating climate" debased "even the Gallic love of pleasure to an unambitious apathy and an untrained sensuality"; "the habit of commanding" slaves, despite the retention of French civility, "induced a certain fierce imperiousness of will and temper"; and instead of the "love of freedom" common to the frontier there developed "an attitude of arrogant superiority over all constraint." In sum, "unrestrained, proud, intrepid, self-reliant, rudely voluptuous, of a high intellectual order, yet uneducated, unreasoning, impulsive, and inflammable—such was the first native-born generation of Franco-Louisianians."

Such a characterization, emphasizing Creole indolence, sensuality, and tolerance of public corruption—faults exacerbated by slavery—informs the whole of *The Creoles of Louisiana* and is recognizable in the gallery of Creole characters in Cable's fiction. He does praise the Creoles for striking "the first armed blow ever aimed by Americans against a royal decree" (*CL,* 51) in their insurrection against the Spanish governor, Ulloa, in 1768. They fell short, however, of establishing a republic on just grounds because they were "wanting in habits of mature thought and self-control," having "not made that study of reciprocal justice and natural rights which becomes men who would resist tyranny" and lacking "the steady purpose bred of daily toil" (*CL,* 71). One of the leaders of this insurrection, Attorney General Lafrénière, like Agricola Fusilier, was a Creole of "commanding mien, luxurious in his tastes, passionate, overbearing, ambitious, replete with wild energy, and equipped with the wordy eloquence that moves the ignorant or half-informed" (*CL,* 60). Cable makes these implicit and explicit comparisons with the movement toward independence in the British colonies to suggest that progress for the Creoles means abandoning their Old World aristocratic thinking and ways and moving "into harmony with North American thought and action" (*CL,* 149).

Cable's analysis of Creole civilization in many ways reflects a New South perspective. He identifies "private enterprise" as "the true foundation of material prosperity" (*CL,* 37) and emphasizes how the French and the Spanish authorities, by restricting such enterprise, limited Louisiana's progress and encouraged pubic corruption. The choice of an agricultural, plantation economy requiring slave labor rather than skilled industrial workers is also portrayed as a mistake. Consistent with New South rhetoric and the *Century* editors' desire for pleasant reading, he avoids discussing either the Civil War or Reconstruction, and while he insists on the debilitating effects of slavery, he asserts optimistically that "there is no other part of Louisiana where the slave has made so much progress, as a mass, toward the full possession of freedom as he has in the 'sugar parishes'" (*CL,* 310). He does fault the more aggressive Americans for their commercial excesses and for their taste in architecture, but for the most part, just as the Creoles advance as they become more Americanized, the Americans decline as they acquire Creole faults and habits. In the matter of not building a levee around New Orleans, for example, he argues that the American was becoming Creolized and converted to common Southern traits of "improvidence, and that feudal self-completeness which looked with indolent contempt upon public co-operative measures" (*CL,* 275). While Cable would soon part radically with the New South proponents on the grounds of the treatment of the freedman, in *The Creoles of Louisiana* his emphasis, with some reservations, is on industry and commerce in combination with Northern political and social ideals as the source of material and moral progress for the South and for the nation generally.[9]

The Creoles of Louisiana was well received in both the Northern and the New Orleans papers, but one wonders (along with Louis Rubin) at Turner's speculation that a "Creole not oversensitive might find, actually, that Cable came closer to violating accuracy through sympathy than severity" (1956, 129; Rubin, 115–16). A trivial controversy over Cable's assertion that General James Wilkinson had been involved in a plot to detach Kentucky territory from the United States and deliver it to Spain became more significant when Charles Gayarré joined in the public debate (Turner 1956, 130). Spurred by Cable's initial defense that he had relied on the celebrated Creole historian for his source, Gayarré suggested that Cable had borrowed without acknowledgment.[10] In this attack Gayarré exhibited an unexpected but long-standing resentment against Cable, which was no doubt based, as Rubin argues, on the novelist— worse an *Américain*—having replaced the elder scholar as the best-known authority on Louisiana and earning money by his writing while the Creole was impoverished (114–15).

Cable's friend Marion Baker, literary editor of the *Times-Democrat,* helped smooth the rift, but it offered another sign that Cable's standing with his Creole neighbors was less amicable than he sometimes thought and claimed it to be. Joseph Pennell, who was sent to New Orleans by the *Century* editors to meet Cable and to provide the illustrations for both the magazine and the book editions of *The Creoles of Louisiana,* wrote that he was "entirely barred out" from meeting certain Creoles because "Cable[,] the only 'Americain' down here who knows them[,] is the most cordially hated little man in New Orleans, and all on account of the *Grandissimes;* and so he can do nothing with the better class" (quoted in Turner 1956, 119).

However accurate its portrayal of the Creoles and whatever its continuing value as history, *The Creoles of Louisiana,* with its mix of fascinating events and people and exotic atmosphere, remains an interesting, immensely readable book—perhaps the last such that he wrote. In some sense it is a rendition of the romance of the region without the fictional overlay, the background without an imagined foreground. For students of Cable's fiction it is an indispensable work, offering the fullest and clearest exposition of his attitudes toward the Creoles and of his understanding of the factors shaping Louisiana and Southern society—except for the factors of race and caste. That exception, of course, is significant, but would soon be addressed, again outside of fiction, in "The Freedman's Case in Equity."

Platform Performer

In addition to generating suggestions and commitments for writing projects, Cable's trip to New York in June 1881 also stimulated his move to become a full-time writer by treating him to a taste of camaraderie with literary celebrities. In letters to both his wife and his mother, he expresses pleasure with the opportunity to meet such well-known figures as Howells, Stowe, statesman-novelist John Hay, sculptor Saint Gaudens, and editor-poet Edmund Clarence Steadman, but his being welcomed and entertained in the circle that included not only Charles Dudley Warner and his brother George but also Mark Twain was clearly a highlight of his trip. On later visits to New York, Boston, and Hartford he would meet John Greenleaf Whittier, Matthew Arnold, Andrew Carnegie, Brander Mathews, Mary Mapes Dodge, George Parsons Lathrop, John Burroughs, actors Joseph Jefferson and Madame Modjeska, and other artists and literary figures.

In New Orleans he also became increasingly sought out by important visitors whom he hosted at his house on Eighth Street. Joseph Pennell later recorded his visit fondly in his autobiography, *The Adventures of an Illustrator* (1925), and Mark Twain similarly celebrated in print his week-long stay in New Orleans with Cable as his guide in late April 1882.[11] One highlight of the visit recorded in *Life on the Mississippi* (1883) was a Sunday afternoon at Cable's house in which Joel Chandler Harris joined the party, and each read from his own work except Harris, who was too shy, leaving Cable and Twain to render Uncle Remus's accents. Later that summer Oscar Wilde visited New Orleans to give a lecture and arranged to meet Cable, having been intrigued, like others before him, by reading his work.[12]

One significance of this social activity was that it seemed to establish Cable as a literary celebrity himself and, therefore, to provide some assurance of his prospects as a professional writer. It also provided him with the sense of belonging to a community or social circle of like-minded individuals. The alienation of the artist in American society is an oft-repeated story in American literary history, and Cable's situation in New Orleans can be seen as another version of this story. Although by mid-1884 he would be, as Turner puts it, "acclaimed on every hand in New Orleans except among part of the Creole population" (1956, 155), it is clear that Cable was not unmindful of this exception, having grown up in the city as an *Américain* sensitive enough to the Creoles' exclusiveness to mock it in his fiction, and his growing acceptance in a literary-artistic society in the North would help encourage his move to Northampton, Massachusetts, a few years later.

More immediately, Cable's involvement in literary-social activity contributed in another way to his emergence as a man of letters. Because of his enhanced reputation and status he received invitations to give public lectures and then readings of his work, which he would embellish with singing Creole songs just as he had at many of the soirées in New York and New Orleans. For more than 15 years Cable would rely on public lectures and platform readings as a major source of income, and although these activities derived from his literary work, they subtracted more time and energy from his fiction writing than had his duties in the counting room.

Cable's first public lecture in June 1882 was a commencement address at the University of Mississippi on the subject of "Literature in the Southern States," in which he called for the South to abandon the thinking of a past blighted by slavery, perpetuated by tenant farming and caste, and embodied in traditional "plantation" fiction. These were the first steps necessary to produce a literature that was not merely sectional but truly national. Although his audience might not have been wholly receptive to his thesis, the response to the speech, both during and after, was generally favorable, and Cable thought that he had been a success. A more rewarding opportunity followed in March 1883, when Cable, on invitation from President Daniel Coit Gilman, delivered six lectures on "The Relations of Literature to Modern Society" at Johns Hopkins University and then was asked to stay and read from his books three days later. The lectures were well received, but the reading was by all accounts a sensation, generating comparisons with Charles Dickens's readings earlier in the century.

By this point, encouraged especially by Roswell Smith, Cable was seriously considering platform work as a way to supplement his income. A reading at Hartford in April organized by Smith with the aid of Twain and the Warners was, as Turner describes it, a kind of "coming out party" (1956, 140). Solidly sponsored, well-publicized, and attended by such luminary friends as Osgood, Gilder, Waring, Warner, and Twain, the reading was designed to test Cable's draw and help promote his career as a platform performer. In this and in several more lectures and readings before groups large and small, both North and South, over the next several months Cable experimented with his delivery, timing, and materials. Although the delicacy of his humor and the intimacy of his style seemed to work best before smaller audiences, he employed Franklin Sargent as a voice trainer to help him project to large halls, and he later practiced playing the cornet to develop his lung capacity. In these readings, especially several in Boston, he also enjoyed enormous success in the audiences' enthusiastic responses, in the notices and reviews in the press, and in the troops of notables, such as Francis Parkman, J. T. Trowbridge, T. W. Higginson, Elizabeth Stuart Phelps, and Horace Scudder, who visited him backstage and lavished praise on him and his work.

Although he would complain of the feeling that he was working only for money and of the arduousness and the loneliness of the travel, Cable once again clearly delighted in the attention, in the excitement and gratification of his celebrity. He felt that he had at last "arrived," but he worried about his moral responsibilities. As he wrote to his wife, "I'm the fashion of the moment. God help me to use it for the advancement of truth & righteousness & the blessed things of salvation!"[13] In December 1883 he hired Major James B. Pond to manage his readings, which included not only the round of Eastern cities but such Western stops as Chicago and Ann Arbor. Before he left the lecture circuit in the 1890s he would read throughout the East and Midwest, travel into Canada, visit the West Coast twice—from San Diego to Seattle—and even read before small but dignitary-studded gatherings in London.

The most important and celebrated of Cable's reading tours was a joint enterprise with Mark Twain managed by Major Pond from November 1884 through February 1885. Aided by Cable's recording his experiences and observations in detailed letters to his wife, this "Twins of Genius" tour, as it was billed, offers a fascinating perspective on two of the best-known writers of their age and a backstage glimpse at the nineteenth-century vogue of platform readings. While the two somewhat mismatched personalities got along remarkably well given the amount of time they were forced to share, at the end of the tour there were reports of friction that caused Cable pain when they leaked into newspaper reports. Apart from some professional jealousy, travel fatigue, and worry over money, the source of the difficulty is generally recognized to be Twain's irritation with Cable's religiosity and particularly his sabbatarianism that did not permit him to travel on Sundays, even when that might be more convenient. In a letter to Howells in which he praises Cable's "gifts of mind" and describes him as "pleasant company," Twain also writes, "You will never, never know, never divine, guess, imagine, how loathsome a thing the Christian religion can be until you come to know and study Cable daily and hourly."[14] Given Twain's volatile personality and frequent attacks against religion and piety, it is not surprising that he should have been annoyed at Cable's sabbatarianism, but it is easy to exaggerate the conflict, and both continued to publicly praise each other years later.

Full accounts of the tour can be found in Guy A. Cardwell's *Twins of Genius* (1953) and Arlin Turner's *Mark Twain and George W. Cable: The Record of a Literary Friendship* (1960), but the question of the impact of the tour on Cable's literary career deserves some attention here.[15] In addition to depleting the time and energy he needed to write, the readings also engaged Cable more directly in the concern of shaping his material for popular reception. As both Cable and Twain learned, reading from one's own work is not merely a matter of oral narration but a kind of theatrical performance. In 1883, influenced by his new friend Joseph Jefferson and accompanied by the upright Roswell Smith, Cable had tested his mother's and his religion's proscriptions against the theater by attending a play in New York. He experimented with theatrical effects in his readings, and both he and Twain were very sensitive to what worked and what did not in their program. From his "Drop Shot" days, Cable's narrative manner had employed various subtle devices aimed at dramatic effect, but to achieve similar results with a large public audience required broader strokes. His expressed delight in leaving his audience in tears may be symptomatic of the problem.

Years later both Twain and Pond, who also went along on the tour, observed that Cable's voice training seemed to have altered his platform style for the worse by making it less natural. Even more telling is Cable's awareness of what were the most popular, most affecting parts of his program: his reading the stirring, melodramatic "Mary's Night Ride" passage from his new novel, *Dr. Sevier,* and his singing such Creole songs as "Pov' Piti' Momzelle ZiZi," neither of which reflected the sociopolitical elements of his best fiction.[16] In light of Cable's obvious need for public acceptance of his work, not only psychologically and aesthetically but also economically, the latter a more immediate reality of the lecture circuit, it is reasonable to think that Cable's experience of public readings, especially with Twain, may have contributed to the increasing emphasis on the romantic and sentimental in his fiction—not an abandonment of social concerns but a wider split between conscience and art. In short, beyond the obvious pique there may be something of truth in Twain's comment to his wife near the end of the tour that Cable "is one of the most spoiled men, by success in life, you ever saw" (quoted in Turner 1956, 192).

Reformer

Deeply rooted in his sense of applied Christian service, Cable's interest in reform antedated his career as a fiction writer, but during the period of his emergence as a professional man of letters it became increasingly important, both in the time he devoted to it and in the direction it took. His reform interests also significantly affected *Dr. Sevier,* the first novel he produced after he left the counting room.

Cable's most important reform work in the early 1880s grew out of his role as secretary of a grand jury investigating charges of public corruption and abuse in New Orleans's prisons and asylums.[17] Appalled by the contrast with similar institutions he had visited in New England and assigned to write the concluding report, Cable not only denounced local conditions but called for continuing public action. To this end he organized a Board of Prison and Asylum Commissioners, established by city ordinance in November 1881, and a supporting citizen's committee, the Prisons and Asylums Aid Association. For both the board and the association Cable gained the support of many of the city's most prominent business and professional men, and he was chosen to be the association's unpaid secretary. He also accepted an invitation from the editor of the *Times-Democrat,* Major E. N. Burke, to be the paper's official commentator on the subject of prison and asylum reform.

Cable's leading role in this successful reform movement was widely recognized and applauded both in and outside of New Orleans. He acquired a reputation as an expert in the field of prison reform and a willing public servant, and he was invited to join, help organize, or participate in the activities of a host of other civic, reform, and charitable organizations, such as the Southern Art Union, the Louisiana Historical Society, and the National Conference of Charities. Although he participated willingly in these activities out of a sense of moral and social responsibility, they produced no income and took time away from his writing. However, some opportunity to link his reform interests, literary ambitions and economic needs did arise. From December 1881 through March 1882, Cable contributed seven articles to the *Times-Democrat* on various aspects of prison and asylum reform, describing in detail many of the abuses recently uncovered, analyzing causes and suggesting means of amelioration. He was also invited to give public lectures on issues of reform, and thus his role as a reformer was part of his public persona as a man of letters. The most significant of these lectures from both a political and literary standpoint was delivered at the National Conference of Charities meeting in Louisville in September 1883 and published the next year in *Century Magazine* as "The Convict Lease System in the Southern States." With the appearance of the article in *Century* Cable established himself in the role of a Southern spokesperson directly addressing a national audience on important problems of Southern society.

Cable had become increasingly aware of the evils of the convict lease system through his ongoing investigative activities as a member of the Prisons and Asylums Aid Association. He discovered corruption and mismanagement, distorted sentencing practices, numerous escapes, cruel abuse and suffering of individuals, and unequal treatment based on wealth or social standing, and he deplored the injustice of making prisoners pay for their keep instead of society paying for their rehabilitation. He also discovered a greater, more deplorable injustice in the unequal treatment of prisoners based on race, but in the Louisville lecture he omitted the references to racial inequality so as not to distract attention from his main thesis. The receptions to both the lecture and the article were overwhelmingly positive in the North and in the South, and this evidence of continuing general support for reform activities no doubt bolstered his determination to address the question of the racial injustice when he spoke before the conference again in September 1884. This lecture, published the following year in *Century* as "The Freedman's Case in Equity," produced a far different reaction, and with it Cable entered into a 10-year public debate over race and caste in America that would occupy a good deal of his intellectual energy. At the outset, his past experiences at reform convinced him he could both marshall public support and achieve a measure of success, but in these expectations he was to be painfully disappointed.

Dr. Sevier

When *Dr. Sevier* was published by J. R. Osgood in September 1884, it was for the most part a critical success. Many of the Northern reviewers praised the novel as Cable's best book and again compared its author favorably with Dickens, Hugo, Daudet, James, and Hawthorne. Even the Southern reviews, while beginning to attack Cable on the grounds of his social and racial opinions, frequently praised the artistry of the work. More recent critics, however—Turner, Butcher, and Rubin in particular—have recognized that the novel is a failure and that its weaknesses constitute its greatest interest for modern readers in what they reveal about Cable's indisputable artistic decline.

As Cable's first novel as a full-time man of letters, *Dr. Sevier* is linked to his hopes to succeed in his new profession and also symptomatic of how the career change affected his art. One effect might be seen in the difficulty Cable had in writing the novel from late 1881 to October 1883, owing in part to the distractions of his new celebrity—travel, social activities, speaking engagements, and other writing projects. Cable's involvement in prison and asylum reform had still greater impact both in the time he devoted to it and in its effect on the novel's central theme. Responding to the first draft, a novelette titled "Bread," Richard Watson Gilder complained that it was "the least good work" Cable had done, a "'put up job' . . . in order that the writer can preach his theories."[18] He chided Cable: "You have turned your mind so completely into philanthropical work that for the time being you have lost your sense of art." Although Gilder became more supportive of later versions, it is apparent that to some degree Cable revised the novel by adjusting his reform impulses to the desire of his editors for a work that would appeal to *Century* readers. Therein, for Edmund Wilson and Philip Butcher, lies a major reason for the novel's failure: to the degree that Cable's strength as a writer is in his social realism and that this in turn derives from his reform impulses, *Dr. Sevier* fails because Cable was turned away from the sources of his literary strengths by his editors and the need to earn a living.[19] As Louis Rubin argues, however, such an explanation misrepresents Gilder's directives to Cable, which, if anything, encouraged his interest in prison reform, advising him not to avoid "the inculcation of morality" but to give it "artistic form." While Gilder was certainly not the best editor to guide Cable in the social theme he chose to address in *Dr. Sevier,* the real problem may lie in Cable's unwillingness or inability to follow the direction he received and, even more, in the implications of that choice. The most significant fact about *Dr. Sevier* may not be the centrality of its reform motive but that it is the first of Cable's stories to be set in the recent past outside of the French Quarter and without Creoles or quadroons as main characters: the first, in other words, in which he did not explore Louisiana's "mines of romance" or its tangled social history for imaginative inspiration.

The novel's main action centers initially in the efforts of a young married couple, John and Mary Richling, to establish themselves in New Orleans from 1856 until the outset of the Civil War. Their difficulties stem from the husband's inability to find suitable employment and his initial unwillingness to accept help from the novel's title character, a widowed doctor for women who divides his time between his successful office practice on Carondelet Street and the Charity Hospital. The couple is plagued by a series of economic and other misfortunes, including Mary's recurring bouts of illness, John's incarceration at the Parish Prison, where he contracts the disease that will eventually end his life, and relentless petty borrowing by Dr. Sevier's Creole accountant,

Narcisse. Ultimately, their fortunes decline to the point where John reluctantly sends his wife to stay with her parents in Milwaukee. While there she delivers a child, named Alice after Dr. Sevier's deceased wife, and John begins to prosper as an accountant for a German baker, Reisen, doing so well that he arranges for his wife to return just prior to the outbreak of the war. Her efforts to make her way through both Union and Confederate lines and reunite the family in occupied New Orleans constitutes the central action of the novel's second half. Traveling with her toddler daughter and accompanied by a backwoods spy, dodging bullets through a furious night ride, she is balked and delayed at several points but manages to join her husband only a few hours before his death. After the war she accepts Dr. Sevier's guardianship of Alice, works as a schoolteacher and as an assistant to him in his charity work, and thus forms a kind of family with the doctor, although they never marry.

One immediately noticeable effect of Cable's choice of setting and material in *Dr. Sevier* is the lack of atmosphere or, more accurately, the substitution of the atmosphere of the American sectors—the business district and the Garden District west of Canal Street—for the more exotic atmosphere of the Vieux Carré. There is much less attention to curious architecture or to the surrounding landscape, with these replaced by a few descriptions of busy commercial and industrial scenes and the flora of suburban gardens. In one passage Cable attempts a play with the "mythic" street names near the Garden District—Naiade, Dryades, Bacchus, Melpomene, Terpsichore, and Apollo. The effort is consistent with his usual close referencing of geography and desire to attach action to milieu, but here it is broadly sentimental and cloying. Of course, most of the picturesqueness that modern critics find objectionable or trivial in Cable's work is omitted with these changes, but the result is a general flatness of tone, an absence of the subtle, complex suggestiveness, the sensual appeal and historical associations of the French Quarter.

Similarly, Cable's attempts at mystification and narrative indirection are minimized, and the novel has been praised for a "singleness and directness" lacking in *The Grandissimes* (Turner 1956, 160). More significantly, the mysteries that are evoked—such as Dr. Sevier repeatedly losing track of the Richlings and the hints about their background (he is the son of a wealthy Kentucky plantation owner who disinherits him for marrying a Northern girl beneath his station)—are disconnected from the physical and social milieu. These mysteries emerge not as in "'Sieur George," "Jean-ah Poquelin," and *Madame Delphine,* as curiosities inherent in the locale, but as obvious and conventional literary ploys.

Characterization also reflects the literary departure. In his earlier fiction Cable used regional particularities of manners, customs, appearance, and speech for his most interesting portraits. The upright Anglo-Saxon characters, such as Koppig, Little White, and Frowenfeld ('Sieur George is made interesting by his vices), are less distinctively developed. In *Dr. Sevier* the main characters, the doctor and the Richlings, again lack depth of development and distinctiveness, but to relieve their blandness Cable adds not an array of Creoles but an array of various ethnic types. There is one quadroon woman, the *rentier* Madame Zenobia, and one black man met on Mary's night ride, neither of whom is fully or significantly developed.[20] The one Creole, Narcisse, is somewhat an echo of Jule St. Ange and Raoul Innerarity, a comic stereotype whose vices of indolence, self-centeredness, chain-smoking, and chronic borrowing are supposed to be forgivable, assuaged by his incurable cheerfulness and irresistible charm and ultimately redeemed by his heroic martyrdom during the war. Narcisse's insensitivity to the plight of the Richlings, however, seems less comic than criminal, and their acquiescence to his requests for money is simply absurd.

Consistent with Cable's focus on the economic developments immediately before and after the Civil War, the more important minor characters are German, Italian, and Irish immigrants, each narrowly stereotyped. Cable had, of course, stereotyped his Creole characters before, but generally with a subtle sense of social nuance and significant historical and political implications. There is no apparent depth of social or historical implication in the ethnic stereotyping of the stolid German baker, Reisen, the resourceful Italian, Raphael Ristofalo, or the good-hearted Irish housekeeper, Kate Riley, and in Ristofalo's courtship of Kate there is a good deal of comic condescension. Not surprisingly, Cable individuated these ethnic characters mainly through their dialects, which he rendered with such a devotion to accurate transcription that several lengthy passages—especially Reisen's speeches—are a struggle to read. The one generally acknowledged exception to this is the speech of the Mississippi backwoods spy, Sam, who accompanies Mary on her flight through the Confederate lines and whose dialect is subtly rendered and natural.

In essence, when Cable abandoned the Louisiana "mines of romance," and thus the wealth of historical lore and sociological detail they contained, he drew instead on personal experience and his ongoing investigation of prison abuses for material of literary interest. Dr. Sevier is modeled after his family doctor, Warren Brickell, and the economic problems of the Richlings—John's seeking employment as an accountant, their search for housing, the threat of plague, Mary's illnesses, the question of their separation, the fall of New Orleans, the terrain of southern Mississippi and northeastern Louisiana—are all recognizable as experiences Cable knew firsthand or as part of his parents' history. In making fiction of these experiences he also seems to have come under the spell of Howellsian realism, particularly in its emphasis on the commonplace. For example, he describes the Richlings sitting in their apartment "like so many thousands of young pairs in this wide, free America, offering the least possible interest to the great human army round about them, but sharing, or believing they shared, in the fruitful possibilities of this land of limitless bounty, fondling their hopes and recounting the petty minutiae of their daily experiences."[21] A similar emphasis on the everyday can be found in the apartment search in the opening sections of the novel, which echoes Marcia and Bartley Hubbard's search in Howells's *A Modern Instance* (1881) and anticipates the Marches' later, more famous house-hunting in *A Hazard of New Fortunes* (1890). Cable also shares Howells's interest in the chaste, subdued delights of middle-class marriage as he devotes several lengthy passages to the affectionate by-play between the young couple, but as is sometimes the case with Howells, the sense of interest in these interchanges lies primarily with the parties involved. In too much of *Dr. Sevier,* especially in "recounting the petty minutiae" of the couple's domesticity, the substitution of the commonplace for the exotic yields tedium.

Certain parallels with Howellsian realism—the emphasis on complicity and the moral or ethical implications of economic change—can also be found in Cable's handling of social themes. Some of the best portions of the book are the Dickensian prison, hospital, and court scenes and the exposure of various abuses and corruptions of the penal and hospital systems. These drew on the specifics of Cable's recent research and reform work and reinforce the argument that his literary strength lay not in his imagination but in a marriage of research, careful observation, and an appropriately ironic style. The overall handling of social and economic themes is, however, neither effectively dramatized, sufficiently clear, nor particularly meaningful. John Richling's inability to gain suitable employment is represented as a problem of upbringing and class consciousness. Although willing to work, he is the son of a slave owner, raised to believe that he "was always to be master, and never servant, . . . to go through life with soft hands" (*DS,* 448), and he, therefore, does not know how to seek employment, how to promote himself, when to push, when not to.

In specific contrast with Ristofalo, John has not the knack for seeing and seizing an economic opportunity: he "was educated to know, but not to do" (*DS,* 449). Even when he finds employment, it is somehow not entirely right for him, and he is notably aloof from the other employees, "a recluse, or at least, a dreamer" (*DS,* 121), primarily absorbed in his wife. In his own characterization, John is "the typical American gentle-man,—completely unfitted for prosperity and totally unequipped for adversity" (*DS,* 200). If this typicality were somehow demonstrated or felt in the novel, if his problems were recognizable as a social and eco-nomic pattern, the social theme might be more convincing.

Instead, Richling seems something of a special case. His disconnection from the world around him is both signalled and exacerbated by his being hard of hearing. Although we are given little grounds for the spec-ulation, Cable describes him as potentially an "inventor, . . . a writer, a historian, an essayist, or even . . . a well-fed poet" (*DS,* 122). He is, in other words, something like Cable himself, fired by what Cable saw in his mother as "intellectual ambition," fearful of settling for something less than the full use of his talents but uncertain of earning an adequate living by those talents and, therefore, afflicted with a sense of alienation from his milieu. Rubin has recognized that this alienation is Richling's defining feature, and he argues that it is a reflection of Cable's own growing sense of estrangement from the South because of his opinions on the issues of race and caste (140). For Rubin, Richling only makes sense as a closet abolitionist, and the novel is flawed, therefore, by the author's consciously omitting the issue that was the source of the feeling he was trying to convey. To be sure, the novel suffers from not address-ing questions of race, both in its economic themes—the competition for labor between slaves, freedmen, and immigrants—and, more noticeably, in its treatment of the Civil War. To attempt a novel about the South during this period and not include racial issues is virtually to assure triv-iality. The problem with Richling's character and with the novel's socioe-conomic theme, however, goes beyond the omission of the specific issue of race to a more general lack of adequate grounding.

This generalizing tendency in *Dr. Sevier* seems to have been intention-al and is again connected with Cable's moving the setting out of the unique French Quarter. In writing the book Cable seems to have been attempting the kind of "national" novel, transcending merely sectional interests and perspectives, that he had spoken of in his address at the University of Mississippi and that formed a central part of his literary theory. This intent is most obvious in his efforts to appeal to both Northern and Southern readers, celebrating on both sides the pageantry of war preparations, the heroism and martyrdom of soldiers, and depicting the courageous suffering of the South in defeat while acknowledging the justice of the Northern cause.[22] Omitting nearly all references to slavery and race seems part of this broad effort to heal sectional differences. Similarly, the diminishment of local-color features and the claim of the Richlings' typicality, even the broadened range of ethnic stereotypes, makes the novel seem less regional than national, not a New Orleans but an American novel. Of course, without the well-chosen particulars that embody and reveal the general, the effect is blandness—too much talk and too little substance, the "preaching" and artificiality that Gilder and some later critics complained of.

This weakness is most telling in the development of the novel's major theme, which is charity, the question of how much and in what way to help the needy so that they can survive and not lose either the independence or dignity necessary for later success. Typical of realist novels of the era in which professional men replace clergymen as moral authorities, the central figure for articulating these issues is Dr. Sevier. Like many of Cable's moral spokespersons, the doctor (whose name, Cable said, should be pronounced like Xavier and may suggest a combination of *severe* and *savior*)[23] struggles between excesses of austere moral rigidity and soft-hearted sympathy. He must learn to be ruled less by his head and more by his heart, like a Hawthorne character. Although he is successful in his medical practice, money is secondary to his pursuit of a noble calling. "He waged war," Cable notes, "against malady" (*DS,* 7), both physical and social. One problem with his character is that, like Richling's, it is inadequately dramatized, the sources of his severity in withholding aid from the young man are neither clear nor convincing. Some complication is added to his character by his obvious attraction to Mary, who reminds him of his deceased wife, but the implications of this are again not fully developed.[24]

More important, the economic world of New Orleans is only vaguely suggested in the first half of the novel, and the second half is mostly melodramatic action. Wayne Mixon has argued that Cable attacks New South confidence about the value of economic progress by showing how Richling's struggles and eventual success are ultimately unsatisfying and lead to his death, but this, too, is unclear outside of a general point about the falsity of money-getting as an end in itself (Mixon, 101–102). The most specific detailings of New Orleans's economic life are Richling's seemingly endless job hunts (mostly reports of the days' failures) and Ristofalo's relatively petty enterprises. And, if there were some thought of applying Dr. Sevier's theories of charity to the reconstruction of the South, the connection is feeble and easily missed. Hence, in the absence of a depiction of real economic forces and conditions, the essentially moral and ethical discussions about charity seem vapid, sententious, and irrelevant.

It is not that Cable did not know economic hardship by experience, but that he approached these problems as one, like Richling, who preferred to exchange ideas with men of standing and education, like his officers during the war, the surveying engineers on the Atchafalaya River and the business and civic leaders in Black's cotton exchange. His clarity of moral vision, based on his reading of the Bible and the Constitution, and his ironic sense of social nuance served him well in addressing the questions of the injustice of slavery and the treatment of the freedman, but as evidenced by *Dr. Sevier,* these qualities were less valuable in providing a meaningful analysis of poverty and economic injustice.

In sum, when Cable moved the locus of literary interest in his work to universalize his themes and to broaden his appeal, he created a void that he had neither the imagination nor the right kind of research to fill. Moreover, in writing about what he thought he knew by experience or what he believed by moral abstraction, rather than what he observed as an ambiguously attached but inescapably marginalized voyeur in Creole New Orleans, he lost an essential element of complexity. The problem in *Dr. Sevier* seems less that Cable's conscience was stifled or diluted by his editors but that, like Howells in *A Hazard of New Fortunes* and James in *The Bostonians* (1886) and *The Princess Casamassima* (1886), he tried to write the kind of social novel for which his artistic temperament, vision, and taste left him ill-equipped.

Chapter Five

Civil Rights

In "My Politics" Cable wrote that when he left the cotton business he "hoped to make literature [his] sole calling" and that "literature meant, to [him] belles-lettres, not essays whether political or other" (*NQ,* 18).[1] As he then observed, however, he "made an odd digression from belles-lettres, for all that," and for nearly 10 years after the appearance of *Dr. Sevier* in 1884 he published no original fiction except the three Acadian stories that became *Bonaventure* (1888). During this period his income derived largely from the lecture/reading circuit, and his literary efforts centered in a reform crusade on behalf of the freedman. Cable had previously addressed issues of slavery, race, and caste both in his Creole fiction and, as early as Reconstruction, in newspaper pieces and public lectures, but "The Freedman's Case in Equity," published in *Century Magazine* in January 1885, presented Cable's most direct statement on what he called, speaking as one white Southerner to others, "the greatest social problem before the American people to-day . . . the presence among us of the negro."[2]

Sparked by the controversy this essay aroused, Cable defended and promoted his views through numerous speeches and essays for the next five years and significantly altered the focus and direction of his literary career. When the furor began during his reading tour with Mark Twain, Cable was near the height of his reputation, both North and South, but by its close he would be widely attacked in the South for his politics, and he would have begun to lose nationally some of the audience for his fiction. Nevertheless, the essays he wrote on the Southern question, most of which were published in two volumes—*The Silent South* (1885; expanded edition in 1889) and *The Negro Question* (1890)—constitute Cable's fullest articulation of the issues of race central to his most important fiction. They also represent the most significant defense of civil rights for the freedman written in America from the end of Reconstruction until the end of the century. However else he might be judged, his courage and moral consistency in this defense seem singularly admirable, all the more so because so few voices, none of comparable stature—not Howells, not Twain—joined him publicly in his crusade.

This transition in Cable's literary career was accompanied by another transition in his life: his move to Northampton, Massachusetts, in September 1885. While the move has often been perceived as a forced flight from hostile neighbors, Cable had actually considered moving his family to the North for a number of years before the controversy broke over "The Freedman's Case in Equity." New Orleans summers were enervating, especially for Louise, and Cable also longed to be closer to his publishers and to the stimulating intellectual and cultural life in the North. As early as 1882, in a letter explaining his inability to attend Harriet Beecher Stowe's birthday celebration, he had written that he "had never been home" until his first visit to New England the year before.[3] No doubt the warm reception he had received from his earliest trips north, his sense of celebrity status, had much to do with drawing him away from New Orleans, as did Louise's chronic poor health. It was primarily for the latter reason that he relocated her and their four daughters to Franconia, New Hampshire, for the summer of 1881 and then again in July 1884 (now with a fifth daughter) to Simsbury, Connecticut, where he decided to remain for the entire year and perhaps longer. He rented his home on Eighth Street to his friend Major E. A. Burke, and for a time it was occupied by the poet Juaquin Miller.

Cable retained warm feelings for his native city, but when the storm broke over the freedman article early in 1885 the decision to relocate permanently in the North was, as Philip Butcher suggests, essentially made for him. The New Orleans newspapers were attacking him mercilessly, and he was rebuffed or treated coldly even by some of his longtime friends and acquaintances. He was informed that the loans on his house would not be renewed, and his property was reassessed for taxes at an exorbitantly high value. In January, near the outset of the newspaper attacks, he wrote to Louise about the "state of society" he observed in New Orleans and the South: "The more carefully I study it the less I expect of it; and though there is no reason why I should indulge ungracious feelings toward it I cannot admire it or want my children to be brought up under its influence" (quoted in Turner 1956, 222).

Cable chose Northampton as his permanent home (moving his mother, sister, and sister-in-law there in the summer of 1886) for a number of reasons: it was relatively inexpensive to live; it provided easy access to his publishers in New York and Boston and to towns favorable for platform readings; it offered the opportunity for his daughters to attend Smith College without tuition; and it had a history and reputation for both conservative religion and radical social reform. Cable was readily accepted in his new community and became quickly involved in various civic, church, and social activities that became increasingly the center of his life, apart from writing fiction.[4]

In "My Politics" Cable describes his conversion from ardent Confederate to civil rights advocate as occurring in several stages, beginning with his recognition of the practical folly of secession while he was still in uniform. After the war he was troubled even more by the ease with which so many Southern newspapers abandoned the principle of secession as having been "forever negatived by the arbitrament of the sword" (*NQ,* 5). Interested in principles from his earliest years and believing that the rightness of principles could not be based on military power, he studied "Story on the Constitution" (*NQ,* 6), which convinced him that secession itself had been wrong, leaving slavery as the only justification for the war.[5] When he re-examined the biblical "Onesimus argument" (*NQ,* 7) on which the divine right of that institution had been defended, he concluded that slavery, too, was unjustified in principle, although what seemed to him the apparent "offensiveness" of the freedman immediately after the war left him little doubt about which side he would choose in a "much feared 'war of races.'"

Nevertheless, sympathy for the freedman was sparked in Cable by the sense that "these poor fellow creatures were being treated unfairly" and especially by the arguments he read and heard about "our black peasantry"—arguments he found to be an "un-American, un-Democratic, and tawdry delusion." His sympathy became more pronounced and his rejection of Southern opinion more focused when, on assignment for the *Picayune* in 1871, having earlier reported disapprovingly on an integrated "Teacher's Institute," he observed the practice of integration in the New Orleans public schools. He saw not only that blacks and whites could work and learn together productively and peaceably but also that the black teachers and students exhibited the same intellectual capacity and social refinement as their white counterparts. He saw further, as he reports it in "My Politics," that there was an essential distinction between private life and public rights, that society must be constructed on the basis of equal opportunity to public rights, and that the efforts of the Democratic party to thwart this were in essence an effort to preserve "the old order—minus slavery only—the old rule by race and class . . . hopelessly at variance with the national scheme" (*NQ,* 10).

Outside of arguments with his employers, friends, and associates, Cable's main expression of these discoveries, fired further by his indignation after reading the old Code Noir, was in some of his early fiction.

They form, however, the central perspective of his "first public political utterance" (*NQ,* 14) in September 1875, when a furor over integration prompted by the eviction of nonwhite girls from several public schools spurred him to write a letter in defense of integration that was published in the New Orleans *Bulletin,* signed "A Southern White Man," and accompanied by the editor's lengthy repudiation of his arguments. A second letter responding to the editor's arguments was rejected by both the *Bulletin* and the *Picayune,* and Cable made no further public political utterances until the early 1880s.

The essence of Cable's political evolution as he describes it lay in his measuring all private and public conduct on principle and his testing those principles with his own careful study, observation, and reason. The primary sources of his values he identifies as the Bible, the Declaration of Independence, and the Constitution—Christian ethics and American values of liberty and political equality. Of course, "My Politics" was written in defense of specific attacks made against him and was, therefore, shaped as much by the rhetorical purposes of the debate of 1889 as by his memory of actual experience.[6] He is careful, for example, to clarify that he neither profited by his views nor pandered to Northern audiences: he admits reading *Uncle Tom's Cabin* but credits it with no effect on his views of slavery or race. Similarly, he repeatedly and pointedly identifies the newspapers, which had been vilifying him for some time, as the sources of pernicious errors of both fact and opinion, and he attributes his interest in other reading as the basis of his enlightenment. The story he tells, in fact, reads something like that of the elderly Benjamin Franklin, humbly admitting his various youthful errata—in this case the tenets of Southern opinion—so that his correction of them can be exemplary. In this sense Cable's narrative of his political evolution is an instructive account of moral growth and intellectual independence, the latter gained at the expense of social acceptance but with a clear sense of having risen above the mundane, the mass, the popular.

Cable was encouraged to speak publicly on behalf of the freedman by the reception he received to similar public lectures prior to his presentation of "The Freedman's Case in Equity" in Saratoga, New York, in September 1884. In an address on "The Good Samaritan" before the New Orleans Sunday School Association in April 1881, he identified the Samaritan of his day as "part Chinese, part Indian, part Irish, and part Negro," and he reminded his listeners of their Christian obligation to "love *this neighbor* as [them]selves" (*NQ,* 39). In commencement addresses at the University of Mississippi in June 1882 and at the University of

Louisiana (now Tulane University) in June 1883 he argued that the values of a slave society, perpetuated in "landlordism" and caste, stifled and made obsolete the intellectual and cultural life of the South.[7] His most direct previous appeal for the freedman's civil rights came only three months before the Saratoga speech at the 1884 University of Alabama commencement, and afterward he received the first indication of the hostile press reaction his views could generate. Nevertheless, claiming that many present expressed their "approval and accord," he decided to launch his campaign, "more deeply impressed than ever before with the fact that behind all the fierce and resentful conservatism of the South there was a progressive though silent South which needed to be urged to speak and act" (*NQ,* 22).

The content and strategy of the arguments in "The Freedman's Case in Equity" are framed to specific attitudes and circumstances of the period in which it was written. In 1883 the Supreme Court had declared unconstitutional the Civil Rights Act of 1875 forbidding racial segregation in common carriers, thereby essentially leaving the individual states to settle the question of the status of the freedman. Reconstruction, which had officially ended in 1877, was widely perceived as a shameful era of bad government, its corruptions attributable to immediate enfranchisement of the former slaves under the Fifteenth Amendment, and the economic redevelopment of the South was being celebrated by such New South apostles as Henry W. Grady, of the Atlanta *Constitution,* Francis W. Dawson of the Charleston *News and Courier,* and Henry Watterson of the Louisville *Courier-Journal.* Their visions of progress were predicated on industrial expansion, Northern investment, stable society, and "pure" government, the latter two achievable, they argued, if the South (i.e., the white South)—better qualified by its experience of paternalistic slavery—were permitted to solve the problem of the freedman without interference. Weary of sectional strife, eager to embrace visions of industrial progress, ignorant of and, for the most part, indifferent to the plight of the freedman, most in the North were quite willing to accede to the South's requests.

Cable's address to these circumstances in "The Freedman's Case in Equity" is essentially historical and in that sense similar to his treatment of social issues in his strongest fiction. He recognizes that the responsibility for slavery and its consequences is national but that it falls heaviest on the South. He traces conditions and attitudes in the South of his own day to the fact that slavery, while it "withered away" in the North when submitted to the question of equity, "became the whole cornerstone of the social structure" in the South because it was "overlooked in that aspect" (*SS,* 3). In resubmitting the case to equity, Cable offers the chance for a final withering away and warns of a new petrification if the opportunity is missed. The "sentiment" at the "roots of the question" is the perception of the Negro as "alien" (*SS,* 6), which Cable allows was the case when Africans were first brought to America but which the white Southerner, in order to square an acceptance of slavery with American ideals of liberty, found it necessary to see as an unalterable, natural condition, an axiom beyond reason or need to defend.

Commitment to this sentiment of the negro as alien and menial, not the institution of slavery itself, became the real cornerstone of Southern society, "the absolute essentials" (*SS,* 12) of self-respect, and it is this sentiment that has been left unchanged either by emancipation or Reconstruction. With this sentiment still dominant and freed to go its own way by the Supreme Court and by an indifferent or conciliatory North, the South was thus simply re-establishing the "old relation" between the races without the "peculiar institution." The Negro was, as Cable put it, "Freed—Not Free," and he demonstrates this with considerable evidence of mistreatment of the freedman in public transportation, in the legal and penal systems, and in the schools. His discussion of the legal system reflects his careful research and documentation of conditions discovered through his prison-reform activities, and his analysis of the schools repeats his earlier observations of integrated classrooms and the distinction between civil and social associations. Cable's strategy in these demonstrations is not so much to arouse sympathy for the freedman but to expose conditions that were being publicly denied but whose continuance, once known or acknowledged, ought to arouse the shame of all those professing to be Christians and Americans.

In describing the treatment of the freedman under Jim Crow laws in public transportation and education, Cable raises the question of "social equality." His attitude, discoverable as early as his "Drop Shot" column on the New Orleans streetcar, is consistent with that of his 1875 letter to the *Bulletin* and underlies his treatment of race in his fiction. Cable insisted that he did not advocate social equality, and he was definitely not egalitarian in his views. His arguments against segregation were based specifically on a principle of class distinctions defined by character and refinement, not birth. In fact, the final impetus for his speaking out on racial issues, as he claimed later in "My Politics," was an incident also recounted in "The Freedman's Case in Equity," in which a young black woman and her small daughter, both neat, quiet, and respectable, were forced to remain in the same car with a chain gang dressed "in filthy rags, with vile odors and the clanking of shackles and chains" (*SS,* 28). Cable was so repulsed that he quickly moved, but the woman was refused the same opportunity "not because [she] was, but because she was *not,* engaged at the moment in menial service." Cable's offense at having even briefly to share a compartment with such "melancholy and revolting company" as the convicts is obvious, just as it would be sometimes in his complaints to Louise of having to suffer vulgar train companions while traveling in the Midwest and West.

Cable's recounting this incident, however, seems aimed to stir in his audience, especially in the South, some residue of gallantry leading to indignation that a woman and child should also suffer so: an appeal to class consciousness to override race consciousness. Cable points to the inconsistency of segregation laws in public transportation throughout the South, but he was also clear that "separate" was in practice—as it was meant to be—"unequal," designed to encode and ensure the freedman's alien, menial status. The color line, as he had dramatized in his fiction and as he would repeat in later essays, in fact forced a more offensive "social equality" than it prevented because it arbitrarily forced together not only the meanest with the most refined black person but also someone like himself with the most detestably vulgar white person: "it actually creates the confusion it pretends to prevent. It blunts the sensibilities of the ruling class themselves. It waives all strict demand for painstaking in either manners or dress of either master or menial, and, for one result, makes the average Southern railway coach more uncomfortable than the average of railway coaches elsewhere" (*SS,* 24).

Many of Cable's statements in "The Freedman's Case in Equity" and in other of his civil rights essays, in which he denies advocating either social equality or racial mixing, invite charges of racism. He makes a point of agreeing with those who see Africans as "one of the most debased races on the globe" or, more simply, "an inferior race" (*SS,* 3). There is not a shred of cultural awareness or sensitivity in his description of the African slave's arrival in the New World as "a naked, brutish, unclean, captive, pagan savage, to be and remain [in the slaveholder's mind] a kind of connecting link between man and the beasts of burden" (*SS,* 6). As noted earlier with regard to Cable's fiction, that he should harbor and articulate views in the 1880s recognized as racist in the 1990s is neither surprising nor necessary to defend, but in his civil rights writing this issue is more problematic than in his fiction and even more interesting.

Most of Cable's civil rights essays were written as implicit or explicit debates with a recognizable counter-opinion that he hoped to win over by dint of reason and reasonableness, the "cunning" he had Frowenfeld encourage in Honoré, f.m.c. If, as Philip Butcher suggests, Cable was taking up the mantle of abolitionists such as William Lloyd Garrison, Wendell Phillips, and Frederick Douglass, his aim was not like theirs to inform and arouse Northern opinion against Southern slavery but to convert the Southern opinion that was by consent or by silence instituting a new slavery (1962, 83). Cable professed to write as a Southerner to his fellow Southerners, and his comments on the inferiority of the "Negro race" can be recognized as part of a pragmatic strategy of establishing common ground with his audience. These comments are also intended as an acknowledgment of the general economic, educational, and social condition of the freed slaves, the problem demanding solution.

To identify Cable's rhetoric as only conciliatory, pragmatic, realistic, or racist is, however, to miss a good deal of the subtlety and irony of his strategy, especially in "The Freedman's Case in Equity." When he describes the condition of the slave upon arrival in America, he notes, "Sometimes he was not a mere savage but a trading, smithing, weaving, town-building, crop-raising barbarian" (SS, 6). Such distinctions, however, were lost on "our fathers" (the white Southern patriarchy), whose "sentiment went blind" (SS, 7). So fixed was the idea of the African as alien that no "occasional mingling of his blood with that of the white man," no number of "Generations of American nativity," no process of enculturation could change it: "He [the African] accepted our [white] dress, language, religion, all the fundamentals of our civilization, and became forever expatriated from his own land; still he remained, to us, an alien." Cable's point is to identify the irrational rigidity of the Southern race sentiment in the presence of obvious facts, and in so doing he subtly mocks the South's failure to recognize and value the evidences of its own civilizing influence.

Cable uses this irony even more cleverly when he praises the freedman for not accepting the New South's offer of restoring "that one old relation" of paternalistic dependency, because "the very nobility of civilization that had held him in slavery had made him too much a man to go back to that shelter" (SS, 15). Such a statement both strokes and chides Southern pride and honor, and it suggests a dissolution of the category of race, even as he invokes it. In all his writing, Cable is rather clearly ethnocentric, stereotyping and in some cases denigrating Latins, Chinese,

Jews, German and Irish immigrants, Native Americans, and Catholics, placing Protestant Anglo-Saxon values and culture above all others. He argues against white fears of domination by blacks precisely on the grounds of his confidence in the ultimate superiority of the Anglo-Saxon "race." Yet the logic of his ethnocentrism did not apply to individuals, and it implicitly eliminates the boundaries of race: if the "inferior" can *become* like the "superior," then it is neither irrevocably inferior nor unalterably alien. Hence he is skeptical of the existence of a natural "race instinct," but even allowing its existence, he derides the use of instinct for moral authority and points out that those who believe in a race instinct should trust it to keep the races apart without the aid of law.

Cable's arguments in "The Freedman's Case in Equity" have been justly praised as "beautifully rational" and his "understanding of the sins of others sweetly reasonable."[8] Although these qualities are certainly important, the tone or manner of his writing offers more than a straightforward appeal to reason. The subtle manipulation of the social-equality issue just described gives some measure of Cable's more complex rhetorical strategy, as does his admonitory use of history. "Slavery was a dangerous institution," he observes. "Few in the South to-day have any just idea how often the slave plotted for his freedom" (*SS*, 9). Hence, without adding anything as inflammatory as a direct threat of race war, he nevertheless clearly hints at the prospect of future violence if, as in the antebellum period, the South remains silently unwilling to submit to equity the question of the treatment of the freedman.

As Arlin Turner points out, Cable's technique was often to observe "the irony of history or of the contemporary situation" (1956, 197), and in "My Politics" Cable describes the tactic "of arguing entirely from such admissions" as his opponents "let slip against themselves": that is, "getting the enemy to furnish the ammunition" (*NQ*, 11). The ironic tone and tactics, along with what Turner calls "the overtones of moral condemnation," contribute a great deal to the power and interest of "The Freedman's Case in Equity" and much of the other political essays, particularly as these elements exist in tension with the surface of calm reasonableness and accommodation, as if the real tenor of Cable's feelings, his genuine outrage and condemnation, were being held in check. Irony had characterized his style from his first "Drop Shot" columns, and he had, as well, the long-standing habit of writing positively and cheerfully to his family, regardless of circumstance, occasionally chiding his wife when she failed to do the same. However much he tried not to antagonize his audience, it is easy to see how, as Turner describes it, "Cable's way of seeing and saying a thing evoked the resentment he hoped to prevent."

In the South the reaction to the *Century* publication of "The Freedman's Case in Equity" was swift, angry, and nearly unanimous denunciation. Virtually every Southern newspaper began printing attacks on Cable, once again labeling him a traitor to the South who pandered to Northern audiences and advocated miscegenation, social collapse, and race warfare. His friend the literary editor Marion Baker remained guardedly supportive, but Baker's brother, Page, led the attack on Cable as main editor of the *Times-Democrat*. Two of his more vitriolic opponents, representing the unreconstructed Old South, were poet Paul Hamilton Hayne and historian Charles Gayarré, the latter already embittered over Cable's usurpation of his role as the authority on Louisiana history. These attacks were widely reported in the Northern press, and Cable, still on tour with Twain, was frequently sought out for interviews.

The *Century* received so many letters on "The Freedman's Case in Equity" that it decided not to print them and to ask Henry W. Grady to write in defense of the opposing view. Grady's essay, "In Plain Black and White," appeared in the April 1885 issue of *Century,* representing a broad base of Southern opinion, particularly that associated with New South progressivism. Compared with the newspaper diatribes and with the attacks of Hayne and Gayarré, it is a model of restraint and reason. Grady insists that Cable's views are not shared in the South, but he allows that they are honestly held. He admits the wrong of slavery, accepts voting rights for the freedman (although skeptical of its wisdom), and agrees to equal opportunities for Negroes in the schools, churches, courts, and public transportation. Believing, however, in an "ineradicable and positive" (Turner 1980, 80) race instinct "bred in the bone and blood" (78) that creates an inevitable "antagonism" between the races whenever they are indiscriminately mixed, he insists that keeping the races separate is a "wise and proper" policy. He warns that accepting Cable's views will lead to social and political chaos and to the "unspeakable horrors" (79) of amalgamation. Typical of the exaggerated New South optimism, he describes the progress in race relations that had been made as a result of the separate-but-equal policy. He invokes images of the defeated and maligned South to appeal for sympathy, and, most importantly and most adamantly, he insists that the right of the South to settle the race problem is based on "the clear and unmistakable domination of the white race in the South, . . . the right of character, intelligence and property to rule" (87).

Cable's rebuttal of Grady's essay, "The Silent South," originally planned to appear simultaneously in the *Century,* was delayed by his various speaking engagements until September. Even more than the Freedman essay, "The Silent South" illustrates Cable's delight in "getting the enemy to furnish the ammunition," for it is largely a countering of the charges made against his views by Grady and others. Responding to the claim of white fairness and goodwill in the South, he adds considerable evidence of unequal treatment of the freedman in public accommodations and particularly in the courts and the penal system. White claims that neither race wants desegregation are refuted by the numerous letters and personal expressions of support and encouragement he had received from individual Negroes and Negro groups. The evidence of black opinion opposed to Cable offered by a letter from "one 'Jack Brown, colored'" (*SS,* 67) to the Selma "Times" is exposed as a ludicrous sham by the paper's inability to produce the individual despite Cable's efforts to locate him.

The "tap-root of the whole trouble" Cable identifies as the white South's wanting to cling to the prerogative "of holding under [its] own discretion the colored man's *status,* not as a freedman, not as a voter, but in his daily walk as a civilian" (*SS,* 49). The "sticking point" of disagreement between himself and his opponents is the belief that "Civil Rights means Social Equality" (*SS,* 53), and he reiterates his own view that "social equality is a fool's dream" (*SS,* 54), that the crucial distinction is between "*impersonal right*" and "*personal choice*" (*SS,* 55). He also specifically denies advocating racial amalgamation as a solution to the problem and points to the bountiful evidence that miscegenation has occurred most under conditions of segregation. To Grady's claim that if race instinct did not exist by nature "the South 'would, by every means in its power so strengthen the race *prejudice* [Cable's added emphasis] that it would do the work and hold the stubbornness and strength of instinct,'" Cable responds with evident scorn, asking, "Could any one more distinctly or unconsciously waive the whole question of right and wrong? Yet this is the standpoint on which it is proposed to meet the freedman's case *in equity*" (*SS,* 58).

Cable's most powerful and effective point in "The Silent South," however, may be his attack on Grady's claim for the necessity of white supremacy on the grounds of "the right of character, intelligence and property to rule." Grady's argument was related to white conservative interpretations of Reconstruction and the need for a "Solid South" to prevent the abuses and manipulation of a solid, one-party "Negro vote." Cable argues that the solidarity of the Negro vote was actually a reaction to obvious white hostility and would disappear with a promise of equal treatment. More tellingly, he points out that White Rule is rule by race and caste, not by character, intelligence, and property, since it gives the right to white persons without these qualities and excludes black persons with them. This "domination of one fixed class by another without its consent" is un-American, not a residue of European aristocratic sentiment, but "Asian antiquity and tyranny" (SS, 57).

Finally, to those who would argue to go slowly, Cable reminds them of the bloody consequences of the South's going slowly in eliminating slavery. Echoing Thomas Jefferson's arguments against manufacturing in Notes on the State of Virginia, he warns that if "the black man is to furnish the labor" in New South factories, separated therefore from the "bright amiable influences" of his previous pastoral realm, "how urgent is our necessity for removing from him all sense of grievance that we may rightly remove" lest he learn "the evil charms of unions, leagues, secret orders, strikes and bread riots" and become "the dangerous and tractable animal that now he is not" (SS, 108). In this formulation the "Black Beast" joins the anti-immigrant, antilabor demon in rhetorical service to the cause of civil rights for the freedman.

"The Silent South," along with "The Freedman's Case in Equity" and "The Convict Lease System in the Southern States," were published by Scribners as The Silent South in November 1885, but except for two brief rejoinders to critics in the Century (added as an appendix to the 1889 edition), he published no more direct answers to his attackers. While platform reading remained his main source of income, however, he studied the Southern question diligently and continued to lecture and write on it for the next seven years. Cable received encouraging support from his family and from some of his closest friends, especially Roswell Smith, who shared his interest in social reform. Richard Watson Gilder, who differed with Cable on both the need for his crusade and on the freedman's potential, and whose editorial philosophy and policies aimed at reducing sectional strife, nevertheless doubled Cable's payment to $500 for the "The Silent South." Based on his earlier reform efforts and on his moral and intellectual elitism, Cable was initially stirred to speak out on behalf of the freedman in the belief that open, rational discussion of obvious wrongs could first enlighten and then mobilize the right-minded "best" of the community to effect practical reform.

Despite the virulent attacks, which he attributed mostly to the Democratically owned newspapers, Cable maintained his faith in this "Silent South" and hoped to arouse it by keeping a rational discussion open. He was encouraged in this belief by visiting the South prior to delivering a commencement lecture in June 1887 at Vanderbilt University in Nashville, at the invitation of Professor William Malone Baskervill. Although plans for a larger Southern lecture tour of the South had to be canceled because of the timidity of local managers, the personal reception Cable received, except in New Orleans, was generally friendly and supportive, respectful of his sincerity and honesty if not in full agreement with his ideas or his means of achieving them. The Vanderbilt talk, subsequently revised and published in England as "The Negro Question in the United States,"[9] also provoked the kind of temperate, open response that Cable had hoped for, even from those who disagreed with his views. The willingness of many of Cable's opponents, including Henry Grady, to grant certain concessions of principle helped further to convince him that a "Silent South" did exist and could be won over.

The basic themes and arguments of Cable's first two essays reappear in the later ones, although he becomes less focused on the particular instances of racial injustice and more on the general, national consequences of laws and practices designed to assure segregation and white rule. Beyond simple equity, the case for helping the freedman was based on the "American" principle that only by raising the level of its lowest strata could the society as a whole truly progress and prosper. He emphasized education as a particular key to social uplift, arguing that because funds were inadequate to maintain dual systems in many rural areas, no public education existed there at all. Therefore, he reasoned, the penalty of the prejudice fell on poor whites and blacks alike. In "The Southern Struggle for Pure Government"[10] he argued against various measures for ballot qualification on the grounds that to do so would leave a large segment of society, including both blacks and whites, unprotected by the ballot from other segments. Without such protection a "free government" did not exist, corruption was inevitable, and therefore a "pure government" was not possible. Many of these arguments seemed to challenge specifically the New South celebrations of progress in the South, for Cable argued that without a base in social justice real or lasting progress was doomed. In "The Negro Question" he describes the New South as "only the Old South re-adapting the old plantation idea to a peasant labor and mineral products."[11]

In speaking and writing to black audiences, Cable praised the signs of advancement and refinement that he saw, and he urged their embracing the cause of civil rights (including his own denials of any desire for social equality, amalgamation, or block voting) as a key to their continued progress. Although he had received much behind-the-scenes support and private praise from Booker T. Washington, Cable differed sharply from the black leader's compromise policy of delaying demands for civil and social rights in exchange for economic uplift through such industrial and agricultural education as was offered at Tuskegee Institute.[12] Anticipating somewhat W. E. B. Du Bois's famous critique of Washington's "Atlanta Exposition Address," Cable held that "no people can ever catch step with the world's progressive march, moral or material, by consenting to political bondage," and that if the freed slaves accepted partial citizenship they were in essence accepting partial humanity and proving that "they never deserved to be anything but slaves" (NQ, 234).[13]

By 1890, however, Cable began to recognize the intransigence of the white South, and he proposed his own compromise measures as well as the possible need for federal intervention if no progress were visible within a prescribed period. Six of his essays of this period, previously published as magazine articles ("The Negro Question," "National Aid to Southern Schools," "What Shall the Negro Do?" "A Simple Southern Question," "What Makes the Color Line?" and "The Southern Struggle for Pure Government"), were collected as The Negro Question in 1890. The most clearly focused and effectively developed of these, perhaps Cable's best crafted political piece, is the title essay.

Cable's desire to cultivate discussion with and within a Silent South had its most concrete form in the Open Letter Club he helped organize with Baskervill in 1888. The design of the club was for members to write, exchange, criticize, and revise brief essays on some aspect of the Southern question and then publish them in a symposium. With its headquarters in Nashville, the membership was composed of distinguished professional men—university presidents, professors, doctors, ministers, lawyers—primarily from the South and included, as perhaps the most familiar name to modern readers, Charles W. Chesnutt. Cable's role, as it had been in earlier reform organizations, was ostensibly peripheral but actually central—the driving, organizing force behind the endeavor. For clerical help he enlisted the service of Adelene Moffat, a young schoolteacher and aspiring artist who had heard Cable speak at Monteagle, Tennessee, the previous summer and had initiated a correspondence with him praising his work. Cable had invited her to move to Northampton to work as his secretary and attend art school with funds he loaned to her, and she became a longtime friend, assistant, and member of his household. The first symposium, "Shall the Negro Be Educated or Suppressed?" was published in the February 1889 *Independent* with contributions from eight writers, including Cable and Baskervill, but plans for a second publication never came to fruition.

The collapse of the Open Letter Club owed partially to financial considerations and partially to the hardening of conservative opinion undermining the progress of debate, but ultimately it was caused by the outrage expressed through newspaper editorials over Cable's eating dinner as a guest at the home of a black lawyer, J. C. Napier. Cable had frequently met with black groups and individuals, and only a month before he had been entertained in Chesnutt's home. He had attended all-black church services on occasion, visited black high schools, and lectured at Berea College, an integrated school to which he also contributed financially. Breaking bread with Napier and his wife, however, refueled the argument that Cable advocated social equality and demonstrated "his preference for the Negro race."[14] Cable responded quickly and with unmistakable moral indignation in three letters to the Nashville *American* (31 December 1889, 12 January 1890, and 9 February 1890). In the second letter he explained that he had accepted the invitation to dine—in fact, initiated it after a late business meeting in the Napier home—to relieve his hosts' dilemma "between asking a white man to sit at their board and sending him away supperless" (quoted in Turner 1956, 269). "We broke bread together," he explains. "Was I wrong in that? To anyone who answers yes, I can only reply, Shame on you! Shame on you!!" He goes on to reiterate his basic views on social equality and racial mixing, pointing sarcastically to the fact that "probably not one in a thousand" of the persons of obviously mixed blood "owes his or her mixture . . . to anyone suspected of advocating 'social equality.'"

Finally, Cable recants none of his previous statements on "the race problem" and proudly asserts, "If the friendship of any friend of mine North or South, old or new, hangs on the condition that I must never do again what I did the other day in Nashville, I bid such a friendship goodbye. I will break bread with the murderer in his cell if I choose. I have no fear that I shall lose all my friends but I know that I shall keep my self-respect." Usually restrained and careful not to antagonize, in this

"OK-then-I'll-go-to-hell" statement, Cable offered perhaps the clearest public view of his moral strength and fervor and certainly achieved one of his finest, most admirable moments. Baskervill, however, who had become increasingly conservative in his views, found Cable's reputation in Nashville so damaged and the threat to his own reputation so palpable that he—along with several others—withdrew from the Open Letter Club and returned all the papers to Northampton, thus assuring an end to the enterprise.

After the demise of the Open Letter Club, Cable redirected his reform energies into the Home Culture Clubs, which he had organized in Northampton in 1886. The aim of these clubs was to help elevate members of society, primarily workers, through group reading and study at individual members' homes. Beginning with one four-member club, the organization grew to include 54 clubs by 1894, requiring both a significant organization budget and a regular newsletter, the *Letter*. Adelene Moffat served as secretary until 1907 when she was pressured to resign. For Cable, the success of the clubs was a matter of particular pride and satisfaction after his failure to turn the tide of segregation, and he remained active in the organization and its related activities, such as the home garden competitions, for much of the rest of his life.

During the late 1880s Cable also became more active in church activities, and he published a number of articles, collected in *The Busy Man's Bible* (1891), on the teaching of religion and the relation of religious teaching to everyday life. Despite the orthodoxy of his earlier years, which had kept him from the theater and at times irritated Mark Twain, Cable's writings on religion, as anticipated by his fiction, are generally humanitarian and distinctly not dogmatic or doctrinaire. He became increasingly impatient with most of the sermons he heard in their preoccupation with theological niceties and conventional morality. After a class in Bible study that Cable had taught in 1887 at Boston's Tremont Temple and that included much of the message of *The Busy Man's Bible,* the comment of one student is particularly telling: "He sets tradition at naught. He tramples on conventionality. He sees with his own eyes, thinks with his own mind and decides with his own judgment" (quoted in Biklé, 201). Cable's changes of religious and racial attitudes followed parallel courses in which inherited, unexamined, and conventional views were converted to a basic humanitarianism by thorough study, independent thought, and adherence to principle.

The significance of Cable's political writing is not, of course, in its immediate effect, for in that respect it failed miserably. Unable to marshall public support for his views or even to slow the tide of segregation and racial oppression, he was essentially driven from the field. Although some of his arguments seemed prophetic and especially pertinent to the renewed civil rights debates of the late 1950s and 1960s, their relevance to current issues is problematic. Many modern readers will be uncomfortable with his repeated insistence on the superiority of Anglo-Saxons and with his purposefully not emphasizing lynchings, burnings, and other forms of racial violence, even though he is clearly aware of their occurrence. Cable's thinking on race relations and civil rights is not sophisticated, either philosophically or politically, but it is rigorous and compelling in its adherence to reason and moral principle. Cable's political writings address—in relatively general terms and within the limits of his own prejudices—what he saw happening in the South and in the nation, and he so clearly and cannily argues for fundamental justice and exposes the blind illogic and obfuscation of the opposition that the effect is frequently both dazzling and powerful.

The phenomenon of his taking up the crusade, both as a Southerner and without much reinforcement in the North, has also been identified as significant. Of course, in a recognizable sense, by the 1880s Cable was, at best, in Louis Rubin's phrase, a "Southern heretic," unsympathetic to, if not scornful of, prevailing Southern political and social opinion, his sensibilities more at home in Northampton regardless of his warm feelings for individuals and places whose customs and history he had mined for romance. There were a few other well-known liberal reformers speaking out, such as Albion Tourgée and Frederick Douglass (whose arguments in speeches and essays of this period closely resemble Cable's),[15] but Cable was unique in that he was the lone "mainstream" writer to publicly challenge the overwhelming drift of the nation toward racial segregation. While in doing so he was entirely consistent with his well-established views of Christian duty and his interest in social reform, he does not seem by background or social habit an unconventional man.

Joel Williamson characterizes Cable as "a latter-day saint" (99) in his capacity to sympathize with the freedman as he had earlier with the Creoles, but Cable also exhibits a degree of genteel, stiff-backed contrariness centered in his Christian ethics, bolstered by what Louis Rubin aptly calls his "remorseless and impeccable logic" (184) and driven by an elitism founded on "intellectual ambition," a disdain for mere expediency and mass opinion.[16] Whatever the source, Cable's capacity for independence of thought in his political writings is truly remarkable, and the play of that independence—sometimes fierce indignation, love of irony, and subtly manipulated surface decorum—makes these essays, after *The Grandissimes* and some of the *Old Creole Days* stories, the most interesting, impressive work Cable produced. They deserve to be better known and more thoroughly studied, not just for their political content but for their complex strategies of thought and feeling.

Chapter Six
Politics and Fiction

In late 1889 Charles Chesnutt sent Cable a manuscript of a story, "Rena Walden" (an early version of *The House Behind the Cedars*), and asked for the novelist's suggestions. Cable and Chesnutt had been corresponding since the previous year and were at the time working on an essay Chesnutt was preparing for the ill-fated second symposium of the Open Letter Club. Aware of Chesnutt's generally unknown mixed racial ancestry, Cable advised the aspiring author to remember that his audience was white and "that the greatest element of strength is to yield all ground you honestly can to the possible prejudices of your reader."[1] Although he later counseled Chesnutt, who was piqued over the story's rejection by Richard Watson Gilder, to maintain the honesty of his vision, Cable's initial comment suggests his susceptibility to pleasing the tastes of Gilder and the readers of the *Century* and apparently signals an unhappy divergence in his writing between politics and fiction.

Cable's editors and others had been encouraging him to produce another novel, but while Cable was engaged in his civil rights crusade, he devoted little time to fiction. When he did manage to produce *Bonaventure* in 1888, he seemed intent on keeping his politics out of fiction. Nevertheless, both the Acadian stories and *Strange True Stories of Louisiana* (1889), although it is neither political nor entirely fictional, do reflect his social concerns of the period. And *John March, Southerner* (1894), written after the reform crusade had failed, is fully a "purpose" novel in which he attempted to give dramatic embodiment to his analysis of the problems facing the South in the aftermath of Reconstruction.

Place Congo

The question of divergence between Cable's "political" and "literary" writing bears interestingly on two essays published in the *Century* in the midst of the Southern debate. "The Dance in Place Congo" (February 1886) and "Creole Slave Songs" (April 1886) obviously touch on issues of race, but they reflect literary interests and treatments consistent with his earliest fiction. Cable had wanted to incorporate some of the Creole songs in *Old Creole Days* and *The Grandissimes,* and he did include them as a popular part of his platform performances. Thus the publication of the essays in collaboration with *New York Times* music editor Henry Edward Krehbiel, illustrated by E. W. Kemble, represents a culling and reusing of material from his longtime study of Louisiana history and folkways.[2] Cable drew on several published sources of linguistic and anthropological information, which he acknowledged in the essays, along with the contributions of Lafcadio Hearn, Joel Chandler Harris, and Louis Gottschalk, the Creole composer who had popularized "The Bamboula," but he also relied on his own memories and impressions of growing up in New Orleans.

Cable's respectful attention to ethnic diversity, to the purposes and feelings, sometimes subversive, behind the music, has been justly praised (Turner 1956, 230; Butcher 1962, 90), but however accurate and valuable as folklore, the descriptions in these articles, especially in "The Dance in Place Congo," are more striking for their picturesque appeal and exotic sensuality. In the first article Cable establishes the scenes and atmosphere of Old New Orleans in terms that would be familiar to readers of *Old Creole Days* and *The Grandissimes.* He develops a contrast between the Place Congo and the Place d'Armes in terms of a polarity between wilderness and formal-garden imagery, savagery and civilization, and this in turn shapes the overall representation of the Africans as primitives, characterized by wildness, strength, vigor, lack of inhibition, primal rhythms, deep passions, physicality, and pagan animal worship. Cable's mixture of fascination and condemnation is apparent in his descriptions of "the furious Bamboula"[3] with its orgiastic climax ("What wild—what terrible delight! The ecstasy rises to madness") and of the more frankly erotic Counjaille songs ("Sweat streams from the black brows, down the shining black necks and throats, upon the men's bared chests, into dark, unstayed bosoms" ["Congo," 526]).

At the same time, reflecting his concern with the civil-rights controversy, Cable evokes sympathy for the Africans with references to their suffering and degradation under slavery, the Code Noir and the quadroon caste system.[4] Thus part of the fascination of these articles is the apparent conflict between Cable's political ideology and his literary modes insofar as these modes identify Africans as exotic savages. The ideology requires the Africans' refinement and conversion to civilized ways, but the literary mode preserves and exploits their "primitive origins." "Times have changed," he observes, "and there is nothing to be regretted in the change that has come over Congo Square. Still a glamour hangs over its dark past" ("Congo," 528).

Bonaventure

Of all Cable's fiction published before 1894 his collection of three Acadian stories called *Bonaventure* has been the most readily dismissed by modern critics. William Malone Baskervill's characterization of the book as "that pure white flower standing alone in the turbid pool of partisan controversy" (Turner 1980, 111) suggests the tone and basis of many early reviewers' appreciation and also a major reason for the later critical neglect. Turner finds the book's appeal in the "charm of the Acadian villages," and while impressed by its "total picture . . . of gentle people, delightful in their simplicity and heroic in their minor way," he observes that "the book has no characters and no scenes to stick in the reader's mind" (1956, 237). Butcher calls the novel "slight," concluding that the blend of romance and realism in it "is notable for sweetness rather than potency" (1962, 93). Most harshly, Louis Rubin claims that "there is scarcely anything in *Bonaventure* that rises above the level of romantic, pastoral melodrama and sentimentality" (194). The underlying complaint is that the novel lacks a significant social message, a particularly egregious error in light of its appearance during the midst of Cable's civil rights crusade. While Cable seems intent on avoiding controversy in *Bonaventure,* just as he had in removing the politics of the Civil War from *Dr. Sevier,* it is less tedious than his preachy prison-reform novel, more interesting in what it attempts. Certainly *Bonaventure* does not succeed, but because it is more consistent in its aims and techniques with his earlier and best work, it is at least as instructive as *Dr. Sevier* in how its weaknesses help clarify its author's strengths.

Cable's interest in the descendants of French-speaking refugees from Nova Scotia who settled in the bayou and prairie country of southwest Louisiana began at least with his days as a surveyor on the Atchafalaya River after the war and was revived with his work on the U.S. Census. On his several trips to the region he stayed with local residents and observed and recorded numerous details of language, custom, landscape, and culture that were not used in the census report but form the essential background and texture of the published stories. Cable submitted a draft of a story about the Acadians as early as 1883, but "Carancro" did not begin in *Century* until January 1887, followed by "Grande Pointe" in March and "Au Large" starting a five-month run in November. Thus, although the novel made by collecting the three stories appeared in 1888, its literary impulse is closer to the era of the Creole stories.

As the publication history might suggest, one of the weaknesses charged against *Bonaventure* is a lack of narrative coherency. Each of the stories has a separate plot centering on a love conflict and a conflict between the rustic Acadians and the larger world. In "Carancro" the orphaned young Creole, Bonaventure Deschamps, in love with his foster-sister, Zoséphine Gradnego, and jealous of her interest in an athletic, fiddle-playing horseman, Athanase Beausoleil, delivers him to Confederate conscript officers and then, wracked by guilt, tries to locate his missing rival after the war. Mistakenly believing that 'Thanase has gone to sea, he returns on their wedding day, and then taught by a kindly, progressive curé, he converts his self-interest to helping others through education.

In "Grande Pointe" Bonaventure is sent to teach in a remote Acadian village, where he is welcomed by some and ignorantly feared by others. He falls in love with one of his older pupils, Sidonie Le Blanc, but he finds himself again in a conflict between self-interest and serving others when another of his students, Claude St. Pierre, asks him for romantic advice about the same girl. In a dramatic demonstration of his students' spelling prowess, he proves his worth as a teacher and the value of education to the provincial community, and he wins the heart and hand of Sidonie.

"Au Large" centers on the "fretted love" of an older Claude St. Pierre and Zoséphine's daughter, Marguerite, and also that of Zoséphine, widowed at the end of "Carancro," and George Washington Tarbox, the spurious judge of the spelling performance in "Grande Pointe." The ordeals of all four are set against the transformations of the Acadian world by the railroad, agriculture, and other signs of progress. Bonaventure appears, but it is mostly as a shadowy apotheosis of selflessness.

Typical of most of Cable's fiction, the individual love plots are conventional and banal. "Carancro" lacks dramatic tension, and the sentimentality and melodrama of the educational demonstration in "Grande Pointe" is, frankly, ludicrous. But "Au Large," longer and more complex, is more satisfying in its plot development, and the combination of the three stories, which Cable described later as a design "favored" by "the pastoral nature of the subject" ("After-Thoughts," 18), achieves something more than a loose association of characters, themes, and milieu.

There is a general movement from the remote prairies of "Carancro" and the backwaters of "Grande Pointe" to the environs and streets of modern New Orleans in "Au Large." The characters introduced in two groups in the first two stories are drawn together in the third. Hence if "Au Large" is thought of as the central narrative, with "Carancro" and "Grande Pointe" as semi-self-contained preludes, the coherence of *Bonaventure* can be better felt. That coherence depends less on the title character than on the evocation of the Acadian milieu and the themes of its relation to the larger world.

Cable's accuracy in portraying the Acadians, much as he had the Creoles, has generally been identified as his primary aim and most significant accomplishment in *Bonaventure.* Merrill Skaggs credits Cable for having created the stereotype of the Acadians "Athena-like," without "literary ancestors somewhere" (146) but with specific descendants in the Acadians of Grace King and Kate Chopin. As Turner had earlier, Skaggs emphasizes the "great care" (150) with which Cable describes the lives of Acadians, "their sources of income, their daily routines, their amusements, even the varieties of their food and of the plants in their gardens." The Acadian dialect, although sparingly used (the Acadians usually speak French to each other, which Cable represents as standard English), is often masterful, clearly distinct in linguistic features and tone from the rendering of Creole dialect in *Old Creole Days* and *The Grandissimes.* In addition, Cable does suggest some differences between the "two different types of Acadians" (Skaggs, 148)—the more prosperous herders and farmers of "Carancro" and the hunters, trappers, and sugar-cane workers of "Grande Pointe"—but these distinctions are slight and mostly tonal.

In fact, the accuracy of Cable's portrait seems less an effect of abundant social and cultural detail than an overall impression of the Acadians' personalities, their charm as peasants, their shyness, gentleness, and simplicity, and this leads to some flatness and monotony in characterization. The most interesting Acadian characters are the elder St. Pierre, who is torn between his love for his more progressive son and his own traditions, and the pot-hunter who kills 'Thanase and then flees to live alone and die in the swamps, tortured by guilt into destructive paranoia. The most striking character in the novel, however, may be the Anglo-Saxon encyclopedia salesman and good-hearted confidence man, G. W. Tarbox. Described by critics as something out of Dickens or Mark Twain (e.g., Colonel Sellers), he seems also—in the rhythms of his speech—an ancestor of W. C. Fields (albeit sans vinegar).

The absence of a rich and subtle examination of manners and customs is partly explained by the fact that the Acadians lack the social
consciousness of the aristocratic Creoles, and while Cable notes the
Creole-Acadian contrast at several points, it is not used for dramatic
tension in the way the Creole-American contrast figures in his earlier
fiction. He does render the sense of the Acadians' remoteness and isolation from the larger world and from each other with considerable
artistry. Much of this derives from the descriptions of landscape, which
include a characteristically accurate and detailed verbal map of the
region but, more importantly, evoke a sense of distance and space: in
"Carancro" the vastness of prairies dotted with the "*îles*" of Acadian
"homestead groves"[5] and in "Grande Pointe" the hushed enclosure of
the eerily beautiful swamps and bayous. The directness of the narrative
style is also appropriate to the Acadians' peasant simplicity, making the
evocation of their world a product less of sociology than of a particular
harmony of landscape image and tone.

The terms in which Cable renders the Acadians are central to his
moral-social themes, which center on progress and which seem—rather
than sociological fidelity—his major interest in writing *Bonaventure*. The
Acadians' lack of social consciousness gives them a moral advantage
over the Creoles and others in the Southern aristocratic tradition which
G. W. Tarbox at one point makes specific: "They're the only white people that ever trod this continent—island or mainland—who never on
their own account oppressed anybody" (*B,* 197). Theirs was not a slave
economy or culture, and thus they have little at stake in the Civil War
and are victimized both by marauding, antislavery Jayhawkers and
Confederate conscript officers. Still, if they lack a stake in the South's
cause, they do have a stake in the nation's material and moral progress.
The negative side of the Acadians' isolation and lack of social consciousness is their provinciality. Out of the larger world they are rescued from
some of its vices, but they are also particularly susceptible to some of its
false representations. Hence we have Tarbox's ability to present himself
as a man of the world and State Superintendent of Education in
"Grande Pointe" and to sell the "Album of Universal Information" in
"Au Large." Hence we have Claude St. Pierre's misreading of
Marguerite's sophistication in New Orleans. Hence, too, and more seriously, we have the susceptibility of Catou and Chat-oué to a parish
priest's arguments that Bonaventure's teaching English poses a threat:
"Discontent," he warns. "Vanity. Contempt of honest labor . . . good-by
to the faith of your fathers" (*B,* 99).

The more narrow-minded Acadians' seem as perverse and malignant as Agricola Fusilier in their desire to cling to the old ways at all costs. And the pot-hunter, who "by choice . . . would not have harmed any living creature that men call it wrong to injure" (*B,* 277), nevertheless has killed and would kill again in the ultimate isolation of his paranoia. He is destroyed because he misinterprets the signs and cannot understand the language of the outer world when it invades his swamp. In each of the stories Cable makes clear that the Acadians' isolation, for all its charm, is ultimately a liability, and the key to their advancement is education: "Knowledge is power," and with it comes self-control and service to others.

The tension between the nostalgic appeal of the Acadians and the argument for progress adds significance to Cable's subtitling his novel "A Prose Pastoral of Acadian Louisiana," making it something more than the expression of vague sentimentality claimed by the critics. As Leo Marx argues in *The Machine in the Garden,* the paradigm of nature employed in interpreting and directing American experience was not the vitalizing wilderness of primitivism but the "middle landscape" of pastoralism, "the ideal reconciliation of nature and art which had been depicted by writers of pastoral since Virgil's time."[6] Cable establishes the pastoral image not only in the obvious depiction of the Acadians as gentle herders ('Thanase's fiddling, carried on by his daughter, seems a part of this convention) but also in the sense of their world as a middle ground between New Orleans and the ever-present, forbidding wilderness of swamp and forest. The Acadians' harmony with nature, their naturalness, is clearly a source of their appeal, and insofar as they are not separated from its more beneficent influences by slavery, it is a source of their virtue (note the similar Jeffersonian argument at the end of "The Solid South").

If, however, nature can be beautiful and gentle, as Cable makes clear in many of his descriptions, it can also be powerful, violent, and chaotic, and he uses these less benign images to reflect moral or psychological states, for example, when Bonaventure wrestles with his conscience in the swamp and when the pot-hunter struggles with his fears during the storm and crevasse. Cable's point in these renderings is suggested in one of his most painfully sententious passages: "'Subdue the earth'—it is being done. Science and art, commerce and exploration, are but parts of religion. Help us, brothers all, with every possible discovery and invention to complete the conquest begun in that lost garden whence man and woman first come forth, not for vengeance but for love, to bruise the serpent's head" (*B,* 292).

All the novel's main action can be interpreted within this ideology of lovingly subduing nature: Bonaventure's instincts for selfishness (perhaps his heritage as a Creole) must be twice subdued and converted to social good; Claude St. Pierre similarly must overcome his childish infatuations and timidity to gain education and serve humanity through his inventions; the river must be contained by the levees; the Acadians, like the elder St. Pierre, must overcome their narrowness to find some accommodation between their past world and its virtues and the new world of progress. In short, the extolling of progress centered in rationalism and technology is figured within a paradigm that idealizes nature. For all the novel's movement of action and characters toward the city, the final vista, "the one small part of New Orleans" (*B,* 110) he wishes to take with him, is "the Old Carrollton Gardens," including the levee and the sight of the Mississippi and pecan groves beyond.

This is not to say the novel lacks social comment altogether. As some early reviewers complained, Cable does seem to plea for federal aid to education. It is also possible to see parallels between his depiction of the Acadians and his arguments for the necessity of uplifting the freedman, as suggested by Philip Butcher's observation that "it is the Acadian's potential, what he may become, rather than what he is, that wins the author's respect" (1962, 237). The one black character in the novel, used as a local-color device in "Grande Pointe," forms a working partnership with the elder St. Pierre in "Au Large," and the novel does implicitly address the consequences of slavery by presenting the appeal and potential of a culture pointedly *not* based on slavery or caste subjugation. There is also a subtle critique of New South ideology in the qualification of technological progress by a Jeffersonian idealization of nature. Similarly, the apostle of progress, G. W. Tarbox, will need some of his vulgar edges softened (presumably under the gentle feminine influence of Zoséphine) before he can represent a palatable image of a New South society.

Such implicit or oblique social commentary lacks force, however. There is no strong indictment of public wrong or appeal for reform, and the apparent lack of controversy makes the work something of an anachronism, similar in method and interest to the *Old Creole Days* stories. For example, Cable's exploration of the pot-hunter's irrational fears, the demonstration of his capacity for violence, and the attempt to project his psychology through the exterior images of violent nature parallels the subtle treatment of 'Sieur George's corruption. Had *Bonaventure* been written in the same period it might be more highly regarded, but the novel has a more fundamental weakness than the lack of strong social content. Despite the Darwinian overtones of the storm scene, Cable's use of pastoralism, his exploration of the moral value of nature, seems dated and ultimately without conviction or power. If we compare *Bonaventure* with another "pastoral" novel of the same era, *The Adventures of Huckleberry Finn*, we might note the lack of an equivalent to Huck's unfaked, unschooled reverential awe in the presence of natural beauty and natural power, recorded in language at once plain and lyrical. While knowledgeably detailed and often visually effective, Cable's descriptions of nature bear too much the stamp of genteel romanticism and cultivated moral feeling, of a man who would write a home-gardening book a few years later and who enjoyed the prospects of swamp and forests as distanced fringes.

Put differently, the tension between nature and civilization in *Bonaventure* is inadequately represented, unconvincing because it appears to have been inadequately felt. Cable sides too much with progress, and this is particularly telling in his representation of the interior dilemma of the Acadians, their feeling for their world—including nature—that was fast disappearing. Cable had studied the Acadians of his day with his usual diligence, but he makes little use of their history and, having not grown up among or closely beside them, he lacks the kind of knowledge born of experience and the tension of relationships that he had with the Creoles.[7] *Bonaventure* is more serious, complex and interesting than has been generally recognized, but it is not compelling. Once again, the combination of knowledge, feeling, material, and method, not just the absence of political or reform purpose, was not conducive to Cable's best art.

Strange True Stories of Louisiana

The seven stories included in *Strange True Stories of Louisiana* are based on manuscripts and documents that Cable had collected over several years and in some cases purchased. He bought three of the stories from Mme Sidonie de la Houssaye, a Creole widow living in the Acadian Parishes who had published several books in French and with whom Cable had consulted extensively in writing *Bonaventure*. Three others were well-documented legends of the region, two having already appeared in newspaper or other published accounts, and the last was a diary recounting the siege of Vicksburg written by Dora Richards Miller, a former school teacher in need of money whom Cable helped by purchasing this and other manuscripts but who later publicly complained of not having received sufficient acknowledgment or compensation. The stories, including an introductory essay, "How I Got Them," were first published separately in *Century* over a 12-month period beginning in November 1888 and then collected as a single volume in 1889.

The degree to which the stories reflect Cable's authorship in the telling varies considerably, and consequently they also vary in quality and interest. Despite their disparity, Cable suggests they have a "coherent sequence,"[8] and he attempts to link many of them with internal references to characters and events from one to another, generally around themes of immigration, tragic and mysterious pasts, and race relations. The lesser stories present such exotic experiences as Indian attacks and cannibalism ("The Young Aunt with White Hair"), escape from French and Haitian revolutions ("The Adventures of Françoise and Suzanne" and "The History of Alix de Morainville"), and exploring the Louisiana landscape ("The Adventures of Françoise and Suzanne"). "Attalie Brouillard," which Philip Butcher accurately identifies as unique because it was based on oral accounts and, therefore, was the most "fictional," converts the dilemma of a quadroon's efforts to secure her rightful inheritance into a playful farce. The lengthy "War Diary of a Union Woman in the South" is interesting in its detailing of the terror of the siege, in its Unionist point of view, and in Cable's comment that it reflects "the woman's side of that awful war" (*STSL,* 17). The most enduring of the narratives are "Salome Müller, the White Slave" and "The 'Haunted House' in Royal Street," in both of which Cable plays a significant role as storyteller.

"Salome Müller, the White Slave" is based on an actual Louisiana court trial and subsequent appeal of 1844–45 in which a German immigrant girl, who had been taken into slavery as a child some 26 years earlier, was eventually declared white and free. As a first-person narrator, Cable summarizes the history of the Müllers and other redemptioners, relating conversations with some of the persons involved and also quoting newspaper and court records at some length. The description of the Müllers' ordeal in emigrating to New Orleans and then to the Attakapas region echoes his account of the Frowenfeld family in *The Grandissimes,* and he specifically parallels the Müllers' immigrant experience with that of Françoise and Alix in earlier tales in the collection. He also attempts to heighten the drama of the account by characterizing some of the courtroom actors, particularly the lawyers for the defense, and by building suspense before the decisions are announced.

Cable's greatest interest in the story, however, is clearly the issue of racial identity. He points to the moral perspective induced by slaveholding that permitted Salome's master to hold in bondage not only her but several others who "had every appearance of being . . . white, without ever having seen the shadow of a title for any one to own [them], and with everything to indicate that there was none" (*STSL,* 177). Similarly, he mocks the public outrage over the "unparalleled hardship, cruelty, and oppression" (*STSL,* 170) of Salome's 20-year ordeal because it was based only on the grounds that she had no African ancestry, "which, be it ever so faint, would entirely justify, alike in the law and in the popular mind, treatment otherwise counted hard, cruel, oppressive, and worthy of the public indignation." The efforts to determine the racial identity of the woman known as Sally Miller (Salome) are exposed as ludicrous, unaided by any details of appearance or by a witness's claim of an inexplicable "instinct" for determining race. "This man's 'instinct,'" Cable points out, "nor that of any one else, either during the whole trial or during twenty years' previous knowledge of the plaintiff, was of the least value to determine whether this poor slave was entirely white or of mixed blood. It was more utterly worthless than her memory" (*STSL,* 177–78).

Even the evidence of birthmarks, known only to her family and certified as authentic, was insufficient to persuade the first judge "to take away a man's property" (*STSL,* 183), although his negative decision was reversed by the state Supreme Court. Cable clearly explores the issues of the case "in view of current beliefs of to-day" (*STSL,* 177)—that is, the freedman debate—and with it he exposes both the absurd arbitrariness of the color line and the greater, pervasive moral blindness and corruption in the use of it to justify subjugation and mistreatment. Alice Hall Petry has recently argued that Cable's avoidance of authorial commentary in the story and his exploration of documentary versus imagined or subjective truth challenges "the boundaries between fiction and non-fiction in ways that anticipate Joyce, Dos Passos and the metafictionists of our own time."[9] Most readers, however, are likely to find that the source materials are simply not translated or digested enough to create a wholly successful narrative, but there is some dramatic power, and the social and political implications are clearly brought out with effective irony and indignation.

"The 'Haunted House' in Royal Street" draws on two separate incidents associated with a building on the corner of Royal and Hospital streets, infamous in Cable's day and still a regular stop on walking tours

of the Vieux Carré. The first incident, recounted earliest by Harriet
Martineau in her *Retrospect of Western Travel* (1838) but often retold in
print, concerns Mme Lalaurie, who in the early 1830s maintained a
facade of extravagant Creole elegance while brutally torturing the slaves
she kept imprisoned in her house. When the full extent of her brutality
was discovered during a fire set purposely by the cook, a crowd of out-
raged citizens broke into and ransacked her house, forcing her to flee the
region and ultimately to France. The second incident was the attempt in
1875 to oust "colored" students from the integrated Girl's High School
housed in Mme Lalaurie's restored former home—an event that had
induced Cable to write two letters in protest to the *Bulletin*. Cable
gained inside information on this incident from reading Dora Miller's
account as one of the school's teachers.

Cable's authorial manner is very nearly that of his first Creole stories,
lacking mostly the excesses of indirection and whimsy. As in *Madame
Delphine,* he opens the narrative in the role of a tour guide pointing out
the picturesque sights of the Vieux Carré, including the scenes of some of
his own stories, and he is careful throughout to establish the action within a map of the region that highlights its tourist appeal. The point of the
technique is that, as in *Madame Delphine,* "'Sieur George," and "Jean-ah
Poquelin," Cable engages and implicates the reader's interest in a conventional, essentially Gothic mystery associated with a locale—in this
case the stories that the house was haunted—and by exposing the history behind the mystery, reveals a more powerful and "real" social horror,
sustained into his own time by illusions, conventions, and irrational
fears. The tourist is led to look beyond both the modernity of New
Orleans and the superficial interest in its picturesque past.

The horror of Mme Lalaurie is that she made such a show of wealth,
refinement, decorum, and social elegance while committing atrocities
forbidden even under the old Black Code. "One would hope" (*STSL,*
207) she was insane, Cable observes. This horror pales, however, before
the "passive complicity" of her husband and the society generally who
knew or had heard the rumors of her mistreating her slaves but refused
to act or investigate because she was a Creole needing protection from
American aspersions, or because she was a lady, like Faulkner's Emily
Grierson, and "enough allowance can hardly be made in our day for the
delicacy society felt about prying into one of its own gentleman or lady
member's treatment of his or her own servants." Even when the officials
were forced to act, after a young servant girl fell to her death in view of a
neighbor, they committed the absurdity of confiscating her slaves only to

permit her to buy them back. When a mob surrounded and entered her house, rescuing the living slaves and exhuming the dead, two of the survivors were killed by being given "food and drink in fatal abundance" (*STSL,* 211), and the others were "tenderly carried" to prison and left on display, while Mme Lalaurie brazenly made her escape by the front door "in all her pretty manners and sweetness of mien" (*STSL,* 213).

In his account of these events, Cable makes clear that the source of both Mme Lalaurie's insane brutality and the crowd's ultimately mindless, amoral violence was slavery, the horror never fully acknowledged by the indignant citizenry. Mme Lalaurie "was only another possibility, not a type" (*STSL,* 202) of the slaveholder, and in a specific linking of her story to that of Salome Müller, Cable observes, "The moral of the two stories—if you care to consider it—is the same: a public practice is answerable for whatever can happen easier with it than without it." The brutalities of Mme Lalaurie, like the suffering of Salome Müller were, if not caused, made easier by slavery, and the society as a whole is accountable for the wrongs.

The image of the house as "a ghost-ridden monument" (*STSL,* 219) to the "horridest possibilities" of slavery then becomes an effective device for linking the Southern past to the "dark romance" of Cable's own day: the fundamentally, if not so visibly, brutal actions of the White League in trying to enforce segregation. Cable introduces the second narrative with a brief account of Reconstruction, essentially the analysis found in "The Freedman's Case in Equity" in which he allows the "corruption and misrule" (*STSL,* 220) of the period but ascribes it to slavery's ill-preparing the freedman for the responsibilities of citizenship and to the former masters' determination to maintain white rule. Most important, he insists that "no serious attempt was ever made by the freedman or his allies to establish any un-American principle of government," therefore distinguishing them from the White League and other proponents of caste rule.

Similar also to his political arguments as early as the *Bulletin* letters, Cable calls attention to the initial peace and harmony of the integrated schoolrooms "without the enforcement of private social companionships" (*STSL,* 222), and he draws the ironic contrast with the history of race relations whose "ghosts" were still present in the rooms in which the classes were conducted. These ghosts were then resurrected in the race sentiment that drove the "Conservative" party to try to override the actions of the temporarily ruling "Radical" party, resulting in such violent mob actions as the White League's waterfront battle with the metropolitan police in 1874 and their invading the school at Mme Lalaurie's house to drive out the students "tainted" with African ancestry. In the questioning of the girls to determine their racial identity, Cable underscores the inconsistency of the League's judgments, imperiously rejecting the meek or acquiescent but quailing before one who claimed relation to "a high Democratic official" (*STSL,* 228) and before another "of much African blood" who insisted she was Spanish and threatened that her brother would "*call on*" her interrogators to "*prove it.*"

These actions suggest the mindlessness of the 1834 mob, and there are other ironic parallels: where the mob in the first narrative came to rescue the abused slaves and punish their tormentor, in a sense the White League came to rescue the tormentor's sentiment and abuse the slaves' descendants. Where Mme Lalaurie outwitted the crowd by her bravado, the girls have to be escorted out meekly under the protection of a school official. By the time of Cable's writing, the Girl's High School had been reintegrated, then resegregated, moved, and closed, and the building had been converted to a Conservatory of Music, "but," he observes with pointed reference to the then current state of race relations, "the ghosts were all there, . . . [trooping] thickest and fastest . . . when a passionate song thrilled the air with the promise that 'Some day—some day / Eyes clearer grown the truth may see'" (*STSL,* 232).

In some ways "The 'Haunted House' in Royal Street" is a dramatized version of his major arguments against slavery and segregated schools. The opening narrative ploy, the use of Gothic conventions, the symbolic setting, the subtle characterization of Mme Lalaurie and the studied irony make it in spots at least as literary and artistic—as *artificed*—as any of his previous novels and stories. But, it is not fiction, as Cable thought of the art, and that Cable chose to write "strange, true" instead of fictional stories at this time has interesting implications. To some degree the challenges to his claims about the South growing out of his civil rights debates may have encouraged the somewhat defensive posture of his insistence on the factuality of the stories of racial injustice. More generally, Cable's introductory essay supports Arlin Turner's comment that Cable welcomed the opportunity to write something more factual than fiction and more imaginative than history (1956, 237–38). This suggests how much these stories, his early fiction, *The Creoles of Louisiana,* and "The Dance in the Place Congo" all derive from a common, multistranded literary impulse—reality, romance, and social and moral benefit.

The more interesting point, however, may be the distinction between the "treatment" Cable claims to have limited himself to as "story-teller"

and the "tampering of the fictionist" (*STSL,* 1) that has been warned off
by the "charms" of these "natural crystals." In "The 'Haunted House' in
Royal Street," at least, that treatment involves considerable shaping of
material and manipulation of reader response to achieve "that harmony
of values and brilliant unity of interest" constituting an "artistic whole."
But it does not include the imposition of a sentimental love story or the
invention of characters to illustrate or mouth heroic ideals. That this
might be the "tampering" he meant is unfortunately too often illustrated
by his fiction, especially after he withdrew from the civil rights debate.
All of the narratives in *Strange True Stories of Louisiana* are spared such
treatment, but not all are successful as "gems in the rough." "The
'Haunted House' in Royal Street" is easily the masterpiece of the collection and one of the most powerful and effective stories Cable wrote.

John March, Southerner

While Cable worked on his new novel between 1889 and 1894, his life
continued to be active, varied, full of competing interests, and characterized by transition. Much of his time was occupied in his lecture and reading tours, which took him to the West Coast in 1892 and 1893, and
included joint appearances with Hamlin Garland, Harriet Monroe,
James Whitcomb Riley, and others in Chicago and Eugene Field on
tours of the East and Midwest. By 1892, having given up both his overt
political campaign for the freedman and his Sunday-school teaching, he
devoted more of his time to the Home Culture Clubs and to his personal and civic life in Northampton. With his daughter Dorothea's birth in
1889, his family had grown to include seven children (a son, William,
had been born in 1885), and although his mother, Rebecca, died in
1890, he remained actively involved in the second Cable household that
included his sisters, Mary Louise and Nettie, and Nettie's children.

In 1892 Cable moved to a house he would call Tarryawhile, on the
edge of Paradise Woods not far from Smith College, and he became
active in both the remodeling and the landscaping. When his oldest
daughter, Louise, married James Chard in 1894, he celebrated with an
elaborate reception and party that included dancing until late—a sign of
his liberalized morality. Through all this activity and despite the fact that
by 1892 he owed the Century Company more than $4,000 in advances,
Cable published only a few miscellaneous pieces, including two short
narratives ("A West Indian Slave Insurrection" and "The Taxidermist")
collected in later volumes, a reminiscence of his boyhood days in New

Orleans for *St. Nicholas,* an appreciation of Robert E. Lee and Stonewall Jackson, and *A Memory of Roswell Smith* in tribute to his close friend and supporter who died in 1892. While his reform zeal had been redirected into other activities, however, his interest in the Southern question remained and formed the central thesis of his major literary effort, a novel first called *Johnny Reb.*

If *Dr. Sevier* is sometimes used to demonstrate the negative effect of Richard Watson Gilder and the Gilded Age on Cable's art, *John March, Southerner* has offered an even better example. Gilder's reaction to the first version he read in 1890 was that he could "weep for disappointment" (quoted in Turner 1956, 291). He found it "a tract, not a story" into which Cable had put "much of [his] most serious thought on public, political and humanitarian questions," and, as with *Dr. Sevier,* he complained that this was done at the expense of "literature" (quoted in Biklé, 213). *"Beware of the Fate of Tolstoi,"* Gilder warned, hoping for a return to books like "Bonaventure the Beautiful" (quoted in Turner 1956, 291). Stung by these comments, Cable nevertheless continued to revise the manuscript, submitting two more versions to the Century Company with little more success. In rejecting the novel for a third and last time, Gilder wrote of the "innate disagreeableness that seems to pertain largely to the conditions described" and that "there is an apparent effort to conceal the salutary purpose in the book—but it is there, all the same,—running along in an irritating way" (quoted in Turner 1956, 292).

Turner notes that Gilder's own views on the freedman and the South had become increasingly conservative, but his objections to overt moralizing, direct social and political commentary, and general disagreeableness were long-standing. Because the original manuscript is not available, it is difficult to assess fully Gilder's impact on this novel and on Cable's art generally, but Lucy Biklé's observation that "Mr. Gilder was right, my father was convinced" (213) is suggestive. Rubin observes that Gilder's objections to the novel were less its political content than its *"unpleasantness"* (229), and Cable's comment written as he was finishing the novel— that he hoped the completed work would offer "a pleasing story of the heroic in imagined lives" ("After-Thoughts," 23)—indicates that he concurred. We can only speculate about what Cable added or took out of the first version to make the novel more pleasant, but given Cable's previous practice of fiction, it is likely that the elements that weaken the novel were present in some portion from the outset. Gilder was clearly not the best editor to encourage and develop Cable's strengths as a realist and social observer, but Cable too much shared his editor's tastes not to limit or weaken his work on his own. Although it was unacceptable to the editors of *Century,* Cable was, with their permission, able to begin publishing *John March, Southerner* in *Scribner's Monthly* in January 1894, and after some further revision the book appeared in February 1895 (dated 1894).

The basic plot of *John March, Southerner* concerns the efforts of the central character in the aftermath of Reconstruction to develop the family estate, Wildwood, left to him by his father. John March's plan, also a family legacy, is not to create a new plantation but a community of people whose wealth derives from the abundance of mineral resources in the land. To do this he becomes involved in the general commercial and industrial development of the region. He naively joins in a complicated capitalization scheme that includes a significant reliance on Northern investors and travels to the North and ultimately to Europe in search of immigrants to form the new community. In many scenes, through both dialogue and action, Cable directly addresses the issues of the New South and Redemption that were part of the Southern debate in the late 1880s when the novel's plot was born. He includes commentary on the sources of corruption under Reconstruction, the convict lease system, government aid to education, the role of the newspapers in distorting truth, segregated schools and church congregations, the need to elevate the lower economic orders, and similar topics.

In the novel's concluding action the capitalization scheme is exposed as corrupt and exploitive, the outside investors flee with their profits, the community is left with half-built factories and jobless workers, and John March loses his land (albeit temporarily, since it is returned by a deus ex machina title mix-up). Thus Cable effectively attacks the New South proponents on the grounds of their inflated claims of economic development and of their arguments that commercial and industrial progress meant social and moral progress as well. John March's early struggles to overcome his baser impulses and feelings—not only his quick temper, self-centeredness, and "Southern" imperiousness, but also his resentment toward blacks after being beaten by an angry ex-slave, Cornelius Leggett—formulate Cable's message to the South, for in the end a "totally diffe'nt"[10] John March, aware of the corruption all about him, including the unjust treatment of the freedman, stays on to help develop his region for social good, not personal gain. He also wins the hand of Barbara Garnet, daughter of the president of his college, Rosemont, and the man who becomes his business partner and finally tries to rob him of his land.

The range of issues Cable addresses in the novel creates an impressive and satisfying complexity, although the business machinations are difficult to follow and ultimately lack dramatic effect. Arlin Turner's description of the action as gaining complexity "less from intricacy of plot than from the succession of crowded scenes" (1956, 294) points to one source of this weakness. Many of the social and political ideas are presented in the speeches of individual characters without authorial comment and without anyone to clearly speak for the author, as if Cable were in part letting the opposition "furnish the ammunition" that would expose them. This may be a sign of Cable's withdrawal from controversy, but the technique seems more an effort at dramatic presentation, an attempt not to preach. The more serious problem is that it does not work: the issues and ideas in the speeches are not made central to the dramatic conflict. A comparison can be made with the second half of William Dean Howells's *The Rise of Silas Lapham* (1885), in which Lapham's business affairs and decisions are made the focus of suspense, the center of dramatic and thematic tensions. Despite some powerful and melodramatic scenes, *John March, Southerner* lacks this development of dramatic tension centering in its social, economic, and political ideas. In addition, the love plot, which dominates the second half of the novel, is trivial and tedious, and it generally distracts from the dramatic potential of the narrative of economic development, offering a clear sign of Cable's susceptibility to genteel taste.

The choice of setting is more problematic. The inspiration for the novel is linked to Cable's visit to Monteagle, Tennessee, in 1887, and, according to Philip Butcher, its plot is based on the unsuccessful efforts of John Moffat, Adelene Moffat's father, to colonize and industrialize land he held on Cumberland Mountain and to found a "collegiate and normal institute" (Butcher, 120) like that of Rosemont in the novel. Cable returned to this region to interview locals and to gather information and impressions that he recorded in a notebook, but with the plot already in mind he moved the locale deeper into the South to the region around Marietta and Cartersville in northwest Georgia, again visiting the area to record details and observations. The specifics of the two regions, particularly the latter, give some substance to an imaginary setting called Suez in the "State of Dixie, County of Clearwater" (*JM*, 1). For Cable, this choice of locale is significant both because it is not Louisiana and because it is a fictional place designed to represent the postwar, industrializing New South as a whole. Butcher correctly observes that "Louisiana, with its Creoles, Acadians, and quadroons, had a unique history and special problems that made it inappropriate for his purpose" (121), but the relocation and the use of the imaginary setting pushes the novel toward allegory.

In some passages Cable does provide descriptions of street scenes based on his notes of Cartersville that ring true with concrete, characterizing detail, reminiscent of similar descriptions of backwoods towns in Twain's *Life on the Mississippi* or *The Adventures of Huckleberry Finn*. But, like his descriptions of Acadian Louisiana in *Bonaventure,* these passages do not reflect the intimacy of knowledge and complexity of feeling found in his characterizations of Creole New Orleans. The descriptions of landscape, while appropriate to the region and studded with plant names, are fairly generalized and, outside of the initial sight of battle-scarred fields, they are little used to convey feeling or develop atmosphere and ideas. The scenes on trains and in the North are even flatter, despite his including descriptions of Paradise Woods and other locales near his home in Northampton.

In freeing himself from the ready-made, familiar auras and associations of his native New Orleans, Cable may have allowed a broader address to Southern problems and saved his novel from inappropriate romantic elements, but he also robbed it of a satisfying concreteness and fullness of detail, a psychology of landscape and the social and historical resonance of actual places. Cable's Dixie is too much a region of social and political ideas, not enough a region like William Faulkner's significantly *mythical* and concretely real Yoknapatawpha. The setting alone does not ruin the novel, but its effect is more significant and more weakening than most critics have recognized.

Despite the weaknesses of plot and the problem of setting, *John March, Southerner* is, as Rubin observes, "ambitious," and much of its interest lies in its characterizations. As in *The Grandissimes* and *Dr. Sevier,* he includes a broad range of social and personality types identified with the milieu: a dignified, land-poor Southern gentleman; an unreconstructed Old South slave owner; an itinerant preacher–turned–college president; a dashing ex-Confederate officer–turned–New South editor; a plantation owner–turned–scalawag; a Southern belle; a genteel Southern poetess; an "Uncle" and an "Aunt"; a rascally politician and several other "Negroes"; a few gun-toting, bootlegging "hill people"; plus scrupulous and unscrupulous Northern investors, a disapproving Englishman and several others, less distinct. Most of the characters are well defined, although primarily through their speeches and, for some, their behavior. Cable uses dialect with the Old South and black characters, which helps identify them, but in some instances the use of dialect in long speeches makes important ideas difficult to follow. Also, most of the characters, somewhat like Honoré Grandissime, are not distinctive or memorable in their appearance, another effect, perhaps, of the generalized locale and of a less luxuriant narrative style, more sparing in its use of imagery.

In addition to the range of types, the comic treatment of most of the characters is one of the novel's more interesting and appealing features, as if for this novel "Drop Shot" resurrected Felix Lazarus. Cable's reference to a man who "had smashed a window, . . . by accident, and clearly the fault of the bar-keeper, who shouldn't have dodged" (*JM,* 234), offers one instance of the humor, but there are other, broader examples: his description of a revival meeting; the courting of "Daphne Dalrymple" (Mrs. March) by Dinwiddie Pettigrew; a burlesque love encounter between Pettigrew and Mrs. March's servant, Daphne Jane (dressed in her mistress's clothing). If Cable was under the spell of Howells in writing *Dr. Sevier,* he seems to have been influenced by Twain in the first half of *John March, Southerner,* or at least by the same tradition of Southwestern and Western humor in which Twain wrote.

Consistent with the humorous treatment, all the characters in the novel, with the exception of Barbara Garnet, exhibit significant measures of human failing, but even the worst is more than a cartoon villain. As most critics have noted and as Cable himself was aware, he had been largely unsuccessful in creating believably virtuous characters in his earlier work. But John March's initial self-centeredness, romanticism, stubborn pride, and quick temper are both credibly represented and linked to a home in which his mother emotionally manipulates his kindly but ineffectual father, and more generally with the defensive inwardness of the fallen South. Even more striking, Cable shows March to be capable of actual violence without his committing any unredeemable acts. This capacity is made both psychologically plausible and thematically significantly as a part of the pervasive violence of the region but, more specifically, as a festering wound from the unwarranted beating he receives as a boy from Cornelius Leggett, an ex-slave who has just been unjustly beaten himself. Cable's point, as it was with most of his earlier heroes—most notably Frowenfeld, Vignevielle, and Bonaventure—is the necessity of self-mastery and, at least with the Southerners, overcoming negative cultural conditioning, without becoming an apostate.

March's transformation begins with believable flaws and is, for the most part, realistically portrayed as a slow, difficult process, although his prolonged willingness to trust Garnet does strain credulity. When he overcomes his resentment of Leggett and rescues him from a lynch mob, the action is melodramatic but thematically significant. More broadly, one of the necessary changes for him is to convert an essentially sentimental attachment to the idea of the South, schooled by his mother's insipid poetry, into a more realistic commitment, grounded in an awareness of the wrongs of the past and present, still centered in feeling and not personal profit, dedicated to reform. To the degree that this change is linked to the conversion of his feelings from infatuation with Fannie Halliday to true love for Barbara Garnet, the transformation is sentimentalized.

The role of religion, however, is played down and ultimately made satiric by March's trip to the "mourner's bench" in a comic revival scene. The transformation is also vaguely associated with his trips to the North, suggesting further, as most modern critics have recognized, that March's growth of understanding parallels Cable's own. March's ultimate refusal to leave the South may reflect Cable's second thoughts about moving to Northampton, but more likely it dramatizes the kind of involvement in Southern affairs and concern about the region's future that he had shown in his civil rights crusade. John March is perhaps Cable's most convincing hero, but even with him Cable is better at representing vice than virtue, and his moral reform is more thematically clear than psychologically credible.

Cable's success in depicting human failing is best illustrated by Major Garnet, whose evil, as Turner puts it, is "of a deep cast" (1956, 294). The list of his corruptions is long and impressive, including not only the shady business practices, the lying, scheming, manipulating, exploiting, and betraying that are central to the main action, but also his apparent philandering and his violence, both to his former slave and to his daughter. The frankness and starkness with which these corruptions and those of some of the other characters are presented is another of the novel's striking features, making it, if not quite seamy, a good deal coarser and earthier than Cable's other work. More significantly, Garnet's character is defined in terms of his milieu. Raised in genteel poverty and educated to be a minister, he is a circuit rider before the war, marries a woman whose land enables him to found a college, Rosemont, and returns after the war, an officer covered with a "wealth of gold braid" (*JM*, 13), his wounded arm in a sling, to become a college president, businessman, and civic leader. He broods over the Lost Cause, is "addicted to rhetoric," and speaks as if "his very flesh seemed to feel the smartings of trampled aspirations and insulted rights" (*JM*, 27). His racial attitudes are made

apparent when he beats Leggett for suggesting emancipation had given
them "a sawt of equality" (*JM*, 33) and then reproaches himself with the
ungentlemanly show of passion forced on him by the "vile ingrate" in
"exercise of the only discipline, he fully believed, for which such a race of
natural slaves could have a wholesome regard" (*JM*, 38).

W. M Baskervill's complaint about Cable making a villain of "an old
Confederate, plucky enough to fight to the end and brave enough to
save a comrade at the risk of his own,"[11] indicates how much he departs
from the stereotype of the honorable Southern aristocrat embalmed in
antebellum plantation fiction and kept on display by Thomas Nelson
Page. In fact, Garnet's character seems drawn to undermine that fictional image by exposing the brutality and damaged ego underlying his
convictions of white supremacy, as well as the New South background,
ambition, and rapacity underlying the Old South bearing, show of
manners, and rhetorical flourish. It is significant, too, that he is identified with evangelical religion, for as Philip Butcher discusses at greater
length, Cable satirizes religious practices throughout the novel, target-
ing the emotionalism, preoccupation with dogma, and social irrelevancy
of churches that he had criticized in some of his writings on religion and
that led him to give up teaching Sunday school. In sum, something of a
cross between Colonel Sartoris, Flem Snopes, and Elmer Gantry, he
offers a clear illustration of Cable's argument that the fundamental
wrong of slave culture, its "ethos" of subjugation, had been kept alive
and thereby made more desperately corrupt through Reconstruction
and after.

Some of the other characters are less striking in their virtues and vices
but are interesting nevertheless. Portrayed at one point "with his silver-
shot curls dancing half-way down his shoulders, a six-shooter under each
skirt of his black velvet coat, and a knife down the back of his neck"
(*JM*, 55), Launcelot Halliday is vividly rendered, an audacious oppor-
tunist whose self-interest coincides with public good. Recognizing the
unviability of his cotton plantation after the war, he sells to a Yankee,
becomes a cotton factor in New Orleans, and then returns to Suez to
reclaim the mortgage and set up a freedman's agricultural colony,
Leggettstown, on his former plantation, apparently operating on a crop-
lien basis. Although qualifying as a scalawag for cooperating with the
Radical government, he is not corrupt, but he lacks the moral purpose
and genuine conviction of a true Southerner like John March. He is,
therefore, an ineffectual agent of social change.

Jeff-Jack Ravenel, dashing and charming as a war veteran, is shown to have genuine feeling for his fallen comrades-in-arms, but he drinks excessively enough to be barred from his wife's sleeping compartment on their wedding night. While he is not directly involved in the corrupt schemes of Garnet and others, he boosts Suez through his newspaper by exaggerating the progress, makes no attempt to reform the corruptions he sees, and thus is an indirect accomplice to the eventual collapse. In him Cable seems to get back at the Southern newspaper editors whom he had previously blamed for much of the criticism of his civil rights crusade, but the mildness of the attack compared to that directed against Garnet and his ilk suggests that he had come to recognize the resistance as more broad-based.

Given the overall depiction of flawed humanity in *John March, Southerner* it should not be surprising that the black characters are also not idealized, but this has troublesome implications for this novel. Critics have generally agreed that by creating purposely unsentimentalized black characters Cable aimed to counter the charge that he preferred blacks to whites and always treated them more sympathetically in his fiction. Cornelius Leggett in particular seems to represent such a balanced treatment, for he is shown to be a shrewd businessman, a pragmatic champion of the freedman, a spokesperson for some of Cable's views on education and against white supremacy, and at the same time a cruel, heavy-drinking, libidinous, cowardly, and venal rascal. Cable's treatment of Leggett's character, however, goes beyond realism to the kind of minstrel-show stereotyping that is also apparent in the characters of "Aunt" Virginia and "Uncle" Leviticus. Examples of this can be seen in the depictions of Leggett's courting behavior or of his being so paralyzed by fear on the edge of a ravine that John March has to carry him to safety, but the "stage-darky" quality is more evident in drolleries of speech. For instance, mixing the serious with the comic, he tells John March, "Ef you wants to make a rich country, you ain't got to make it a white man's contry, naw a black man's country, naw yit mis the races an' make it a yaller man's country, much less a yaller woman's; no, seh! But the whole effulgence is jess this: you got to make it a po' man's country! Now, you accentuate yo' reflections on that, seh!" (*JM*, 121). To some degree, these comedy devices ("whole effulgence," "accentuate yo' reflections") undermine Leggett's appeal and his effectiveness as Cable's civil rights spokesperson. Butcher argues that Leggett's characterization, along with other burlesquing of black physical traits, speech, and personality, the frequent use of the terms "nigger" and "darky," and the novel's posing no solution to the unjust treatment of the freedman, reflects a change in Cable's attitude toward race accompanying his more comfortable life of conformity in Northampton (1962, 125).

Certainly, one of the novel's weaknesses is the absence of educated, refined, and accomplished black male figures such as Cable knew personally, but Butcher's argument does not give full justice to Cable's treatment of race in the novel. As Wayne Mixon observes, "Even the so-called old-time Negroes in *John March, Southerner* know where their interests lie" (Mixon, 107), as illustrated by Garnet's former slaves abandoning him as soon as they are freed. In addition, some of the demeaning comedy comes from the use of dialect, which alone inevitably places the characters who use it on a lower status than the narrator and other characters speaking Standard English. This had earlier contributed to the charge that Cable was denigrating the white Creoles in his Louisiana fiction. Cable's point in insisting on Leggett's flaws is that the freedman's sins merely reflect the far greater corruptions of the white world. If Leggett conforms to a blackface stereotype, reinforcing the Southern view of the freedman, he demonstrates nevertheless a clear perception that "his true interests necessarily lie with the cause of popular government and public education, and he will support anyone, white or colored, who will genuinely work for that cause" (Rubin, 230). Compared with the most familiar late-nineteenth-century, white representations of black character—Harris's Uncle Remus and Twain's Jim or even his Roxanna—Leggett is an extraordinarily strong character, "unique" in Mixon's view because "comical darky, 'uppity nigger,' and artful corruptionist though he be, he fights in the cause of social justice" (107).

Also, consistent with his earlier racial arguments, Cable's most sympathetic black character is a woman, Barbara Garnet's childhood playmate and then maid, Joanna. Unlike the mulatto Leggett, Cable describes her as "very black" (*JM,* 21), as if not to confuse the issues of her portrayal with that of the quadroons in his earlier fiction, whose mixed racial heritage was a source of pathos. Joanna may be "stigmatized" by her dialect like the others, but she successfully resists Cornelius's blandishments, and she is able, steadfast, and conscientious in her work. In the scenes where she dines publicly with John March in the North and where she quietly waits in his office to deliver a crucial letter, her image echoes that of the demure, respectable black woman whose expulsion from a railroad car he described as having moved him to write "The Freedman's Case in Equity."

Joanna's significance is more sharply defined by the contrast with Mrs. March's maid, Daphne Jane. Daphne is distracted from her opportunity for an education by her flirtatiousness, and she becomes "one of Leggettstown's few social successes" (*JM,* 276). Her open interest in men and falling prey to Leggett mark her as more sexual and less chaste than Joanna, but her values and behavior are again specifically identified as a reflection of the white world. Thus the conscious mimicry of her "trying to pomatum the frizzles out of her hair" (*JM,* 276) and of her trying on her mistress's clothing, manners, and poetic style, while recognizable as racist humor of the period, also makes the point that she has, like Leggett, been influenced by the worst in Southern culture: "She minced before the mirror, she sank into chairs, she sighed and whined, took the attitudes given or implied by the other Daphne's portrait down-stairs, and said weary things in a faint, high key" (*JM,* 286). While Joanna has Barbara Garnet for a model, Daphne Jane is shown to aspire to the same vapid, self-absorbed femininity exhibited by her mistress, a literary predecessor of Scarlett O'Hara with the nom de plume Daphne Dalrymple. Moreover, whatever lustfulness is implied by her brazen flirting, it is no more than that suggested of the Frenchwoman, Mademoiselle Eglantine, and perhaps Fannie Halliday as well. Refinement and decorum, in short, follow no color line, and this had been at the center of Cable's views of race since the mid-1870s.

As suggested by the contrast between Joanna and Daphne Jane under the influence of their respective mistresses, Cable includes the white women characters in his critical anatomy of Southern society. Fannie Halliday, who seems at first a typically shallow "Southern Belle" and whose marriage to Ravenel seems grounded more in the appeal of superficial beauty and passion than in practical wisdom, shows some courage and self-control in barring him from her bed on their wedding night and considerable strength later in nursing him faithfully at the risk of her own health. Mrs. March is presented as a caricature of a small-town Southern poetess whose sentimental verse extolling the virtues of the old plantation days and proudly defying Yankee oppression (Garnet asks, "You've seen her last poem: 'Slaves to ow own slaves—Neveh!'" [*JM,* 19]) recommend her to local tastes: "The Pulaski City Clarion reprints her poems," Garnet enthuses, "and calls her 'sweetest of Southland songsters.'" A published collection of her poems fails, however, to attract notice or sales, and thus through her Cable clearly suggests the debilitating effect of the plantation tradition, amateurism, and provincialism on Southern art.

Mrs. March also constructs her own image as a Southern woman within the same sentimental literary conventions, which makes her a vapory, mannered coquette, delicate in health, used to her own way, deeply manipulative and susceptible to the likes of Dinwiddie Pettigrew and even Major Garnet. Her characterization is fully in keeping with the work's comic tone, but it is curious that Cable would make his hero's mother the least attractive woman in the novel. Barbara Garnet, otherwise a fairly conventional romantic heroine, is distinctive in her resilience to her father's physical abuse, in her good sense, and in her ability to engage in the "man-talk" (*JM,* 305) of business affairs. Cable's version of the moral ingredients necessary to a sound transformation of the Old South thus includes not only masculine self-mastery but some degree of feminine self-reliance and strength.

The initial critical reception to *John March, Southerner* was brief and relatively acute.[12] Reviewers noted the change from Cable's earlier materials and manner and either welcomed or regretted it depending on their taste. There were complaints about the excessive complications of plot, some grumbling over the dialect, and general praise for the characters with a recognition of the balance of virtue and vice in them and of their fidelity to observable types. The critical taste of what Richard Brodhead has recently called "the literary institutions under gentry control" (Elliott, 472), however, no longer favored the sort of realistic Southern novel Cable had attempted. Consequently, *John March, Southerner* was quickly dismissed or forgotten until interest in the issues he addressed was revived in the late 1950s. Louis Rubin has claimed the most for what he calls "a flawed but notable novel," arguing persuasively that it offers "an impressive, sometimes even stunning examination of [the] region" (237), and Wayne Mixon has agreed: "more than any Southern writer before the Great Mississippian, Cable in *John March, Southerner* attempted to portray the South's complexity, to show her strengths and weaknesses" (103).

The novel is indeed impressive in what it attempts—the convincing portrayals of human corruption, the use of vernacular humor, the attacks on debilitating and essentially literary structures of personality and values, the open-endedness and irresolution of complex social problems— and it is significant in its flaws—the artificiality of setting, the weaknesses in plot, and the press of ideology in shaping action and character. *John March, Southerner* cannot be placed among Cable's best books, but as a purpose novel it is several cuts above *Dr. Sevier* and in the significance of its concerns more compelling to modern readers than *Bonaventure.* In it, at least in the first half, Cable tried to harmonize his practice of fiction with his social vision, to diminish the romantic elements and even attack, more directly than before, the false romanticism that contributed to the South's moral blindness. But the achievement was at the cost of emotional and psychological complexity, and it was only partial, for in the novel's second half the practice of fiction became once again predominantly the telling of a love story. Unfortunately, this would become the dominant practice in most of the novels he was yet to write.

Chapter Seven

Pure Fiction and the Mines of Experience

Although most of Cable's fiction after *Madame Delphine* can be described as "interesting attempts," modern critics have agreed almost unanimously that Cable wrote little of literary significance after *John March, Southerner*. The standard view is that because of his defeat in the freedman crusade, Cable turned to writing "pure" fiction, abandoning not just political writing but the political in his writing. Nevertheless, over his last 30 years, Cable published 10 more books, five of them novels and one, *The Cavalier* (1901), his only "best-seller," and to understand the nature of his achievement it is useful to explore the source of his failures, particularly in his last three novels, which reflect a conscious effort to return to the vein of his early work.

Cable's activities from the mid-1890s on suggest an increasing retirement, if not from literature then certainly from national affairs. He settled into a comfortable life of domestic pleasures, literary celebrity, and uncontroversial civic projects. Cable's two oldest daughters married in the 1890s—Louise to James Chard in 1894 and Mary to Alfred L. P. Dennis in 1899—and the third, Lucy, graduated from Smith College in 1898 and began a career as literary editor, joining with Mary E. Burt to bring out *The Cable Story Book* (1899), a collection of the author's work selected and revised for young readers. Until Louise's death in 1904 the Cable family remained a tight nucleus with the father actively involved in the children's affairs. Cable was particularly close to his son William, whose weak health kept him from too much activity and independence and who would die at 23, four years after his mother.

The Cable home was also a center for many Northampton social activities, and distinguished visitors, such as Arthur Conan Doyle and Joseph Jefferson, were often invited to plant a ceremonial tree in Cable's garden.[1] The visit of the English novelist James M. Barrie and critic W. Robertson Nicoll in 1896 was important not only because it was a sign of Cable's status as a "must-see" celebrity, but also because it led two years later to his visiting England, where he gave small readings, toured, and was even more elaborately fêted than he had been by the Clemens circle early in his career. He met or visited such luminaries as George Meredith, George Gissing, Walter Besant, Conan Doyle, Rudyard Kipling, and Henry James, whom he had first met in New York in 1883 and with whom he shared a genuine mutual admiration. He stayed a week in Scotland with Andrew Carnegie at Skibo Castle, and there established a friendship that would later have material benefit for himself and for the Home Culture Clubs.

While visiting Scotland, Cable also learned about the annual garden competition Carnegie sponsored at his birthplace, Dunfermline, and he inaugurated his own competition the next year as part of the Home Culture Club activities in Northampton. Carnegie contributed prize money for the first garden competition in 1899, and he later donated $50,000 to build a clubhouse with reading rooms, activity space, and offices, dedicated with an elaborate ceremony in 1905 as Carnegie Hall.[2] Cable remained directly involved in the business and other affairs of the clubs—renamed the People's Institute after 1909—but he was most active in the garden competition, at first conducting them entirely by himself and serving as judge every year until 1922. The competitions were pointedly democratic in their rules and designed to provide social uplift through beauty. Cable also wrote a number of magazine articles on home gardening—its aesthetic and social philosophy as well as its practice—that were collected in 1914 as *The Amateur Garden.*[3] He engaged in a few other public service roles, such as membership in the American Academy of Arts and Letters and in the Simplified Spelling Board. Maintaining his convictions about the injustice of segregation and white rule, he contributed funds and helped promote the all-black Okolona Industrial College in Mississippi. But his devotion to home gardening seems the most visible sign of his having converted his earlier passionate social commitment into something like an extended domesticity.

To what degree this transformation represents a "decline" in "Cable's personal integrity" (Butcher 1962, 119), "emotional exhaustion" (Rubin, 245), or simply advancing age has sparked some speculative debate. It does seem unfair to expect Cable to become the kind of crusader he never was—that is, a lifetime devotee to a singular cause—but it also seems unnecessary to wrap him in the redeeming mantle of defeated-soldier imagery, the civil rights equivalent of Lost Cause pathos. Cable's involvement in specific reform activities followed a consistent pattern in which he would initially lead by calling attention to the wrong to be righted and by organizing the community's most respected and influential citizens into institutions of effective change. While sincere, selfless, and courageous, this method was also pragmatic and alloyed with an "intellectual ambition" to enjoy the support and respect of those he thought of as society's best. Such mixed motives are similar to the irony of his basing his arguments for equal civil rights on the need to maintain appropriate social distinctions, and they bear on the ultimate consequence of his move to Northampton. In the New England town he was able to enjoy the respect and recognition of his neighbors and feel with them a particular harmony of social, moral and intellectual values. Furthermore, that harmony fits the Emersonian dictate that "all things are moral,"[4] and thus, just as his earlier Presbyterian rigor had dissolved into a bland general spirituality, Cable could maintain his political convictions while rechanneling his moral energies into beautifying and educating his own domestic environment.

The Emersonian cast to Cable's outlook during the 1890s can also be seen in his fiction, and especially in his small body of critical-theoretical writing. As editor of the Home Culture Clubs *Letter* and its successor *Symposium* in 1895–96 and of *Current Literature* in New York from April to September 1897, Cable wrote editorials and commentaries on such authors as Howells, James, and Zola, addressing contemporary literary topics (e.g., art for art's sake, naturalism, realism, and the uses of dialect), but, as Arlin Turner observes, his discussions are far too general to be either valuable or interesting (1956, 299). His more extensive theoretical views appear in a series of articles that focus primarily on the office of the storyteller and the relation of fact to fiction.[5] He extolls the value of fiction as "but a refinement of truth harmoniously concentrated and foreshortened," aimed "pre-eminently for, our emotions," which the "right sort" of books "kindle, while they chasten" ("Extracts," 418). The storyteller's office, he insists, "is not the conveyance of exact or complete information, but the more ultimate one of fitting right emotions to facts" ("To See," 62), "to make you feel to-day that you are entertained, and find to-morrow that you are profited" ("Speculations," 90), and, therefore, every storyteller "cannot escape being" a "Romanticist and realist in one," and "in their noblest meanings, religion and romance come to the same thing" ("To See," 66).

Such pieties are broad enough to allow for all of Cable's literary practice, but they certainly do not identify the strengths of his best work. In fact, when he asserts that "an argument may end in a story, but a story should never degenerate into an argument," he seems to chasten himself wryly for the overt political aims of novels like *John March, Southerner* and even *The Grandissimes*. With respect to the battle over literary realism led by William Dean Howells, Hamlin Garland, and others, Cable's statements are not dramatically different from some of Howells' editorial arguments published in *Criticism and Fiction* (1891). Cable, like Howells, always mixed attention to commonplace detail with a measure of romantic idealism, but Cable's emphasis here on feelings, ideal Truth, and the superiority of poetry to science marks him more in the opposite camp of such "Defenders of Ideality" as Gilder, Edmund Clarence Stedman, and Richard Henry Stoddard.

Cable's manner of presenting his literary views in these essays is, however, more interesting and significant than the views themselves. As he makes specific in "The Speculations of a Story-Teller," he writes not as a critic but as a practicing artist, and his method is essentially narrative and descriptive, a conversation with family or friends at Tarryawhile or in adjoining Paradise Woods. One of the reappearing guests, "Smith of New Orleans," a "friend . . . who gets a living by fiction," is obviously Richard Thorndyke Smith, the autobiographical persona he creates to narrate the *Strong Hearts* stories then appearing in *Scribner's Magazine*, and thus some of the conversation is with himself, or between the artist and critic in himself. The use of the Northampton setting is particularly striking, first for the emphasis on nature, the attempt to project concepts or feelings—in this case literary values—through descriptions of landscape much as he had done in *Bonaventure*. Cable obviously echoes Emerson, and he specifically cites Thoreau, Carlyle, and Whitman, thus providing a background for his ideas, a pallid distillation of "transcendental" sentiment, entirely in keeping with the New England locale. Whereas complexity, contradiction, deep psychological ambivalence, and the subtle specifics of oddity mark Cable's esthetic response to New Orleans, Tarryawhile and Paradise woods seem to generate feelings of harmony and homogeneity, a resolution of all values in a mild, idealistic New England haze.

Strong Hearts

The three original stories Cable published in *Scribner's Magazine* during the 1890s—"The Taxidermist" (May 1893), "Gregory's Island" (August 1896), and "The Entomologist" (January–March 1899), which were collected in 1899 as *Strong Hearts*—reflect the tenor of his literary theories. The stories share Richard Thorndyke Smith as their common narrator, but there is no continuity of action between them and only minimal cross-referencing of characters; the collection therefore has less unity of plot than *Bonaventure.* In an initial chapter added to "The Solitary" (as "Gregory's Island" was renamed in the book), however, Cable explains how he conceives that, despite changes "of time, scene, character, this tale of strong hearts is one."[6] Each "sets forth, in heroic natures and poetic fates, a principle . . . so universal that . . . as [Joseph] said to the sovereign of Egypt, 'This thing is established of God.'" Hence each is one because "it illustrates the indivisible twinship of poetry and religion" (*SH,* 4). Such language suggests the general focus of the stories on moral or spiritual truths rather than social and political conflicts. As in *Bonaventure,* the moral theme of each story centers in the individual character's relation to nature, but there is very little sense of milieu, either natural or social, except for the island and gulf scenes in "The Solitary." More than the lack of reforming zeal or political purpose, it is the thinness or absence of social, historical, or (with the one exception) natural *context,* the flatness of texture, that weakens these stories and makes them seem what Allen Tate said Emerson had made of New England literature—a "sip of Cambric tea."[7]

Written second but placed first in *Strong Hearts,* "The Solitary" most clearly reflects Cable's thinking about storytelling. The central action involves the efforts of a weak man, Gregory, nicknamed "Cracked-fiddle," who tries to control his alcoholism by marooning himself on a coastal island in the Gulf of Mexico. Cable uses Gregory's weathering a hurricane, which aborts his premature efforts to return to civilization, and his communion with the beauties of nature to suggest both the terms of his psychological turmoil and his spiritual growth. Insofar as Gregory's gains derive as much from accident and fear as from any religious or natural pieties, and his weakness is shown to be never completely under control, Cable handles his theme with some complexity and understanding.

His achievement, however, is less comparable to Stephen Crane's powerfully existential and ironic "The Open Boat," as Butcher (1962, 137) and Rubin (240) have suggested, than to Lafcadio Hearn's more atmospheric and melodramatic *Chita* (1889). Cable's self-reflexive interest in literary issues is signaled by Smith's sententious observations on storytelling, on the functions of romance in illustrating heroism, on the question of whether Gregory's narrative is sentimental, and on the harmony between reading and nature in Gregory's transformation. In this regard the story's theme of Gregory's gaining self-mastery by narrowing "the circumference of his life to limits within which he might hope to turn *some* of his daily issues into good poetry" (*SH,* 6) seems to reflect Cable's view of his own role in the narrowed circumference of Northampton.

"The Taxidermist" is a story of a humble Creole artisan, P. T. B. ("Pas Trop Bon") Manouvrier, who wins the Louisiana Lottery and uses the funds to build a beautiful home for his wife, but without ever living in it he donates the house to replace a nearby orphanage destroyed in a fire. The main concern is Manouvrier's selflessness, and his strength of character is signaled initially by his harmonizing a love of nature and a devotion to high artistic ideals in his taxidermy. He abhors any wanton destruction of nature but practices his art to capture the souls of animals accidentally killed, such as that of the hummingbird Smith brings to him at the outset. The details of the bird's being unintentionally crushed by Smith's child, Manouvrier's ability to restore the delicate creature to something lifelike, his refusal to accept payment, and his childlessness suggest parallels with Hawthorne's "Artist of the Beautiful," but not in artistry or in depth of aesthetic and psychological insight. The story is slight and sentimental, but like "The Solitary" it reflects Cable's changed consciousness of virtue and the artist's relation to it. Where before Cable had campaigned against the Louisiana Lottery and had depicted its pernicious effects in "'Sieur George," in "The Taxidermist" he shows a good man playing it under control and converting his luck to good purpose. The most strident railing against the lottery's evils comes from the "decent, rich" (*SH,* 62) man who kills a pigeon in order to stuff it, but Smith—Cable himself in some respect—is unmoved by such reforming zeal, although he feels a "vague shame," knowing "as well as anybody that a man without a quick, strong, aggressive, insistent indignation against undoubted evil is a very poor stick" (*SH,* 67). However serious this self-reproach, the story suggests that more social benefit comes from individual acts of heroic selflessness and a mysterious Providence than from any social activism.

The third story, "The Entomologist," is a tediously long account of a flirtation between a young New England woman, married to a volatile Creole, and a boorish, older scientist, a German-born baron, whose trusting wife is a morally refined seamstress. Vain, frivolous, and pretentious, Flora Fontenette is drawn to the entomologist apparently because her formerly wealthy husband now has to earn a living and the scientist, she believes, is romantically ethereal in his pursuit of knowledge. The baron's "avarice of knowledge" (*SH,* 100) is, however, such that he neglects his appearance, eats grossly, keeps himself only "so clean as it comes eassy [*sic*]" (*SH,* 148), and shows no erotic interest. He is not a man of "*perverted* principles and passions" but one in whom the pursuit of truth has not informed his moral life through beauty—that is, one who is "totally undeveloped in all the emotions, affections, tastes, that make life *life*" (*SH,* 103). The two demonstrate that neither her falsely sentimental appreciation of nature nor his scientific study yields spiritual or moral insight. Given such a love object, it is not surprising that nothing comes of Flora's flirtation, and after both die in the yellow fever epidemic of 1878, her jealous husband and his devoted wife are betrothed.

Turner has argued that the manner of this tale's telling, including the use of a meddlesome narrator, suggests parallels with the techniques of Henry James, but the similarities are at best superficial. The "affair" is improbable, ultimately trivialized, and the story's "strong-heart" lesson about nobility and virtue in commonplace acts of selflessness is trite. Worse, when the baron obliviously pursues a prized moth into Flora's sickroom and so frightens her that she goes into convulsions and soon dies, the scene is unintentionally but grotesquely comic. In fact, one of the story's curiosities, perhaps its only interest, is the incongruous mix of mildly steamy melodrama and autobiography. The character of the entomologist is based on Cable's New Orleans friend, Baron Ludwig von Reizenstein, who named a moth after him (*Smerinthus Cablei*), and the plague scenes are those in which Cable, like Smith, lost his son. What, then, are we to make of the suggestions of infidelity and jealousy?

In a comment on Cable's fiction written between the birth of his last child and the death of his wife, Philip Butcher notes that in *John March, Southerner,* "The Entomologist," *Bylow Hill,* and *The Cavalier* "there are incompatible couples and instances of real or suspected infidelity" (1962, 143). More recently, Robert O. Stephens also observes that "notable . . . in his late fiction is a recurring theme of sexual jealousy, particularly in 'The Entomologist' and *Bylow Hill.*"[8] The latter brief novel, written in 1900 and published in 1902, is particularly relevant because it treats jealousy as a form of psychotic behavior and is set in a New England town very much like Northampton. The basic story was told to Cable by S. Weir Mitchell, the doctor-novelist whose "rest cure" for "hysteria" in women contributed to the breakdown Charlotte Perkins Gilman describes in her now-famous "The Yellow Wall-Paper." In Cable's novel the clergyman Arthur Winslow marries a Southern girl, Isabel Morris, "on the rebound" and becomes insanely suspicious that his wife is unfaithful. Finally, after he dreams that he has killed her, he trips, falls down stairs, and dies in a mad flight from his house. The failure of what is generally regarded as Cable's worst novel lies in its sketchiness and limited psychological insight—weaknesses that have been attributed to the author's lack of "personal knowledge of characters and events" (Turner 1956, 320). Given the pattern noted by Butcher and Stephens, however, and given Cable's frequent use of autobiographical material even in his early work, some basis in experience seems likely. As Butcher observes, "The change in Cable's attitude toward matrimony may not seem significant, but it should not be disregarded" (1962, 143).

Indeed, the concern with obsessive jealousy and infidelity in *Bylow Hill* and other fiction of the period can be traced to Cable's own marriage. Cable's biographers consistently praise Louise for her loyal devotion and steady management of a large home through years that included economic insecurity, her own weak health, the loss of their first son, political controversy, and many months of separation. Like others, Rubin describes their relationship, revealed through their many letters to each other, as "intense and passionate" and also "deep and uncomplicated" (249), and Cable was devastated and disorientated by his wife's death. Such a view, however, converts her into a Norman Rockwell stereotype, and those same letters suggest that *her* experience of the relationship, while every bit as intense and passionate, may not have been as uncomplicated as his. She could not, for one thing, be as consistently cheerful as he in the face of what she felt were great responsibilities, her loneliness while he was away, and the nearly constant worries over money. Also, while she admired and supported his success, she was conscious of not being able to express herself as easily as he. Her letters generally focus on everyday domestic matters and not the high-minded ideas to which he devoted himself, especially in the late 1880s. In one letter of this period, she passionately expresses her sense of being misunderstood:

> All my life long, because I would not or could not speak out, my dear parents took it for granted that I was satisfied, or that if I was not, I would surely ask questions, and learn what I wanted.
>
> You too, seem to have felt the same way, and thought that if I did *not* know, I did *not care to know,* so you have given your time to others outside not knowing how hungry your wife was, for just what you were so freely giving away to others.[9]

Louise was particularly upset about her husband's communicating to his secretary, Adelene Moffat, matters not told to her. As she wrote in November 1889, "I don't see how I am to learn anything about the work you want me to take an interest in: you say you are too busy to write me about it and that Miss Moffat will tell me what she is doing, then I ask her as much as I ever can ask, and she says she is doing the work, and then finishes her report of it, sends it off to you without another word to me about it; how can I ask questions, when I don't even know what it is about at all?"[10] She goes on to complain of Moffat's not sharing business correspondence with her and also of her acting as chaperone for their daughters at dances, and while "everything goes on with the greatest pleasantness," she concludes that "all this is no good as far as I am concerned."

Clearly Louise Cable was jealous of the attractive younger woman who effusively praised her husband's nobility and commitment to social causes, who received financial support from him, and who actively shared in his most impassioned crusade. Actual infidelity seems unlikely, and Louise expressed such confidence while making her feelings clear: "I positively deny any thought or intention of charging deceit as you think I did, either on the part of Miss M. or any one else: I *do not believe* at all that *you wish to hide anything* from me; *nor,* little as I like her, *do I consider her deceitful:* you have misunderstood me again."[11] Nevertheless, as Thorndyke Smith observes in "The Entomologist," "Jealousy, . . . once set on fire, burns without fuel" (*SH,* 134), and in a letter of the same period, agonizing over what she fears he must think of her for expressing her feelings, she says, "I feel just miserable, and even dream of insanity & of my becoming insane."[12] Ten years later, after Cable's departure to Europe, she describes to him a dream about a dinner party in which "you talked exclusively *to her,* and when I asked you to make your conversation more general, you got very angry with me, and would not stay at the table at all."[13]

Such expressions certainly seem relevant to Cable's explorations of jealously and infidelity in his later fiction, just as the signs of Louise Cable's dislike of Adelene Moffat must certainly figure in Cable's dismissal of Moffat from her position with the Home Culture Clubs in 1907, not for reasons of finances and reorganization as officially claimed, but because Cable believed she had slandered his deceased wife.[14] Rubin goes so far as to suggest that the dispute may have arisen over Cable's marriage in the previous year to Eva Stevenson, a 48-year-old "gray haired spinster"[15] from Kentucky, because Moffat may have expected to be the second Mrs. Cable (251). The point here is not to assign blame but to expose and partially fill a curious gap in the previous accounts of Cable's life and its relation to his later fiction. As Butcher observes, "If more were known about Louise Bartlett Cable it might be possible to understand more fully the man—not merely the author and public figure—who was her husband" (1959, 196).

The Cavalier and *Kincaid's Battery*

The literary philosophy that Cable articulated in the 1890s and that shapes *Strong Hearts* is also apparent in his most financially successful novel, *The Cavalier.* In fact, the novel began as another character study like those in *Strong Hearts* and uses Richard Thorndyke Smith as its narrator, but through several revisions it grew to a point where separate publication was necessary. *The Cavalier* draws on Cable's own experiences as a Confederate soldier, but there is very little sense of place, and the central plot centers on a complex love triangle. The hero, Ned Ferry, loves a glamorous Confederate spy, Charlotte Oliver—and she him—although she is unhappily married to a murderer whom Ned's sense of duty urges him to bring to justice, even at the risk of his never being able to marry her. Knowing this, Charlotte desperately tries to prevent it. The actual war and its issues are not relevant to these doings, therefore not represented, and the skirmishes in which Ferry and Smith become involved have less blood and grime than a rugby match.

There are echoes of Cable's earlier stories in *The Cavalier.* In Scott Gholson he provides a crazed religionist like Arthur Winslow and satirizes his own earlier sanctimoniousness in Smith. Charlotte, like many of his heroines, has discreet but unmistakable erotic appeal, and like John March, Smith's response to this appeal for a time places him in a jejune rivalry with the more worldly Ferry. Also, becoming ill or wounded, as in "'Tite Poulette" and *The Grandissimes,* again sets up a love connection between an unfortunate young man and his nurse. The evidence of his recent esthetic philosophizing can be seen in some use of the characters to represent heroic ideals and noble sentiments, but even this seems secondary to the melodramatic action and cloying love scenes. In *The Cavalier* more than in any other story Cable wrote, the emphasis on entertainment seems to dominate completely. It is here and in *Kincaid's Battery* that Cable becomes, in Rubin's phrase, "a romancer pure and simple" (245).

The purity of the emphasis on entertainment in *The Cavalier,* distinguishing it even from *Strong Hearts,* is worth noting, for it was the result of Cable's need to make money, a related but different pressure than that of an homogenizing culture.[16] Cable's finances were never wholly secure, and by the end of the century he had neither the energy nor the appeal to continue to support himself as a platform reader. He had earlier accepted the editorship of *Current Literature* in the hope of securing a steady income, but when this did not work out he was faced with living more completely by his pen than he had since he first left the counting room. Royalties from new editions helped some, but he also borrowed against the profits of his next, unwritten novel, and except for *The Cavalier* the returns were generally less than the advances for the rest of his career. Hence, as Elaine Ware has recently noted, despite Cable's protestations that he wrote too slowly to keep up with market tastes, he revised *The Cavalier* with particular attention to his editors' suggestions for what would be successful with his readers.[17] This included some conscious placating of both Southern and Northern audiences and avoiding even the bland, sententious moralizing found in *Strong Hearts*.

To some extent all of Cable's books show evidence of his attempts to adjust to his readers' expectations and not offend them, but in *The Cavalier* the effort is more extreme and results in an emphasis on dramatic action, nearly devoid of either serious issues or textural background. Most of the novel's reviews were positive, and at the time Cable thought it his best constructed work, better in some ways than *The Grandissimes*. However myopic, this view is consistent with what he seems to have meant by "fiction" as distinguished from "strange, true stories" and certainly from "political" novels. The book publication generated a printing of 100,000 copies in a little over two months, but the success may have less to do with its artistry than that it caught a wave of popular interest in romantic Civil War novels at the turn of the century.

The Cavalier's success and melodramatic quality also accounts for its being made into a play with well-known actress-producer Julia Marlowe in the lead as Charlotte Oliver, running from December 1902 through May 1903. After Cable's 1883 conversion to the theater, under the influence of Roswell Smith and Joseph Jefferson, he had become interested in seeing dramatic adaptations of his works, and he tried unsuccessfully to dramatize *Bonaventure*. In the 1890s there were plans for stage versions of *The Grandissimes,* and *Madame Delphine* was performed experimentally as a one-act play in London. From 1901 through 1904 Cable made several more efforts at playwriting: a stage version of "Posson Jone'" and "Père Raphaël" (the latter a pale companion piece to the earlier story, published in *Century* [August 1901] and in *"Posson Jone'" and Père Raphaël* [1909]); his own adaptation of *Madame Delphine*; a play based on *Old Creole Days*; an original play using the story, already begun as a novel, that would become *Kincaid's Battery* (1908). None of these attempts at drama came to fruition, however, nor did still later plans to produce both dramatic and cinematic versions of his works, except for a 1918 Metropolitan Opera Company production of a musical composition based on "The Dance in Place Congo." *The Cavalier* was Cable's only story to be staged with even modest success during his lifetime.

Kincaid's Battery and *The Cavalier,* as books written with both the stage and large sales in mind, are unlikely to appeal to modern readers. Indeed, as a story of the artillery matching *The Cavalier*'s focus on the cavalry, *Kincaid's Battery* is afflicted with many of the same weaknesses— the lack of concern with serious social or political issues, the remoteness of the war itself, the general emphasis on intrigue, sentimental romance, and dramatic action. Turner, Butcher, and Rubin all find the novel to be less interesting than *The Cavalier,* unredeemed even by its modest sales.

Rubin, however, notes that insofar as Cable made his villainess a Creole and his hero and heroine non-Creoles, he "may be said to have reverted somewhat to his earlier habits" (253). He does try to add familiarity and interest by including characters from his earlier stories, such as the Grandissimes, Raoul Innerarity, Jules St.-Ange, Richard Thorndyke Smith, Ned Ferry, and Dr. Sevier. Also, set mostly in New Orleans, *Kincaid's Battery* has a stronger sense of locale than *The Cavalier,* and if Cable avoids representing the real hardships and indignities of "Beast" Butler's rule, he does link the pomp and color of the military companies preparing for war with the elaborate social artifice of the Creoles. Hillary Kincaid, the hero with a reputation as a "ladies man," is also associated with the New South orientation to technology. This grounding of the inflated war sentiment in specific social conditions continues in the contrast between Flora Valcour's Creole coquetting and the more straightforward appeal of Anna Callender. In fact, drawing on the wartime experiences of Dora Miller and of his own mother and sisters, the novel centers considerably in the attitudes and experiences of women, but the emphasis is again less on real hardships than on the women's role in a courtly romance, "ladies" won or lost by their "knights'" heroic exploits.

Cable seems to mock the sentimentality of some of these women's patriotism, but the more interesting aspect of the concentration on the woman's side of war is the sense of repressed feelings. Not only was New Orleans captured early in the war, but the women's role was auxiliary, distant from the centers of action. The repression is felt in the strained manners of the characters, the slow build-up of the war, and the physical remoteness of the actual fighting. Also, in scenes of passion on the eve of battle or separation, the tension between sensuality and genteel decorum seen earlier in Cable's work is again evident. The women in these scenes are the registers of the barely checked passions, and it is significant that the scheming Flora is shown to be capable of physical violence: she could kill. For all this, *Kincaid's Battery* is indeed a weak novel, but in its use of setting and in its gently ironic treatment of Creole manners and the forms of sentiment—aspects of Cable's better work, but not social realism—it becomes more interesting than has been generally recognized, at least more interesting than *The Cavalier.*

Gideon's Band

Like *Kincaid's Battery,* Cable's last three novels reflect a partial return to his earlier style, but unlike any of his work after *John March, Southerner* they also return to his earlier concerns with race. Rubin links this "engagement renewed" to Cable's January 1909 visit to New Orleans, where, in gathering material for his next novel, he must have been dismayed by the evidence that the situation of blacks of all classes had significantly declined, even from antebellum days. Whether in response to these present conditions or simply emboldened by the warm reception he received, in *Gideon's Band* (1914) Cable addresses issues of race, class, immigration, and economic corruption in the 1850s.

The novel's main action occurs on the riverboat, *Votaress,* owned and piloted by the Courtneys, making her maiden voyage upriver from New Orleans to Louisville. The Courtney fleet competes with that of Gideon Hayle, whose wife, three sons, and daughter—Gideon's band—are on board as passengers. As in *The Grandissimes,* the hero and heroine, Hugh Courtney and Ramsey Hayle, must overcome the family rivalry and their own character flaws—his stolidness, her giddiness—in what becomes for them a voyage to true love. More serious conflicts are created by the outbreak of cholera among a party of German immigrants. There is also racial conflict centering on Phyllis, a quadroon whose story, like that of Bras-Coupé in *The Grandissimes,* is presented as a half-suppressed family legend. Her father a Hayle, Phyllis accidentally destroyed a Courtney ship, the *Quakeress,* in a fire and thereby initiated the Hayle-Courtney feud. She was rescued from the fire by the Gilmores, an actor and his antislavery wife, and because she was thought dead, she was able to live for 10 years as a white maid named Harriet.

Other characters on the boat represent various social types: a vulgar backwoods preacher, an elitist Methodist bishop, a democratic Kentucky rifleman, a senator, a judge, a slave, and so on. Cable uses the *Votaress* not only to portray the glamour of an exciting bygone era—one in which his father had played a role—but also to represent an economic enterprise linked to New Orleans's hopes for future prosperity and to the development of the South and the West. Thus in this highly theatrical novel (including many songs and a play performance to keep passengers from panicking), the boat becomes a stage on which the wide range of character types dramatize the relation of social and moral ideals to ultimate progress. The civil war looms as a judgmental certainty both for the romance of riverboating and for the South.

As in many of his earlier novels, Cable carefully traces the movement of the *Votaress* through a specific landscape, naming each point, island, cut-off, and bend in the Mississippi and evoking the scenery of river and shore. In the first half at least, such scenic material helps tie the action to a specific milieu in a way that *John March, Southerner,* for example, does not. Cable describes Hugh Courtney seeing on the landing in New Orleans an "exposition of the vast, half-tamed valley's bounty, spoils, and promise" and "of its motley human life, scarcely yet to be called society"[18]—images that project into and out of the upriver territories. Hence, the issues of democratic freedom and independence associated with the Kentuckian named California, the vulgarity of the Baptist exhorter, and the ignorant social pretensions of the New Carthage newlyweds are more appropriately set in the half-civilized world of the lower Mississippi. In fact, as in "Jean-ah Poquelin," "Belles Demoiselles Plantation," *The Grandissimes, Bonaventure,* and *John March, Southerner,* the central theme of progress is effectively developed in a space partially mastered by art and technology and bordered by the wilderness. In addition, through Ramsey Hayle's naive, instinctive response to the river, apparently inherited from her Kentucky father, Cable develops something like a river myth or ethos, "a realm of poetry and adventure" (*GB,* 32), reinforced by the romance of both the boating action and the scenery. Much as in a James Fenimore Cooper novel, a character's capacity to recognize natural beauty reflects his or her moral nature, but if the novel is therefore reminiscent of both Cooper's *The Pioneers* and Twain's *Life on the Mississippi,* the comparison also suggests the anachronistic feel of his treatment of a progress-versus-nature theme.

In some ways the novel's treatment of social themes also seems dated. Ramsey's father is identified as a Jacksonian Democrat and Hugh Courtney's as a Clay Whig. More significantly, in the Hayle twins, Julian and Lucian, Cable presents caustic versions of how slave culture damaged the master's character. Self-centered, narrow-minded, imperious, devious, sensual, and violent, they first appear drunk and throughout the voyage act as troublemakers, keeping the Hayle-Courtney feud alive. A Southern squire describes "their faults" approvingly as "the faults . . . of all our young Southern gentlemen," "faults of which . . . we may almost be proud" (*GB,* 128), to which the actor's wife scornfully responds, "They're the faults of our 'peculiar institution.' " The twins' younger brother, Basile, more of a Creole like his mother, reflects an even shallower egoism and provincialism: "he seemed yet to have acquired no sense of value for any fact or thought beyond the pointblank range of the five senses. He could not have read ten pages of a serious book and would have blushed to be found trying to do it" (*GB,* 148).

Although Cable depicts Mrs. Hayle as able to embrace abolitionism and, like his own mother, to risk her life attending the sick, the terms in which he presents most of the Southern characters essentially repeat his earlier analysis of how the social and political attitudes of the South inhibit the region's moral and economic progress. He also remounts his attacks on religious enthusiasts such as the exhorter and also on the lack of social responsibility of the more proper bishop. The problem posed by the immigrants, not just the importation of disease but the threat of difference, is more significantly treated in *Gideon's Band* than in Cable's earlier work, although the issues parallel his attacks on the insularity and tribalism of the Creoles in *The Grandissimes* and the Acadians in *Bonaventure.* Cable's overarching concern is the kind of society that will be shaped from the disparate elements of American life, how to meld the virtues of the various regional characters and non-native elements represented in the microcosm of the *Votaress,* how to balance between ideals of freedom and independence and the need for a stable, hierarchical social order. Unfortunately, these social concerns are not made either profoundly universal or clearly relevant to twentieth-century conditions.

Cable's handling of racial themes in *Gideon's Band,* although at times as powerful as anything he wrote, seems similarly dated and even for some critics sadly backsliding (Elfenbein, 32; Butcher 1962, 155). The Hayles' maid, Joy, is comparable to Clemence in the *The Grandissimes* as a representative of the unglamourized, unsentimentalized black masses. While her commentary on white society is not as incisively biting as the marchande's, she responds with effective dignity when a childishly insensitive Ramsey badgers her about how she, being "so out and out black," could be the first cousin of Phyllis: " 'Missie,' sighed the old woman, 'y'ain't neveh in yo' life stopped to think dat niggehs is got feelin's, is you?' " (*GB,* 97). Even "de best" white folks, she goes on, "don't *believe* niggehs is got feelins. . . . Some 'o de bes *believes* dey believes, dat's all." The central racial conflicts, however, involve Phyllis, who is not as vividly portrayed as Palmyre but has much of the latter's burning, righteous anger against slavery and caste. Like Cornelius Leggett, she takes out her anger on the novel's young white hero, who then, like John March, must learn to consider questions of racial justice beyond his personal resentment. The repetition of this paradigm may originate in Cable's memory of his parents' slave, Jane, who frightened the children and who was sold for meanness to another slave, but it also reflects a depth of understanding of black anger, for while he never condoned violence, from the 1870s on he consistently made clear that inevitably the fruits of injustice would be violence and that the wrong of retaliation was less than the wrong that caused it. This is what California suggests when he explains how he might react to having to become black after 10 years living as a white woman: "If I was this girl, this goin' back to be black would mean one or two things: I'd either die myself, aw I'd kill some one, maybe sev'l" (*GB,* 410).

The more problematic issue, however, is the miscegenation that Phyllis obviously represents. Cable again attacks "one-drop" mythologies of racial typing in a variety of ways. The senator and the judge articulate the standard Southern slave laws and sentiments that made persons of any African ancestry powerless before the courts. Ramsey's discovery of her own kinship with Phyllis—the two so closely resembling each other that the ostensible slave can substitute for her red-haired mistress in the theatrical performance—awakens her to the injustice of such laws: to enslave Phyllis is to enslave Hayle "blood." California's wanting to marry Phyllis generates discussions of "race conscience" and the need to keep from mixing "the great races we know apart by their color" (*GB,* 413), to which Madame Hayle responds, "of w'at race has Phylliz the conscien'? An' you would know Philliz's race—ad sight—by the color?" In the ensuing debate Hugh Courtney and his father argue for the necessity of obeying a race instinct that dictates against mixed marriages, and critics have seen their statements to represent Cable's own views, introduced once again to deflect any charges that he advocated miscegenation. As Rubin, puts it, "Cable seems to have written a polemic against racism and caste, and joined it to the statement that purity of race in itself is not an evil idea" (260).

Cable's rejection of racial mixing seems further indicated by the fact that the marriage does not occur because, as Joy explains, "Phyllis ain' gwine. She know' you cayn't make her white by takin' her to whah it makes no odds ef she ain't white" (*GB,* 415). Such a statement seems to confirm the Southern view that blacks obey the same race conscience and wish to remain separate. Her real argument, however, is that Phyllis loves society ("She love' de quality, she love' de crowd") and will not go to "any lan' whah de ain't mo'n one 'oman to de mile." Given that California's proposal was in part a transference of feeling from his initial infatuation with look-alike Ramsey, Phyllis's choice has more to do with her being a woman than being black. Also, Ramsey remains unmoved in her feeling that the so-called race conscience is a "Mrs. Grundy"—a narrow social arbiter—and insofar as Hugh Courtney's formulations seem priggish and are clearly hand-me-downs from his father, Ramsey's passion, in this case, seems the surer moral instinct. Furthermore, because she is a Creole convert to abolitionism and because she exhibits moral integrity and courage in nursing the sick immigrants, Madame Hayle's scoffing at the race conscience idea rings with special authority.

Cable's reluctance to advocate racial intermarriage seems obvious, but it is debatable whether he is appreciably less forthright in *Gideon's Band* than in earlier writings, even in *Madame Delphine,* where he allows a mixed marriage to occur.[19] Here as elsewhere, Cable shades and qualifies his views through dramatic representation, and rather than a complete capitulation to conservative views, the debate can be seen as Cable arguing with himself and even mocking himself for his own timidity. He illuminates the moral truth clearly in Madame Hayle's statement but hedges the question of acting on that truth in the form of marriage and "lighting out for the territories." All of this seems a debate from another era, however, essentially the polemics of his crusade in the late 1880s. In *Gideon's Band* Cable not only renews but repeats his earlier engagement with racial issues, and, therefore, while the social commentary in the novel makes it more serious than his Civil War romances, this value is diminished because the commentary adds little new insight. The problem again is related to the particular importance of milieu to Cable's art, for as a saga of the expansion of the South and West centering on the turbulent era of riverboat traffic in the 1850s, a kind of historical, frontier novel like *The Grandissimes, Gideon's Band* has possibilities and some achievement. Reviewers, in fact, praised the novel's historical and technical authenticity. But as the action becomes artificially encapsulated on the boat moving through the landscape, reverting into a syrupy love story and a stagey debate of period issues, it loses both place and force.

The Flower of the Chapdelaines

Cable's last two novels were written and published hard on the heels of each other, and the first published, *The Flower of the Chapdelaines* (1918), was the second written. Both bear evidence of an aging author, now in his seventies, writing with a pressing need for income. In response to a loan request in 1911, Andrew Carnegie had given Cable $1,000 a year as a pension until he finished *Gideon's Band,* and this enabled Cable to save his home and have a necessary cataract operation. Carnegie also established a trust for both Cable and Eva, guaranteeing them an annual income of $5,000 after the philanthropist's death in 1919. By 1916, however, the income from *Gideon's Band* had not paid off Cable's debts to Scribners, and he had already borrowed the maximum allowed against his next novel, which was completed but waited two years for publication while he sought unsuccessfully to sell the serial rights. To fill the gap, he contracted for another book to be made of three previously published stories fitted into a newly written narrative frame. The result, *The Flower of the Chapdelaines,* is a bad book—perhaps more "tidily woven" (Rubin, 264) than Cable's earlier short-story collections but still a flimsy, contrived patchwork. For students of Cable, however, it is interesting in what it reveals about the limits of his imagination and in its making race a central theme.

The frame narrative in *The Flower of the Chapdelaines,* longer than the three interpolated stories combined, begins in familiar Cablesque fashion with a young Southern lawyer, Geoffrey Chester, catching a glimpse of a bewitching Creole maiden, Aline Chapdelaine, in the Vieux Carré. When he ultimately traces her to the antiquarian bookshop of Ovide Landry, he learns of her desire to publish a manuscript written by her grandmother. Having a manuscript of his own, written by his uncle, Chester offers to help find a publisher for a book made of their manuscripts and another, a collaborative enterprise with obvious parallels to Cable's own *Strange True Stories of Louisiana.* The love story between Geoffrey and Aline, wending its way through awkwardness and misunderstanding, barriers and complications to a happy ending in marriage, is altogether forgettable. In addition, because the frame narrative is written almost entirely in dialogue, Cable's attempt to re-create the atmosphere of old New Orleans falls flat, seeming little more than a list of familiar names and places as in a travel itinerary.

The novel is set in the present, with several references to such signs of modernity as movies, telephones, and airplanes, and there is talk of the war in Europe, in which four of the main characters' sons, including Chester's rival, serve. But much of the conversation, particularly Aline's accounts of her family's history, incorporates Cable's earlier published views of the South—of slavery, the Civil War, Reconstruction, and New South redemption. In this sense the device of creating a book of old materials extends into the frame narrative as well. Also, while there are some efforts to link the issues of the past to those of the crisis overseas, the major emphasis is on publishing, as if in the press to generate a publishable manuscript he simply wrote about what was most immediately on his mind. While such matters as waiting for a publisher's response do not create gripping drama, they do provide an interesting insight into Cable's attitudes toward his own work as a writer, particularly his sense of the pressures that altered his fiction after *John March, Southerner.*

One of the major problems facing the publication project is that, as one character puts it, all the stories "got in them *some*-where, alas! the nigger. The *publique* they are not any longer pretty easy to fascinate on that subjec'."[20] But Ovide Landry, who is black, seems more to reflect Cable's own view when he says, "You can't write a Southern book and keep us out" (*FC,* 14), and, indeed, slavery and race are the obvious common round of the three interpolated stories. The first, "The Clock in the Sky," originally published in *Scribner's Magazine* in September 1901, is a slight tale of slaves, Sidney and Mingo, who are helped to escape to the North by the narrator's innocently teaching them about stellar constellations—the Clock in the Sky—which they use to guide their journey. The third, "The Holy Cross," also published in *Scribner's Monthly* as "A West Indian Slave Insurrection" (December 1892), is an edited version of a manuscript purchased from Dora Richards Miller. It has very little characterization, and while its example of racial violence supports Cable's consistent view that "the most blundering effort for the prompt undoing of a grievous wrong is safer than the shrewdest or strongest effort for its continuance" (*FC,* 219), its depiction of insurrection is relatively tame and thus actually diminishes the potential terrors.

The second story, "The Angel of the Lord," was written for *The House Party* (1901), a collection of stories each written by a well-known but unidentified author and published with the offer of a $1,000 prize to readers who could correctly match the stories to their authors. Cable revised the story to make it an account of how the slave family from "The Clock in the Sky" managed to escape the South. Narrated by

Chester's uncle, a Southern gentleman with his father's race prejudices and his mother's abolitionist sentiments, it is effectively told and in its chase scene rivals the best melodrama in *Uncle Tom's Cabin.* The most interesting aspect of the story is the narrator's wrestling with his own conflicting racial attitudes. When he meets two runaway slaves, he is moved to help the bright and refined young boy, "Euonymous," who is "so manifestly superior to millions of our human swarm white or black," but he would leave behind his repulsive, field-hand sister, "Robelia"; to him they are "evolution and reversion personified" (*FC,* 73). We can recognize in this Cable's own ambivalent racial feelings during Reconstruction and even in the midst of his civil rights crusade.[21] The perception here is complicated further by the fact that when the narrator sees them, not only is he disguised as a woman, but both slaves are cross-dressed as well, so that the refined appeal of Euonymous (Sidney from the first story) has something to do with her femininity and the repulsive coarseness of "Robelia" (actually Mingo) is linked to his masculinity.[22]

Ambiguities also surround the story's extension of its message of the importance of freedom to the inevitable question of racial mixing. The narrator observes that "races have crossed, and made new and better ones" (*FC,* 121), but Luke, the father of Sidney and Mingo and, like Joy in *Gideon's Band,* the apparent voice of unembittered black wisdom, disagrees. Nothing is gained, he says, from crossing a race that has "done-done . . . most all what eveh yit been done, on to anotheh what, eh—." "What ain't neveh yit done noth'n'," says Sidney, completing the thought. Cable seems once again to be warding off charges of advocating miscegenation, but the logic of separation is based on the alterable standard of accomplishment, not genes, and the narrator speculates that Luke "may have merely heard some master or mistress say" (*FC,* 121) what he says, that he may be simply repeating the master's defense of slavery. This speculation was added in revision, suggesting that in 1916–17, Cable felt less inclined to placate his readers' presumed prejudices than in 1901. "The Angel of the Lord" is a minor gem in an otherwise weak novel, and one of the book's most fascinating features is its relatively forthright, overall treatment of racial issues in the context of a plot about publishing that argues readers are no longer interested in the subject. The focus of most of the social commentary is indeed safely on the past, and thus the tone of the renewed engagement suggests less a genuine belief that society might finally be awakened than something like ironic perversity.

Lovers of Louisiana (To-day)

Written so close together, *The Flower of the Chapdelaines* and Cable's last published novel, *Lovers of Louisiana,* both reflect the author's sense of having been generally reaccepted by New Orleans and, following that acceptance, his renewed interest and confidence in asserting his racial and social views.[23] As the title suggests, the novel is a love story set in modern times, but with the playful double meaning of a story about lovers *from* Louisiana and about the love *of* Louisiana. The hero is Philip Castleton, an *Américain* with a Ph.D. from Princeton who returns to his native city to become a professor of history at Tulane, and the heroine is Rosalie Durel, daughter of a Creole banker. There is tension between the two families largely owing to the religious bigotry of Philip's aunt, who had prevented the marriage of Philip's mother to Rosalie's father many years before because he is Catholic. Philip's father, now deceased, was a progressive opposed to lynchings and the Ku Klux Klan, and Rosalie's father, Alphonse Durel, although a conservative, does not condone violence and ultimately is able to moderate his views. In fact, Cable's depiction of upper-class Creoles, such as those he now knew as neighbors when he wintered on Esplanade Avenue, is generally positive, but their pride and antiquated social customs, their exhibiting "good manners" rather than "good nature,"[24] figure centrally in both the love plot and the political themes.

Philip's rival, at least in M. Durel's mind, is Zéphire, a distant cousin and cashier at the bank. Reflecting Cable's earlier attacks on the Creoles, Zéphire not only drinks, gambles, and keeps quadroon mistresses, but he threatens Philip with violence, is caught embezzling, and flees to Mexico. Because the Castletons anonymously rescue the Durel bank with a loan ostensibly from Ovide Landry (here an antiques dealer and accountant), the love path between Philip and Rosalie remains cluttered with pride.

Philip's critical views of Southern politics, however, form the major barrier between the couple, both in their substance and in his expressing them before Northern audiences, thereby offending Rosalie's father. Basing his principles on the New Testament, he attacks the undemocratic, unjust treatment of blacks that has been made the defining condition of Southern civilization. At specific points he denounces "all overriding of law by violence" (*LL,* 77), such as the lynchings, burnings, and other examples of "Kuklux" terrorism, and he ridicules the Creoles' obsessions with racial purity while keeping quadroon mistresses. But his broader concern is with the subjugation of blacks to a permanent position of secondary social and political status: "Whereas . . . our Old South could give him [the black man] no worthy, no American freedom, nor the North give him an American freedom over the New South's head, the New South crowds him half-way down again to his old slavery" (*LL*, 41). The result of this policy of subjugation is that New Orleans, representing "Dixie" generally, has isolated itself socially, politically, and economically from the nation and the world and, thereby, has not realized what Philip insists is its rightful position of leadership. He includes in this an indictment of the crassness of New South industrialism and commercialism, even denouncing Mardi Gras as unworthy of a great civilization regardless of the money it brings in.

Philip's views are given a specifically modern cast in relation to the war in Europe, for not only is the war itself "an awful warning against the risks hidden under the apparent harmlessness of all merely national, imperial, or racial standards of greatness or of a world's need" (*LL*, 318), but if America is to have an "exalted seat . . . in the world's council at the war's end," its politics should be "outwardly clean and inwardly pure" (*LL*, 101). For Philip, "preparedness" to avoid the disaster of such a war is to develop "clear, true principles of justice and magnanimity" (*LL*, 125), and this requires an openness to criticism and to innovation. He deprecates "mere pride of country, that national complacency which is only self-esteem swollen to national dimensions," while he exalts "the patriotism whose ardor demands of one's country that same integrity to all the human race which his mother country requires of him to her" (*LL*, 134). Philip's criticisms of the South are, therefore, portrayed as both doubly patriotic—to the region and to the country—and doubly loving—to Louisiana and to Rosalie. In his mind's eye, the region—represented by New Orleans—and the girl are blended images, and his courtship is pointedly according to the "American plan"—"the Constitution, The Declaration, and the Moral Law" (*LL*, 57).

In these views and in a number of other details, such as his serving on a grand jury, publishing articles in the North, and speaking at a black college, Philip Castleton represents some version of Cable himself, if not what he thought he was or had been, then perhaps, as Butcher suggests, what he hoped his son might have become had he lived (1962, 158–59). Philip's staying in New Orleans through newspaper attacks, social ostracism, and even overt violence can be read, along with similar expressions of loyalty in *The Flower of the Chapdelaines* and *John March, Southerner*, as signs of Cable's regret over his move to Northampton, but, as Rubin points out, the example of Philip's father also staying in New Orleans and dying a broken-hearted martyr to his cause argues the opposite.

Here as elsewhere in Cable's fiction, however clearly he posits the moral vision, the question of social action is made more problematic. Apart from the advantage of remaining in the South and speaking out on social ills, which in this novel seem clearly affirmed, Philip is very much the "political prig" (LL, 84) others call him, not insufferable exactly, but certainly tedious and pedantic. Curiously, Cable has Durel observe that because the young professor's "moral standard'" are "too high," he might be an "unsafe" match for his daughter in "middle life" as compared with Zéphire, who has "been 'up in the balloon, boys,' and come down aggain. He's suck' the h-orange" (LL, 93). Philip also has a temper, like John March, and he nearly kills Zéphire before they are separated. Then, at the novel's end, just before the Lusitania is sunk, Philip does seem to adjust his moral perspective when he admits that the South's faults, though "latently as dangerous as ever," diminish before the larger threat in Europe, "suddenly grown colossal" (LL, 319).

It should also be recognized that the strongest social commentary in the novel is provided by Murray, the Scot who repeatedly warns of future violence unless the racial injustice is dealt with, and by Ovide Landry, who as an educated, capable, uncorrupt black man relegated to being a Vieux Carré shopkeeper, lives the unjust, marginalized life Philip describes in general terms. Murray's frankness unsettles even Philip early in the novel, and his comment that the race question in America is "merely 'possumming" has a trenchant currency: "Ye can't neglect it to death," he says; "the neglect of all America can't kill it. It's in the womb o' the future and bigger than Asia, Africa, and America combined" (LL, 223). When Philip describes blacks as a "race of children" and says "we are disillusioned" by their lack of progress, Landry corrects him to say a "child race," points to the general lack of white interest in their development, and insists on the opportunity for individuals to rise if progress is to occur.

Compared with these positions, Philip's speech before the black college is, as Butcher charges, fairly tame (1962, 160). Although he outrages Zéphire and other Creoles by asking his audience to forget that he is white, his message is basically that blacks should make the best of the situation and take advantage of the opportunities they do have, and the fact that the talk is only modestly received by the black students and educators may not be because they fail to understand it but because they understand it all too well. In short, although Philip's political views significantly reflect Cable's own, they should not be identified too narrowly or too simply. In *Lovers of Louisiana* Cable provides a remarkably full summary of his previously published arguments about race and Southern society with a measure of dramatic interplay and qualification to add complexity and shading.

The overt social commentary does not, however, make the novel of much interest except to students of Cable. The racial views, first of all, are only updated in the sense of his noting the continued general injustice, disinterest, and neglect, and suggesting how this undermines the United States' emerging role as an imperial nation and "protector" of democracy. In large part this generality results from the narrative technique of relying almost exclusively on dialogue to develop the plot. The novel's structure is primarily a series of conversations between various members of a small social set, many in such places as Atlantic City, Bermuda (both recent wintering sites for Cable), and New York, and on boat decks and in railroad cars and parlors—places far removed from the actual conditions under discussion. The problem is not only that the plot and characters do not adequately dramatize the novel's ideas, but that, as in earlier works where Cable purposely diminished milieu for the sake of ideas, from *Dr. Sevier* to *The Flower of the Chapdelaines,* there is a loss of textural richness, psychological complexity, and sociohistorical resonance.

In a sense, Cable here seems conscious of this issue, not only evoking a bit of the atmosphere of old New Orleans at the outset and recording some of the changes in the new city—the pronounced decay of the Vieux Carré, the shifts of population and commerce, the advent of modern technology and the diminished picturesqueness. He even has Philip, a lover of landscape, comment on "an almost tragic quality in [Louisiana's] woods and skies" (*LL,* 50); but, like most matters in the novel, this is stated rather than shown or felt. The absence of the insinuating, ironic narrative voice from Cable's early work also contributes to the flatness of tone, the sense of the novel as a series of speeches. But what is perhaps missing most is the sense of discovery, of vital newness, as well as the sheer abundance of detail that attached to material Cable developed from research.

Conclusion

Even before the publication of *Lovers of Louisiana* Cable was working on another novel, but age and ill health made the writing difficult, and it remains an uncompleted manuscript among his papers. Signaling his standing as a "Great Author" in the company of such figures as Winston Churchill (the novelist), Thomas Nelson Page, and Edith Wharton, there were additional inquiries about making films or plays of his works after the appearance of the two novels in 1918, but nothing came of these schemes. He lived primarily off of the legacy from Andrew Carnegie. For several years he had been spending winters outside of Northampton, which eventually compelled him to resign as president of the People's Institute in 1920, and in 1922 he missed the awarding of prizes in the Northampton flower competition for the first times since its inception. His brother James had died in 1915, followed by his younger sister Mary Louise in 1918, his daughter Margaret in 1920, and then his second wife, Eva, in 1923. Through these ordeals of age Cable remained generally positive in his outlook and animated in person. Six months after Eva's death he was married for a third time, to Mrs. Hanna Cowing, a Northampton neighbor, old friend, and welcome companion. For two years the couple wintered in St. Petersburg, Florida, where Cable died on 31 January 1925. After lying in state for two days in Carnegie Hall, he was buried beside his first wife, Louise, at the Bridge Street Cemetery in Northampton.

Randolph Bourne, in a useful review of *Lovers of Louisiana* for the *Dial* in 1918, identifies Cable with the school of "sectional" writers of the 1880s and 1890s who were no longer interesting to "those of us who began our reading careers after 1900" (Turner 1980, 145), and while he offers praise to the "fine veteran of seventy-five" who has outlasted his contemporaries, he ultimately characterizes the novel as "old-fashioned" (150). At his death, the author who in the 1890s had been regularly placed in ranks of Hawthorne, James, Flaubert, Turgenev, and Daudet was remembered in Northampton primarily for his social work and in the national magazines primarily for having discovered and established the literary interest in old New Orleans and the Creoles. When Edmund Wilson reviewed Lucy Biklé's biography of her father in 1929, he described Cable's reputation as "in complete eclipse," the author considered "a romantic novelist, of a species now obsolete, who made a good thing of exploiting the sentiment and charm, the quaintness and picturesqueness, of a New Orleans long gone to decay."[1]

Wilson recognized even then the importance of Cable's critique of Southern institutions to the value of his work, and this element was certainly the driving force in the major revival of interest in Cable, beginning with Turner's biography in 1956, followed by Wilson's rereading and extended discussion of Cable's "ordeal" in the *New Yorker* (9 November 1957), Richard Chase's chapter on *The Grandissimes* in *The American Novel and Its Tradition* (1957), Butcher's studies in 1959 and 1962, Rubin's biography of 1969, and a steady stream of scholarly and critical articles in academic journals. A second, less sustained revival in the early 1980s was occasioned by the centennial anniversary of *The Grandissimes* and included Turner's collection of critical essays on Cable and the special number of the *Southern Quarterly* devoted to Cable's masterpiece. Many of the more recent studies have explored different aspects of his artistry—his techniques, his sources, his use of conventions—but the main reason for studying Cable's work has been what he has to say about the South and particularly about race. As a result, his place in American literature has remained rather consistently that of an interesting minor writer whose early fiction challenged the traditional representations of the South and thereby broke ground for the stronger, more polished generation of Southern writers who began to emerge in the 1920s.

It would be foolish to suggest that Cable's views on race and other social problems are not important to his art. Without a serious subject on which to focus his intellect and talent, he would seem, as Lafcadio Hearn sniped, a writer of "rare analytical powers on a small scale" (quoted in Turner 1956, 234). The courage and clarity of his arguments on civil rights, his insistence on principle and his prescience about the consequences of allowing the injustice to continue are remarkable achievements given his time. But, to the degree that his political arguments focused on the moral and social implications of the conditions emerging in the South in the 1880s and 1890s, those arguments, however impressive, are somewhat dated. Moreover, as *Dr. Sevier* and *Lovers of Louisiana* make clear, overt social commentary did not alone result in good fiction, and it is certainly arguable that Cable's art did suffer from his reforming zeal and tendency to pamphleteer. When he constructed fiction mostly as vehicles to illustrate or simply state and argue ideas, whether they be sociopolitical ideas or moral platitudes, the works in varying degrees suffered. Cable's ideas do not, as most critics recognize, explain the strength and extraordinary appeal of his best work.

That appeal, in my view, is the result of a particular, almost serendipitous combination of factors. Crucial certainly is the Louisiana material itself—its exotic newness and difference; its complex social arrangements; its deeply rooted conflicts; its array of character types; its mingling of past and present, innocence and corruption, sensual beauty and chaste refinement; its mystery, danger, vulgarity, and glamour—a seemingly endless list of qualities centering on variety, contrast, and plenitude. Cable's relationship to that material as a loving and judging outsider, both accepted and rejected, was also crucial, resonating the tensions of the milieu in his own sensibility. Hence the importance also of his characteristic literary manner—his irony, indirection, whimsy, insinuating intimacy, and lushness of description—as particularly suited to the material and an effective register of his sensibility. That sensibility was itself structured in contradictions and incongruities, such as the tension between sensuality and prudery that most critics have recognized, but other anomalies as well, including his social conscience. Rooted initially in his Protestant moral fervor and sense of duty, in his sympathy for those who have felt the sting of exclusion, in his clear, steady logic and his devotion to principle, especially those of the Declaration, Constitution, and New Testament, Cable's reform impulse was also linked to his intellectual ambition, his valuing of social distinction, and his selective unconventionality—a kind of perverse, genteel individualism suggestive less of Twain than Thoreau.

In *The Grandissimes,* his greatest literary achievement, all of these factors came into play and contributed to its greatness, and in his later work, when he consciously eliminated or repressed one or another aspect of his earlier literary practice, whether in service to social reform, moral idealism or pure entertainment, the result was invariably a diminishment of his art.

Was this diminishment a failure of culture, the result of genteel tastes converting the strong realist into the insipid romancer? Or was it, as Rubin argues, primarily a failure of "artistic intelligence" (275), Cable's ultimate incapacity to explore his own interior life? Certainly Cable was influenced by popular taste and by the genteel editorial standards of Gilder and others at the *Century,* particularly when his pen became his main source of income. He largely shared those tastes, and in trying to stay within them, sometimes but not always under pressure from Gilder, he repressed elements of his art that might otherwise have vitalized it.

The realism-romance dichotomy that has been used to describe Cable's art from his first publications needs, however, to be applied carefully and may ultimately be inappropriate. Cable's attention to historical and sociological detail, his painstaking research and careful recording of data, and even his surveyor's sense of environment are important elements in his best fiction, but what Eric Sundquist has described as "an intensification into mythic, psychological realism" (Elliott, 515) such as one finds later in Faulkner, derives significantly from Cable the romancer. As Richard Chase suggests, the special strength of *The Grandissimes* derives from a larger mix of genres than just romance and realism.[2] Many of Cable's most interesting effects come from his exploration and ironic manipulation of literary conventions, his self-consciousness of literary devices, and turning them against themselves. Cable failed to gain artistic control over the complexity and subtlety that were his strengths; this incapacity to grow includes his lack of self-awareness but also reflects the lack of a full commitment to art.

Despite his limitations and unrealized promise, Cable remains a fascinating figure, a curious, unique phenomenon. His best stories and novels—*Old Creole Days, The Grandissimes, Madame Delphine,* "The 'Haunted House' in Royal Street," and even portions of *Bonaventure* and *John March, Southerner*—are among the finest, most satisfying and important fiction written in the last three decades of the nineteenth century. His civil rights essays in *The Silent South* and *The Negro Question* are valuable not only for their reminder of the necessity of adhering to democratic principle and the folly of expediency but also for their insight into the transformation of slave culture into segregated culture—in other words, for their window on white consciousness, including his own as he tried to negotiate between his Southern feelings and his rational, moral convictions. The key in both kinds of writing is the complex interplay between material and method or strategy of representation from which he derives his most subtle and compelling effects. Cable's career warrants study for what it reveals about the practice of art and the influence of culture in America, in this case the particular problem of an artist of exceptional gifts simultaneously empowered and debilitated by conventionality. His best work deserves to be read, admired, and studied both as a precursor to the Southern literary tradition of Faulkner, Warren, Welty, and McCullers and for the pure pleasure it affords.

Notes and References

Chapter One

1. Benjamin Moore Norman, *Norman's New Orleans and Environs* (New Orleans: B. M. Norman, 1845; rpt., Baton Rouge: Louisiana State University Press, 1976), 73.

2. *History of Louisiana: The French Domination,* 3d ed. (New Orleans: Armand Hawkins, 1885), 2: 282.

3. It should be noted that I am using the term *Creole* as Cable used it to designate a group of white Louisianans, and that this is different from its meaning for linguists (denoting a language category distinguished from Pidgin) and much narrower than now popularly used with reference to various aspects of Louisiana and Caribbean culture, usually implying some European-African mixture. For a fuller discussion of the complex history of this term in reference to a 1970s legal battle over racial categorization, see Virginia R. Dominguez, *White by Definition* (New Brunswick, N.J.: Rutgers University Press, 1986); hereafter cited in text. See also Joseph G. Tregle, Jr., "Creoles and Americans," in *Creole New Orleans,* ed. Arnold R. Hirsch and Joseph Logsdon (Baton Rouge: Louisiana State University Press, 1992), 131–85.

4. *Black New Orleans, 1860–1880* (Chicago: University of Chicago Press, 1973), 201.

5. Rodolph Lucien Desdunes, *Our People and Our History,* trans. Sister Dorothea Olga McCants (Baton Rouge: Louisiana State University Press, 1973), 10; originally published in 1911 as *Nos Hommes et Notre Histoire.*

6. Frances Trollope, *Domestic Manners of the Americans,* ed. Donald Smalley (New York: Alfred A. Knopf, 1949; rpt., London: Whitaker, Treacher & Co., 1832), 13–14.

7. "The Unknown Masque: A Sketch of the Crescent City," in *The Writings of William Gilmore Simms: Stories and Tales,* vol. 5, ed. John Caldwell Guilds (Columbia: University of South Carolina Press, 1974), 198, 199; originally published in *Southern and Western Monthly Magazine and Review* (April 1845).

8. *Life on the Mississippi* (New York: Harper & Brothers, 1907), 329.

9. Lucy Leffingwell Cable Biklé, *George W. Cable: His Life and Letters* (New York: Charles Scribner's Sons, 1928), 2; hereafter cited in text.

10. Arlin Turner, *George W. Cable: A Biography* (Durham, N.C.: Duke University Press, 1956), 12; hereafter cited in text.

11. See "New Orleans," *St. Nicholas* 21 (November and December 1893): 40–49, 150–154, and "Some of My Pets," *Youth's Companion* 75 (September 1901): 427.

12. GWC to Richard Watson Gilder, 17 October 1878; quoted in Biklé, 62.

13. GWC to H. H. Boyesen, 5 November 1878; quoted in Turner 1956, 83.

14. See Anna Shannon Elfenbein, *Women on the Color Line: Evolving Stereotypes and the Writings of George Washington Cable, Grace King, Kate Chopin* (Charlottesville: University Press of Virginia, 1989), 28; hereafter cited in text.

15. See Ted Tunnell, *Crucible of Reconstruction: War, Radicalism, and Race in Louisiana, 1862–1877* (Baton Rouge: Louisiana State University Press, 1984).

16. "My Politics," in *The Negro Question: A Selection of Writings on Civil Rights in the South,* ed. Arlin Turner (Garden City, N.Y.: Doubleday, 1958), 3; hereafter cited in text as *NQ*.

17. *Picayune,* 14 March 1871.

18. *Picayune,* 28 August 1870.

19. *Picayune,* 17 March 1871.

20. See Joe Gray Taylor, *Louisiana Reconstructed, 1863–1877* (Baton Rouge: Louisiana State University Press, 1974), 291–96.

21. *Picayune,* 25 February 1872.

Chapter Two

1. Robert D. Rhode, *Setting in the American Short Story of Local Color, 1865–1900* (The Hague and Paris: Mouton, 1975), 14.

2. "Realism and Regionalism," *The Columbia Literary History of the United States,* ed. Emory Elliott (New York: Columbia University Press, 1988), 508; hereafter cited in text.

3. Helen Taylor, *Gender, Race, and Region in the Writings of Grace King, Ruth McEnery Stuart, and Kate Chopin* (Baton Rouge: Louisiana State University Press, 1989), 21.

4. Wayne Mixon, *Southern Writers and the New South Movement, 1865–1913* (Chapel Hill: University of North Carolina Press, 1980), 8; hereafter cited in text.

5. Louis Rubin, *George W. Cable: The Life and Times of a Southern Heretic* (New York: Pegasus, 1969), 46; hereafter cited in text.

6. The judgment is that of George Parsons Lathrop, writing for William Dean Howells, editor of the *Atlantic Monthly.* See Biklé, 48.

7. Merrill Skaggs, *The Folk of Southern Fiction* (Athens: University of Georgia Press, 1972), ix; hereafter cited in text.

8. See Lafcadio Hearn, "The Scenes of Cable's Romances," *Century Magazine* 27 (November 1883): 40–47.

9. Kjell Ekström (in *George Washington Cable: A Study of His Early Life and Work* [Uppsala: Lundequistska Bokhandeln; Cambridge: Harvard University Press, 1950], 93; hereafter cited in text) provides perhaps the longest list, most of whom are based on references in the "Drop Shot" column.

10. Alice Hall Petry, *A Genius in His Way: The Art of Cable's "Old Creole Days"* (Rutherford, N.J.: Fairleigh Dickinson University Press, 1988), 15; hereafter cited in text.

11. *Old Creole Days* (New York: Charles Scribner's Sons, 1879); hereafter cited in text as *OCD*.

12. This is the putative "First Skyscraper" built by Yves Le Monnier on the corner of Royal and St. Peter in 1811.

13. If such a message was Cable's intention, it bears interestingly on his own family history, for his father (another Mr. George), although apparently an enterprising and upright businessman, nevertheless pursued the dream of rapid wealth to New Orleans, gained and lost substantial amounts on the grounds, in part, of luck and speculation, and appeared to be, even by the family accounts, a man who enjoyed sensual pleasures.

14. The suggestion of mixed racial ancestry can be seen as one of several references in Cable's fiction to the Creoles' reputation for miscegenation, or it might indicate that Kookoo is not a "real" (i.e., white) Creole but like many other offspring of *plaçage*—free persons of color—has inherited property from his white father and become a *rentier* in the French Quarter. In either case he is not an aristocrat but, like the neighborhood itself, a decayed remnant of the aristocracy.

15. Petry's argument of a possible influence for the incest theme in the real life scandal underlying Molière's *L'Ecole des Femmes* is interesting but unpersuasive.

16. Philip Butcher, *George Washington Cable* (New York: Twayne, 1962), 35; hereafter cited in text.

17. These views, it should be added, include ethnocentric disparaging of the French, the Italians and, very subtly, the Spanish.

18. *Life on the Mississippi* (1883; New York: Harper & Brothers, 1907), 351. See also William Dean Howells, *Literary Friends and Acquaintance: Personal Retrospect of American Authorship,* ed. David F. Hiatt and Edwin H. Cady (Bloomington: Indiana University Press, 1968), 321.

19. See Edward Stone, "Usher, Poquelin, and Miss Emily: The Progress of Southern Gothic," *Georgia Review* 14 (Winter 1960): 433–43, and Bill Christophersen, "'Jean-ah Poquelin': Cable's Place in Southern Gothic," *South Dakota Review* 20 (Summer 1982): 55–66.

20. GWC to Scribner, Armstrong & Co., 9 February 1878; quoted in Biklé, 58.

21. Butcher's claim that "always the male partner belongs to a race commonly regarded by Americans at the time as superior to the race of the woman" (1962, 40) has been specifically challenged by Rubin as "not strictly accurate" (57). Also, given the anti-Irish sentiment of the times and Cable's aspersions against the Irish in "Jean-ah Poquelin," it is hard to feel the sense of "racial superiority" Butcher sees at issue in the marriage.

Chapter Three

1. In his "After-Thoughts of a Story-Teller" (*North American Review* 158, no. 1 [January 1894]: 16–23; hereafter cited in text as "After-Thoughts") Cable notes (and settles) the question of pronunciation when he writes, "In *The Grandissimes*—three syllables, yes, not four—" (18).

2. GWC to H. H. Boyesen, 6 March 1878; quoted in Arlin Turner, "A Novelist Discovers a Novelist: The Correspondence of H. H. Boyesen and George W. Cable," *Western Humanities Review* 5 (Autumn 1951): 358–59; hereafter cited in text.

3. Robert O. Stevens, "Cable and Turgenev: Learning How to Write a Modern Novel," *Studies in the Novel* 15 (Fall 1983): 237–48.

4. Michael Colacurcio, *The Province of Piety: Moral History in Hawthorne's Early Tales* (Cambridge and London: Harvard University Press, 1984), 20.

5. *The Grandissimes: A Story of Creole Life* (1880; New York: Penguin, 1988), 15; hereafter cited in text as *G*.

6. Charles Swann, "*The Grandissimes:* A Story Shaped World," *Literature and History* 13 (Autumn 1987): 257–77.

7. Tipping Schölin, "'The Sinking Plantation House': Cable's Narrative Method in *The Grandissimes*," *Essays in Poetics* 13 (April 1988): 63–80.

8. See Robert O. Stephens, "Cable's Grandissime Saga," *American Literary Realism* 20 (Fall 1987): 3–17.

9. "Citizen of the Union," in *Critical Essays on George Washington Cable,* ed. Arlin Turner (Boston: G. K. Hall, 1980), 150; hereafter cited in text. This originally appeared in *New Republic* 57 (February 1929): 352–53.

10. Wallace Stegner, Introduction to *Selected American Prose, 1841–1900: The Realistic Movement* (New York: Holt, Rinehart & Winston, 1958), xi.

11. Cable acknowledged that this usage was an anachronism by "some months" but used it for the "convenience" (*G,* 107).

12. See Edward Everett Hale, "Mr. Cable and the Creoles," *Critic* 7 (September 1885): 121–22 (quoted in Turner 1980, 89–91); Edward Larocque Tinker, "Cable and the Creoles," *American Literature* 5 (January 1934): 313–26; Kjell Ekström, "Cable's Grandissimes and the Creoles," *Studia Neophilologica* 21 (Autumn 1949): 190–94; and Ekström 1950, 111–42.

13. *History of Louisiana: The American Domination,* 3d ed. (1886; New Orleans: Armand Hawkins, 1885), 4: 57.

14. Robert O. Stephens (in "Cable's Bras-Coupé and Merimée's Tamango: The Case of the Missing Arm," *Mississippi Quarterly* 35 [1982]: 387–405) provides an account of the Louisiana facts and legends that Cable used in constructing his story, and although the manuscript of "Bibi" has never been located, he posits how Cable revised his original version in response to reading Mérimée's similar account of an untamable African prince. Barbara

Ladd (in "'An Atmosphere of Hints and Allusions': Bras-Coupé and the Context of Black Insurrection in *The Grandissimes,*" *Southern Quarterly* 29 [Spring 1991]: 63–76) traces the background further to accounts of heroic marronists or insurrectionists in the West Indies.

15.   "Lions Rampant: Agricola Fusilier and Bras-Coupé as Antithetical Doubles in *The Grandissimes,*" in *The Grandissimes: Centennial Essays,* ed. Thomas J. Richardson (Jackson: University Press of Mississippi, 1981), 74–80; hereafter cited in text. This essay originally appeared in *Southern Quarterly* 18 (Summer 1980).

16.   "Humor in Cable's *The Grandissimes,*" in *The Grandissimes: Centennial Essays,* 51–59. This essay originally appeared in *Southern Quarterly* 18 (Summer 1980).

17.   William Bedford Clark, "Cable and the Theme of Miscegenation in *Old Creole Days* and *The Grandissimes,*" *Mississippi Quarterly* 3 (1977): 604.

18.   Michael Kreyling, Introduction to *The Grandissimes,* xvi.

19.   Alfred Bendixen, "Cable's *The Grandissimes:* A Literary Pioneer Confronts the Southern Tradition," in *The Grandissimes: Centennial Essays,* 23–33. This essay originally appeared in *Southern Quarterly* 18 (Summer 1980).

20.   Newton Arvin, in *Critical Essays on George Washington Cable,* 180–84. This originally appeared as the Introduction to *The Grandissimes* (New York: Sagamore Press, 1957), v–xi.

21.   Thomas Richardson, "Introduction: Honoré Grandissime's Southern Dilemma," in *The Grandissimes: Centennial Essays,* 1–12. This essay originally appeared in *Southern Quarterly* 18 (Summer 1980).

22.   Richard Chase, "Cable's *Grandissimes,*" in *The American Novel and Its Tradition* (Garden City, N.Y.: Doubleday-Anchor, 1957), 167–76; hereafter cited in text.

23.   See, for example, William Dean Howells, "Novel-Writing and Novel-Reading: An Impersonal Explanation," in *Selected Literary Criticism, Volume III, 1898–1920,* ed. Ronald Gottesman (Bloomington and Indianapolis: Indiana University Press, 1993), 231.

Chapter Four

1.   *Madame Delphine* (New York: Charles Scribner's Sons, 1881), 3; hereafter cited in text as *MD.*

2.   As an example of such arguments against the absurdity of racial segregation, Shelley Fisher Fishkin (in "The Tales He Couldn't Tell: Mark Twain, Race, and Culture at the Century's End: A Social Context for *Puddin'head Wilson*") quotes P. T. Barnum in an 1865 address to the Connecticut legislature lampooning those who express "great love for the white blood" and would keep it as a condition of voting: "Will they enslave seven-eighths of a white man because one-eighth is not caucasian? Is this democracy?" (in David E. E. Sloane, ed. *Mark Twain's Humor: Critical Essays* [New York and London: Garland, 1993], 364).

3. See Joel Williamson, *New People: Miscegenation and Mulattoes in the United States* (New York: Free Press-Macmillan, 1980), and George Fredrickson, *The Black Image in the White Mind: The Debate on Afro-American Character and Destiny, 1817–1914* (New York: Harper & Row, 1971).

4. James Kinney, *Amalgamation! Race, Sex, and Rhetoric in the Nineteenth-Century American Novel,* Contributions in Afro-American and African Studies, Number 90 (Westport, Conn.: Greenwood Press, 1985), 135.

5. Elfenbein identifies *Madame Delphine* as "the work generally conceded to be Cable's masterpiece" (65), but this seems to stretch considerably the praise generally accorded its "finish." In an early brief review for the *Times-Democrat* (24 July 1881) Lafcadio Hearn also described the work as Cable's "masterpiece," but the term is otherwise not widely used to characterize *Madame Delphine.*

6. Donald A. Ringe (in "The 'Double Center': Character and Meaning in Cable's Early Novels," *Studies in the Novel* 5 [1973]: 52– 62) argues that the critics' frequent concern about the inadequacy of Cable's spokespersons misses the point that he usually divides this role between two characters whose interaction develops the moral arguments. In *Madame Delphine* the "double center" multiplies to include Père Jerome, Vignevielle, Madame John, and even Jean Thompson and Dr. Varrillat.

7. GWC to William Dean Howells, 8 October 1891; quoted in Biklé, 73.

8. *The Creoles of Louisiana* (New York: Charles Scribner's Sons, 1884), 39; hereafter cited in text as *CL.*

9. See Mixon, 98–99, for a discussion of Cable's reservations about industry and commerce as a cure-all for Southern problems in *Old Creole Days* and *The Grandissimes.*

10. Cable had supplied Waring with elaborate documentation that was removed from the published census report and never restored. Louis Rubin counts "more than thirty authorities in preparing the history, as well as periodical and newspaper files" (113).

11. A law professor from the University of Moscow, Waldemir Kowaledsky, visited Cable in June, but his write-up after he returned to Russia was less pleasing to Cable, for Kowaledsky quoted him slighting H. H. Boyesen's artistry. Cable publicly denied that he had made such a slight, but undoubtedly, as Turner observes, "Kowaledsky's article had at least a slight cooling effect on the friendship of Cable and Boyesen" (1956, 123).

12. See Mary Cable Dennis, *The Tail of the Comet* (New York: E. P. Dutton, 1937), 34.

13. GWC to Louise Cable, 9 December 1883; quoted in Biklé, 113.

14. Mark Twain to W. D. Howells, 27 February 1885, in *Mark Twain-Howells Letters: The Correspondence of Samuel L. Clemens and William Dean Howells, 1872–1910,* ed. Henry Nash Smith and William M. Gibson (Cambridge: Harvard University Press, 1960), 2: 520.

15. Twain's gain from the association, at the very least, came in Cable's urging him to read Malory's *Morte d'Arthur,* which led to *A Connecticut Yankee in King Arthur's Court* (1889). Less concretely, in writing *The Adventures of Huckleberry Finn* Twain may have been influenced by Cable's attitudes toward the freedman and by his arguments on prison reform. See Cardwell, 68–77, and Victor A. Doyno, *Writing Huck Finn: Mark Twain's Creative Process* (Philadelphia: University of Pennsylvania Press, 1991), 233–34.

16. In addition to other even more innocuous passages from *Dr. Sevier,* Cable's program also sometimes included "Aurora and Honoré, Courtship Scene" and "Raoul Innerarity Announces his Marriage" from *The Grandissimes.* Earlier Cable had used scenes from the popular "Posson Jone'," and sentimental passages from *Bonaventure* would be later favorites. Twain's part of the program included scenes from the novel-in-progress, *The Adventures of Huckleberry Finn,* but these passages, like the "Jumping Frog" and "Blue Jay's Mistake" yarns, were hardly controversial. Both clearly geared their programs to broad popular taste, and they were understandably not interested in provoking unwanted controversy.

17. See Arlin Turner, "Cable's Beginnings as a Reformer," *Journal of Southern History* 17 (May 1951): 135–61.

18. *Letters of Richard Watson Gilder,* ed. Rosamond Gilder (Boston and New York: Houghton Mifflin, 1916), 389–90.

19. Butcher 1962, 72, and Edmund Wilson, *Patriotic Gore: Studies in the Literature of the American Civil War* (New York: Oxford University Press, 1962), 581–82; hereafter cited in text.

20. Louis Rubin's claim that "save for the quadroon landlady, there are no Negroes in *Dr. Sevier*" (140) is not quite accurate.

21. *Dr. Sevier* (Boston: J. R. Osgood, 1884), 74; hereafter cited in text as *DS.*

22. Despite his efforts to be even-handed, Cable's assertion in *Dr. Sevier* that the Union soldiers' "cause is just" and that "since nigh twenty-five years have passed, we of the South can say it!" (*DS,* 377) was grounds for some to view the novel was anti-Southern. As a prelude to the larger controversy soon to break over the freedman essay, the comment prompted a brief letter exchange in the *Century,* in which Cable defended his position. See "We of the South," *Century Magazine* 29 (November 1884): 151–52.

23. Cable's comment on the pronunciation of Dr. Sevier's name can be found an in interview published in the St. Louis *Republican* (11 January 1885) and reprinted in Fred W. Lorch, "Cable and His Reading Tour with Mark Twain in 1884–1885," *American Literature* 23 (January 1952): 481.

24. Interestingly, again for a man whose mother and sister had to survive the loss of husbands, Cable suggests that not only Mary Richling but also to a lesser degree Kate Riley and Mrs. Reisen are more independent and better able to endure hardship than their husbands. Alice Sevier's absorption in her husband, like Richling's in his wife, is also presented as a debilitation. While

they do not make the novel any more readable, the issues of gender in *Dr. Sevier* are interesting but have yet to attract critical discussion.

Chapter Five

    1. Written as a preface to the 1889 edition of *The Silent South,* this important essay was omitted as too personal. Portions of the essay were quoted in Biklé's biography, but it was not published in full until its inclusion in Turner's selection of Cable's civil rights writings, *The Negro Question.*

    2. "The Freedman's Case in Equity," in *The Silent South: Together with The Freedman's Case in Equity, The Convict Lease System, The Appendix to the 1889 Edition, and Eight Uncollected Essays on Prison and Asylum Reform,* ed. Arlin Turner (Montclair, N.J.: Patterson Smith, 1969), 1; hereafter cited in text as *SS.*

    3. Boston *Evening Transcript,* 15 June 1882; quoted in Turner 1956, 222.

    4. For the fullest account of these activities see Turner's biography and Philip Butcher, *George W. Cable: The Northampton Years* (New York: Columbia University Press, 1959); hereafter cited in text.

    5. Cable's reference is probably to Joseph Story's *Commentaries on the Constitution* (1833), which includes a strong defense of national sovereignty. It is interesting and suggestive that Cable would cite Story in this context, for while he was insisting on his Southern origins, he identifies his constitutional authority as the Supreme Court justice from New England who, according to one recent commentator, "was regarded in the South as the sinister mind behind the relentless thrust of Yankee oppression" (James McClellan, *Joseph Story and the American Constitution: A Study in Political and Legal Thought* [Norman: University of Oklahoma Press, 1971], 301).

    6. For a fuller study of how Cable shaped "My Politics" as both a personal and public document, see James Robert Payne, "George Washington Cable's 'My Politics': Context and Revision of a Southern Memoir," in *Multicultural Autobiography: American Lives,* ed. James Robert Payne (Knoxville: University of Tennessee Press, 1992), 94–112. Payne also sees analogies between "My Politics" and such spiritual autobiographies as St. Augustine's *Confessions* and Jonathan Edwards's *Personal Narrative.*

    7. The Mississippi speech was published in Arlin Turner's "George W. Cable's Revolt against Literary Sectionalism," *Tulane Studies in English* 5 (1955): 5–27, and the Louisiana speech was printed in New Orleans by the Board of Administrators of the University of Louisiana (New Orleans, 1883). Portions of both are in *The Negro Question,* 51–53.

    8. Joel Williamson, *The Crucible of Race: Black-White Relations in the American South Since Emancipation* (New York: Oxford University Press, 1984), 98; hereafter cited in text.

    9. *Contemporary Review* 53 (March 1888): 443–68.

10. Originally a pamphlet distributed by the Massachusetts Club (Boston, 1890).

11. *The Negro Question* (New York: Charles Scribner's Sons, 1890), 52.

12. See Philip Butcher, "George W. Cable and Booker T. Washington, *Journal of Negro Education* 18 (Fall 1948): 462–68.

13. Originally published as "What the Negro Must Learn," *American Missionary* 45 (January 1891): 8–13.

14. Editorial in the Nashville *American,* 6 December 1889; quoted in Turner 1956, 268.

15. See, for example, "The Color Line," "The Civil Rights Case," and "The Condition of the Freedman" in Philip S. Foner, *The Life and Writings of Frederick Douglass: Reconstruction and After* (New York: International Publishers, 1955), 4:342–52, 392–403, 403–10.

16. For a less sympathetic assessment of Cable's reform activities see Mary Graham, "The Protest of Writers and Thinkers," in *The Rhetoric of Protest and Reform, 1878–1898,* ed. Paul H. Boase (Athens: Ohio University Press, 1980), 304–308. Among the reasons for Cable's failure as reformer, Graham asserts that "he lacked of full compassion for the oppressed," that "he was incapable of understanding a class of people whom he considered to be inferior," that "he was a rigid person," and that his "nasal tenor voice did not carry conviction" (308).

Chapter Six

1. GWC to Charles W. Chesnutt, 25 September 1889; quoted in William L. Andrews, *The Literary Career of Charles W. Chesnutt* (Baton Rouge: Louisiana State University Press, 1980), 25.

2. A shared interest in the Creole and slave music was the basis of Cable's initially friendly relationship with Lafcadio Hearn, and the two collaborated in the collection of the materials for several years. Due to Cable's piety clashing with Hearn's hedonism, to Hearn's fickleness alone, or to Hearn's jealousy over Cable's greater access to music sources, the interest also helped divide them, so that by 1885 Hearn, who had previously been one of Cable's staunchest supporters at the *Times-Democrat,* apparently joined Page Baker in attacking him.

3. "The Dance in Place Congo," *Century Magazine* 31 (February 1886): 523; hereafter cited in text as "Congo."

4. According to Turner (1956, 230), Cable's editors excised an even more scathing passage, that seemed to reflect a spill-over of his feelings from "The Freedman's Case in Equity" composed at about the same time.

5. *Bonaventure: A Prose Pastoral of Acadian Louisiana* (New York: Charles Scribner's Sons, 1888), 10; hereafter cited in text as *B.*

6. Leo Marx, *The Machine in the Garden: Technology and the Pastoral Ideal in America* (New York: Oxford University Press, 1964), 87.

7. Although noting the author's objectivity rather than the novel's weakness, Skaggs observes that "Cable seems to have approached the Acadians with few deeply felt attitudes toward them" (147). It is precisely Cable's "deeply felt attitudes" toward the Creoles that makes them so interesting.

8. *Strange True Stories of Louisiana* (New York: Charles Scribner's Sons, 1889), 2; hereafter cited in text as *STSL*.

9. "The Limits of Truth in Cable's "Salome Müller," *Papers on Language and Literature: A Journal for Scholars and Critics of Language and Literature* 27 (Winter 1991): 22. Petry's essay, while it claims too much for the story, is provocative and offers the fullest treatment of the background and issue of the story. She also provides a useful discussion of what *Strange True Stories of Louisiana* suggests about Cable's attitude toward fiction and nonfiction at this point in his career.

10. *John March, Southerner* (New York: Charles Scribner's Sons, 1894), 507; hereafter cited in text as *JM*.

11. "George W. Cable," *Southern Writers: Biographical and Critical Studies* (Nashville: M. E. Church, 1902), 1: 352. Baskervill calls *John March, Southerner* "one of the most dismal failures ever made by a man of genius."

12. Five of these reviews can be found in Turner 1980, 95–103.

Chapter Seven

1. The first to be honored in this way was Henry Ward Beecher, whose "Beecher's Elm" was planted at Cable's first Northampton home, the Red House, and subsequently moved to Tarryawhile.

2. Another noteworthy name associated with the People's Institute was a young lawyer, Calvin Coolidge.

3. For specific discussions of Cable's gardening philosophy and his use of gardens and natural imagery in his fiction, see Alfred Bendixen, "George W. Cable and the Garden," *Louisiana Studies* 15 (1976): 310–15; Thomas Hubert, "The Gardens of *Old Creole Days*," *Revue de Louisianne/Louisiana Review* 9 (1980): 154–61; and my own "College Girl Wildness: Nature in the Work of George Washington Cable," *Markham Review* 5 (Winter 1976): 24–30.

4. Ralph Waldo Emerson, "Nature," in *Ralph Waldo Emerson: Essays and Lectures* (New York: Library of America, 1983), 28.

5. The essays comprising this brief theoretical canon are "After-Thoughts of a Story-Teller," *North American Review* 158 (January 1894): 16–23; "The Speculations of a Story-Teller," *Atlantic Monthly* 78 (July 1896): 88–96; "Extracts from a Story-Teller's Dictionary, *Chap-Book* 5 (September 1896): 411–23; "To See Our Life as Romance Sees It," *Symposium* 1 (November 1896): 59–66; "At the Edge of the Woods," *Bradley: His Book* 1 (November 1896): 3–7; "Art and Morals in Books," *Independent* 49 (December 1897): 1643–44. These essays are hereafter cited in text by abbreviated title.

6. *Strong Hearts* (New York: Charles Scribner's Sons, 1899), 3; hereafter cited in text as *SH*.

7. "Emily Dickinson" in Richard Sewall, ed., *Emily Dickinson: A*

Collection of Critical Essays (Englewood Cliffs, N.J.: Prentice-Hall, 1963), 18; reprinted in *Collected Essays,* ed. Allen Tate (Denver: Swallow Press, 1932).

8.   "George Washington Cable," in *Fifty Southern Writers before 1900: A Bio-Bibliographical Sourcebook,* Robert Bain and Joseph M. Flora (New York: Greenwood Press, 1987), 82.

9.   Louise Cable to GWC, [1889?], in The George Washington Cable Papers, Manuscripts Collection 2, Manuscripts Department, Howard-Tilton Memorial Library, Tulane University, New Orleans, Louisiana, 70118-5682; cited below as Cable Collection. The letter is undated but written on "Red House" stationery. Turner seems to cite this letter in commenting on "her inability to speak or write her feelings," and although admittedly feeble evidence, the context of his discussion, as well as the letter's location in the Cable Collection, suggests the 1889 date.

10.   Louise Cable to GWC, 21 November 1889, in Cable Collection.

11.   Louise Cable to GWC, 30 November 1889, in Cable Collection.

12.   Louise Cable to GWC, [1889?], in Cable Collection. The letter is undated, but written on "Paradise Road" stationery like those dated in November 1889. Someone, perhaps Lucy Biklé, has added 1889? in parentheses at the head of the first page.

13.   Louise Cable to GWC, 26 April 1898, in Cable Collection.

14.   See Butcher 1959, 221–45, for the fullest discussion of the controversy. Rubin's interpretation of the incident is less favorable to Moffat (250–52), and Stephens has recently suggested that Butcher may have been "biased by informants involved in controversies of Cable's later career" (Bain and Flora, 83).

15.   GWC to Louise Cable, 15 December 1901; quoted in Turner 1956, 336.

16.   I have suggested earlier that Cable gravitated toward the latter day dissolution of new England transcendentalism into Brahmin gentility, but Alan Trachtenberg's argument about a more pervasive and economically grounded culture of incorporation in which literary realism was a mediating rather than resisting force usefully applies to Cable as well. See *The Incorporation of America: Culture and Society in the Gilded Age* (New York: Hill & Wang, 1982).

17.   Elaine Ware, "George W. Cable's *The Cavalier:* An American Best Seller and Theatrical Attraction," *Southern Literary Journal* 19 (Spring 1987): 70–80.

18.   *Gideon's Band* (New York: Charles Scribner's Sons, 1914), 6; hereafter cited in text as *GB.*

19.   Salome Müller's marriage to a black man, which Butcher sees as a sign of integrity lost in the later stories, does not count, since in that case he was reporting, not imagining. Butcher compares Müller's case with that of Fortune, a white woman mistaken as a slave in *The Flower of the Chapdelaines,* and he suggests that Cable's judgment is reflected in the words of a Creole character that Fortune was "too good and high-mind' to be marrie' to any white man wha'z willin to marry a nigger" (Butcher 1962, 155). But, the Creole is Mme Lefevre, Fortune's former owner, and her words are being quoted by another, more progressive Creole, M. Beloiseau, in part to challenge them. Certainly Cable never

advocated mixed marriages, but to what degree his inclusion of characters' statements against it reflect an impassioned conviction or what he felt was an obligatory, half-hearted disclaimer is unclear, shaded by context. In most cases he identifies the impassioned conviction with conservative Southern sentiment and notes the ironic contrast with the abundant racial mixing already evident.

20.   *The Flower of the Chapdelaines* (New York: Charles Scribner's Sons, 1918), 65; hereafter cited in text as *FC*.

21.   "Euonymous" is a play on Onesimus and therefore an allusion to the biblical defense of slavery that, upon re-examination, convinced Cable that slavery was not divinely justified (*NQ*, 6–7). Also, in a letter to his wife from Nashville, Tennessee (31 July 1887), Cable describes "the Saturday night outpour of the town's black squalor." He says, "I moved through the throng trying constantly to avoid being touched by the vile rags that hung upon the larger part of the noisy crowd." His point typically is not merely to register his revulsion: "The south can never take rank in the great march of progress until she has uplifted this lower class—the lowest lower class in Christendom—out of the mire." Cable did sympathize with those suffering degradation, but here as elsewhere the argument for uplift centers more on deploring the conditions than sympathy for the sufferer.

22.   The scene in which the narrator discovers Euonymous's real sexual identity, when he turns her over after the front of her shirt has been ripped off by a dog, moves Cable's recurrent voyeurism closer to genteel soft-porn.

23.   In 1915, on invitation from the Louisiana Historical Society, Cable spoke to a packed house (many Creoles included) in the Supreme Court room of the Cabildo, and he was enthusiastically received. Grace King, who had begun her own writing career on a challenge to represent the Creoles more faithfully than Cable, kept the minutes of the meeting and several years later observed, "I understand him now. I would say he wrote too well about the Creoles . . . . I am so glad that at last he got this compliment from New Orleans. He deserved it, not only as a tribute to his genius but as compensation for the way we treated him" (interview in the Boston *Evening Transcript,* 29 September 1923; quoted in Turner 1956, 350).

24.   *Lovers of Louisiana (To-day)* (New York: Charles Scribner's Sons, 1918), 81; hereafter cited in text as *LL*.

Conclusion

1.   Edmund Wilson, "Citizen of the Union"; quoted in Turner 1980, 149. This review was originally published in the *New Republic* 57 (13 February 1929): 352–53.

2.   Chase, 167–76. See also Harry B. Henderson III, "Cable and the Holist Tradition," *Versions of the Past: The Historical Imagination in American Fiction* (New York: Oxford University Press, 1974), 204–209.

Selected Bibliography

PRIMARY WORKS

Note: For Cable's numerous, uncollected publications in newspapers and other periodicals, see under Secondary Works the Turner (1956) and Roberson (1982) bibliographies; for published correspondence see Biklé (1928), Cardwell (1953), and Turner (1970), plus Ekström (1950) and Turner (1951). The largest collection of Cable's letters, manuscripts, notebooks, and other materials is in the Cable Collection at the Howard-Tilton Memorial Library, Tulane University, New Orleans.

Novels

Bonaventure: A Prose Pastoral of Acadian Louisiana. New York: Scribners, 1888.
Bylow Hill. New York: Scribners, 1902.
The Cavalier. New York: Scribners, 1901.
Dr. Sevier. Boston: Osgood, 1885.
The Flower of the Chapdelaines. New York: Scribners, 1918.
Gideon's Band: A Tale of the Mississippi. New York: Scribners, 1914.
The Grandissimes: A Story of Creole Life. New York: Scribners, 1880; rev., 1884.
    Rpt. New York: Penguin, 1988.
John March, Southerner. New York: Scribners, 1894.
Kincaid's Battery. New York: Scribners, 1908.
Lovers of Louisiana (To-day). New York: Scribners, 1918.
Madame Delphine. New York: Scribners, 1881. Included in *Old Creole Days* after
    1883.

Story Collections

The Cable Story Book: Collections for School Reading. Edited by Mary E. Burt and
    Lucy Leffingwell Cable. New York: Scribners, 1899.
Old Creole Days. New York: Scribners, 1879.
"Posson Jone'" and Père Raphaël. New York: Scribners, 1909.
Strange True Stories of Louisiana. New York: Scribners, 1889.
Strong Hearts. New York: Scribners, 1899.

Essays

The Amateur Garden. New York: Scribners, 1914.
The Busy Man's Bible and How to Study and Teach It. Meadville, Pa.: Flood &
    Vincent, Chautauqua-Century Press, 1891.

The Negro Question. New York: Scribners, 1890.
The Silent South. New York: Scribners, 1885; expanded 1889.

Miscellaneous

The Creoles of Louisiana. New York: Scribners, 1884.
A Memory of Roswell Smith. New York: De Vinne Press, 1892.

Collections

Collected Works. Edited by Arlin Turner. 6 vols. American Author Series. New
    York: Garrett Press, 1970.
Creoles and Acadians: Stories of Old Louisiana. Edited by Arlin Turner. New York:
    Doubleday, 1959.
The Negro Question: A Selection of Writings on Civil Rights in the South. Edited by
    Arlin Turner. Garden City, N.Y.: Doubleday, 1958.
The Silent South. Edited by Arlin Turner. Montclair, N.J.: Patterson Smith,
    1969.

SECONDARY WORKS

Bibliographies

Note: See also the bibliographies in Turner (1956) and Butcher (1959).

Adam, Anthony J., and Sara McCaslin. *"The Grandissimes:* An Annotated
    Bibliography (1880–1979)." In *The Grandissimes: Centennial Essays,* edit-
    ed by Thomas J. Richardson, 81–94. Jackson: University Press of
    Mississippi, 1981. Includes books, essays and contemporary reviews in
    English.
Roberson, William H. *George Washington Cable: An Annotated Bibliography.*
    Metuchen, N.J.: Scarecrow Press, 1982. Most thorough bibliography
    available. Includes all editions of primary works, uncollected newspaper
    and magazine articles, brief descriptions of holdings in library special col-
    lections. Secondary works include books, parts of books, articles, and
    theses.

Books

Berzon, Judith R. *Neither Black nor White: The Mulatto Character in American
    Fiction.* New York: New York University Press, 1978. Useful back-
    ground study of tragic mulatto theme with brief discussion of *Madame
    Delphine* and *The Grandissimes.*
Biklé, Lucy Leffingwell Cable. *George W. Cable: His Life and Letters.* New York:
    Charles Scribner's Sons, 1928. First Cable biography, includes many letters.

Blassingame, John. *Black New Orleans, 1860–1880.* Chicago: University of Chicago Press, 1973. Excellent social history.

Butcher, Philip. *George W. Cable.* New York: Twayne Publishers, 1962. Important critical study emphasizing significance of Cable's social criticism and reform impulse to his art.

————. *George W. Cable: The Northampton Years.* New York: Columbia University Press, 1959. Fullest study of Cable's social work and life in Northampton.

Cardwell, Guy A. *Twins of Genius.* East Lansing: Michigan State College Press, 1953. Argues Cable's influence on Twain's *The Adventures of Huckleberry Finn.* Includes many letters.

Dennis, Mary Cable. *The Tail of the Comet.* New York: Dutton, 1937. Cable's daughter's appreciative memoir of her father and life in the Cable family.

Desdunes, Rodolph Lucien. *Our People and Our History.* Translated by Sister Dorothea Olga McCants. Baton Rouge: Louisiana State University Press, 1973. Originally published in 1911 as *Nos Hommes et Notre Histoire.* Important early account of free persons of color in Louisiana.

Ekström, Kjell. *George Washington Cable: A Study of His Early Life and Work.* Uppsala: Lundequistska Bokhandeln, 1950; Cambridge: Harvard University Press, 1950. Early study useful in analysis of Cable's treatment of Creoles.

Elfenbein, Anna Shannon. *Women on the Color Line: Evolving Stereotypes and the Writings of George Washington Cable, Grace King, Kate Chopin.* Charlottesville: University Press of Virginia, 1989. Explores Cable's treatment of race and gender and their convergence in tragic mulatto theme.

Garrayé, Charles. *History of Louisiana.* 4 vols. 3d ed. New Orleans: Armand Hawkins, 1885. Began as lecture published in 1848. Primary source for Cable. Offers interesting comparison in romantic treatment of history.

Hair, William Ivy. *Bourbonism and Agrarian Protest: Louisiana Politics, 1877–1900.* Baton Rouge: Louisiana State University Press, 1969. Useful discussion of political climate in which Cable produced major work and conducted civil rights crusade.

Kinney, James. *Amalgamation! Race, Sex, and Rhetoric in the Nineteenth-Century American Novel.* Westport, Conn.: Greenwood Press, 1985. Includes short discussion of Cable's treatment of racial mixing in larger survey of miscegenation themes and images in American fiction.

Norman, Benjamin Moore. *Norman's New Orleans and Environs.* New Orleans: B. M. Norman, 1845; rpt. Baton Rouge: Louisiana State University Press, 1976. Fascinating guide written at time of Cable's birth and now available in reprint.

Petry, Alice Hall. *A Genius in His Way: The Art of Cable's "Old Creole Days."* Rutherford, N.J.: Fairleigh Dickinson University Press, 1988. Only full-length study of Cable's artistry. Thorough and insightful analyses of individual stories.

Rhode, Robert D. *Setting in the American Short Story of Local Color, 1865–1900.* The Hague: Mouton, 1975. Useful discussion of local color writing and its emphasis on background over foreground. Includes commentary on " 'Sieur George" and other Cable stories.

Richardson, Thomas J., ed. *The Grandissimes: Centennial Essays.* Jackson: University Press of Mississippi, 1981. Originally published as Special Feature issue of *Southern Quarterly* 18 (Summer 1980): 1–80. Includes useful new studies of *The Grandissimes* and an annotated bibliography.

Ridgely, J. V. *Nineteenth-Century Southern Literature.* Lexington: University Press of Kentucky, 1980. Places Cable in context of the emergence of southern literature after the Civil War and the desire for reconciliation.

Rubin, Louis D., Jr. *George W. Cable: The Life and Times of a Southern Heretic.* New York: Pegasus, 1969. Provocative study, important for analysis of Cable's artistic achievement and weaknesses, his relationship to genteel tradition, and his place in southern literature.

Taylor, Helen. *Gender, Race, and Region in the Writings of Grace King, Ruth McEnery Stuart, and Kate Chopin.* Baton Rouge: Louisiana State University Press, 1989. Although not focused directly on Cable, useful discussion of regionalism, local-color writing, and creation of quadroon/octoroon stereotypes.

Tunnell, Ted. *Crucible of Reconstruction: War, Radicalism, and Race in Louisiana, 1862–1877.* Baton Rouge: Louisiana State University Press, 1984. Valuable political background.

Turner, Arlin, ed. *Critical Essays on George W. Cable.* Boston: G. K. Hall, 1980. Valuable collection of early reviews and commentaries plus several recent studies.

———. *George W. Cable: A Biography.* Durham, N.C.: Duke University Press, 1956. Remains definitive biography and includes sound critical judgments of Cable's works. Indispensable work for Cable study.

———, ed. *Mark Twain and George W. Cable: The Record of a Literary Friendship.* East Lansing: Michigan State University Press, 1960. Primarily prints Twain-Cable correspondence.

Articles and Parts of Books

Campbell, Michael L. "The Negro in Cable's *The Grandissimes.*" *Mississippi Quarterly* 27 (Spring 1974): 165–78. Study of Cable's ambivalent attitudes toward black characters in *The Grandissimes.*

Chase, Richard. "Cable's *Grandissimes.*" In *The American Novel and Its Tradition,* 167–76. Garden City, N.Y.: Doubleday, 1957. Originally published as "Cable and His *Grandissimes.*" *Kenyon Review* 18 (Summer 1956): 373–83. Classic study of realism and romance in American novel; identifies Cable's achievement in particular blend of genre effects in *The Grandissimes.*

Christopherson, Bill. "Jean-ah Poquelin: Cable's Place in Southern Gothic." *South Dakota Review* 20 (1982): 35–61. Extends Edward Stone's argument to insist that Cable thematically adumbrates Faulkner's "A Rose for Emily."

Clark, William Bedford. "Cable and the Theme of Miscegenation in *Old Creole Days* and *The Grandissimes*." *Mississippi Quarterly* 3 (1977): 597–609. Overview of miscegenation theme in works from " 'Tite Poulette" to "The Haunted House in Royal Street."

Cleman, John. "The Art of Local Color in George W. Cable's *The Grandissimes*." *American Literature* 47 (November 1975): 396–410. Argues that local-color elements enhance rather than detract from Cable's art.

———. "College Girl Wildness: Nature in the Work of George Washington Cable." *Markham Review* 5 (Winter 1976): 24–30. Study of the way images of and attitudes toward nature shaped Cable's art and are reflected in his social philosophy.

Eaton, Richard Bozman. "George W. Cable and the Historical Romance." *Southern Literary Journal* 8 (Fall 1975): 82–94. Explores difficulties of novel in terms of its mixing genres—bildungsroman, realism, and historical romance.

Ekström, Kjell. "The Cable-Howells Correspondence." *Studia Neophilologica* 22 (1950): 48–61. Correspondence between Cable and novelist-editor who led the battle for literary realism in America.

Fredrickson, George M. "The New South and the New Paternalism, 1877–1890." In *The Black Image in the White Mind: The Debate on Afro-American Character and Destiny, 1817–1914,* 198–227. New York: Harper & Row, 1971. Discusses Cable's civil rights crusade and fiction in context of larger pattern of evolving white attitudes toward blacks in America.

Henderson, Harry B., III. "Cable and the Holist Tradition." in *Versions of the Past: The Historical Imagination in American Fiction,* 204–209. New York: Oxford University Press, 1974. Useful discussion of Cable's uses of history, suggesting basis of his anticipating Faulkner.

Hubbell, Jay. "George W. Cable." In *The South in American Literature, 1607–1900,* 804–22. Durham, N.C.: Duke University Press, 1954. An overview; important as early recognition of Cable's place within and against prevailing literary tradition in the South.

Kreyling, Michael. Introduction to George Washington Cable's *The Grandissimes.* New York: Penguin, 1988. Valuable commentary on backgrounds of novel, Cable's divided sensibility, the importance of race theme, and critical assessments of Cable's work.

Martin, Jay. "George Washington Cable." In *Harvests of Change: American Literature, 1865–1914,* 100–105. Englewood Cliffs, N.J.: Prentice-Hall, 1967. Brief but valuable analysis of *The Grandissimes;* explores the array of culture conflicts the novel exposes.

Mixon, Wayne. "George W. Cable and the Fiction of Uplift." *In Southern Writers and the New South Movement, 1865–1913,* 98–109. Chapel Hill: University of North Carolina Press, 1980. Important study of Cable's dissention from New South views and imagery. Includes valuable discussions of *Dr. Sevier* and *John March, Southerner.*

Petry, Alice Hall. "The Limits of Truth in Cable's 'Salome Müller.'" *Papers on Language and Literature: A Journal for Scholars and Critics of Language and Literature* 27 (Winter 1991): 20–31. Explores Cable's self-consciousness about documentary vs. imaginary truth in "strange, true" story, ambitiously converting it into postmodern metafiction.

Richardson, Thomas J. "George W. Cable's 'Jean-ah Poquelin': Folklore and the New South." *Mississippi Folklore Register* 21 (Spring–Fall 1987): 81–88. Persuasive argument about the tensions in Reconstruction between an irretrievable past and an unredeemable present causing Cable to bifurcate his art between political polemics and romantic escape.

Ringe, Donald A. "The 'Double Center': Character and Meaning in Cable's Early Novels." *Studies in the Novel* 5 (Spring 1973): 52–62. Argues Cable's developing moral arguments in *Dr. Sevier* and *The Grandissimes* through artistic use of paired characters (e.g., Honoré Grandissime and Frowenfeld) rather than a single spokesperson, thereby adding greater complexity and depth.

————. "The Moral World of Cable's 'Belles Demoiselles Plantation.'" *Mississippi Quarterly* 29 (Winter 1975–76): 83–90. Argues that the tale's theme is Christian brotherhood rather than divine justice.

————. "Narrative Voice in Cable's *The Grandissimes.*" *Southern Quarterly* 18 (Summer 1980): 13–22. Reprinted in *The Grandissimes: Centennial Essays,* edited by Thomas J. Richardson, 13–22. Jackson: University Press of Mississippi, 1981. Explores Cable's use of narrative voice as guide to milieu and its relevance to social issues of the present.

Schölin, Tipping. "'The Sinking Plantation House': Cable's Narrative Method in *The Grandissimes.*" *Essays in Poetics* 13 (April 1988): 63–80. Persuasively explores different narrative structures in *The Grandissimes* and the way they serve needs for discovery, distancing, and denial.

Skaggs, Merrill. "Stereotyped Characters" and "The Creole." In *The Folk of Southern Fiction,* 141–88. Athens: University of Georgia Press, 1972. Sections are not exclusively devoted to Cable, but important in describing his role in defining Creole and Acadian stereotypes and thereby influencing subsequent depictions of these characters.

Stephens, Robert O. "Cable's Bras-Coupé and Merimée's Tamango: The Case of the Missing Arm." *Mississippi Quarterly* 35 (1982): 387–405. Important attempt to reconstruct the process of revision from the missing "Bibi" to "The Story of Bras-Coupé" in *The Grandissimes.*

————. "Cable and Turgenev: Learning How to Write a Modern Novel." *Studies in the Novel* 15 (Fall 1983): 237–48. Study of Turgenev's influence on Cable's literary realism.

————. "Cable's Grandissime Saga." *American Literary Realism* 20 (Fall 1987): 3–17. Argues against perception of *The Grandissimes* either as kulturroman or overt political commentary, rather that in theme and structure the novel presents history in the form of family saga, both biblical and Hawthornean in character.

————. "Cable's *The Grandissimes* and the Comedy of Manners." *American Literature* 51 (January 1980): 507–19. Valuable study of Cable's use of comedy of manners genre, focused on the Creoles rather than the politics of the Creole-American conflict.

————. "Cable's *Madame Delphine* and the Compromise of 1877." *Southern Literary Journal* 12 (Fall 1979): 79–81. Interprets Cable's treatment of race in *Madame Delphine* with regard to political controversy over Hayes-Tilden election and the end of Reconstruction.

Stone, Edward. "Usher, Poquelin, and Miss Emily: The Progress of Southern Gothic." *Georgia Review* 14 (Winter 1960): 433–43. Important study placing Cable's story in Southern Gothic tradition from Poe to Faulkner on basis of plot and characterization.

Swann, Charles. "*The Grandissimes:* A Story-Shaped World." *Literature and History* 13 (Autumn 1987): 257–77. Valuable study of the uses of history and myth in the novel, pointing to the way narratives enclose and structure our understanding of ourselves and our experiences.

————. "The Prince of Charm: The Heroines of *The Grandissimes*." *Essays in Poetics* 13 (April 1988): 81–88. Explores Cable's exposing the myths of femininity through the Nancanous.

Tregle, Joseph G., Jr. "Creoles and Americans." In *Creole New Orleans,* edited by Arnold R. Hirsch and Joseph Logsdon, 131–85. Baton Rouge: Louisiana State University Press, 1992. Valuable discussion of Creole-American and white-black relations in Louisiana and of Cable's role in this history.

Turner, Arlin. "A Novelist Discovers a Novelist: The Correspondence of H. H. Boyesen and George W. Cable." *Western Humanities Review* 5 (Autumn 1951): 343–72. Letters provide significant insight into Cable's attitudes toward literature at the outset of his writing career.

Ware, Elaine. "George W. Cable's *The Cavalier:* An American Best Seller and Theatrical Attraction." *Southern Literary Journal* 19 (Spring 1987): 70–80. Full discussion of composition, publication, and theatrical adaptation of otherwise critically ignored Cable work.

Williamson, Joel. "George Washington Cable and Secular Liberalism." In *The Crucible of Race: Black-White Relations in the American South since Emancipation,* 93–107. New York: Oxford University Press, 1984. Monumental background study. Discusses Cable's civil rights crusade and basis of his championing freedman.

Wilson, Edmund. "Novelists of the Post-War South: Albion W. Tourgée,
     George W. Cable, Kate Chopin, Thomas Nelson Page." In *Patriotic Gore:
     Studies in the Literature of the American Civil War,* 548–87 and 593–604.
     New York: Oxford University Press, 1962. Originally published as "The
     Ordeal of George Washington Cable." *New Yorker,* 9 November 1957,
     180–228. Review of Turner's biography; argues that the strong social
     novelist in Cable was destroyed by Gilder and the tastes of the Gilded
     Age.

Index

The Author

John Cleman is a professor of English and former department chair at California State University, Los Angeles. He received his A.B. from Stanford University, his M.A. from Washington State University, and his Ph.D. from the University of Wisconsin, Madison. He has published articles on Edgar Allan Poe, William Faulkner, and Charles Brockden Brown, and his previous work on Cable includes "The Art of Local Color in George Washington Cable's *The Grandissimes*" and "College Girl Wildness: Nature in the Work of George Washington Cable."

The Editor

Nancy A. Walker is Director of Women's Studies and Professor of English at Vanderbilt University. A native of Louisiana, she received her B.A. from Louisiana State University and her M.A. from Tulane University. After receiving her Ph.D. from Kent State University in 1971, she taught American literature, American Studies, and Women's Studies at Stephens College, where she also served as Assistant to the President and Chair of the Department of Languages and Literature.

A specialist in American women writers, Walker is the author of *A Very Serious Thing: Women's Humor and American Culture* (1988) and *Feminist Alternatives: Irony and Fantasy in the Contemporary Novel by Women* (1990), which won the first annual Eudora Welty Prize. She has published numerous articles in such journals as *American Quarterly, Tulsa Studies in Women's Literature, American Literature,* and *American Literary Realism,* and several essays on women's autobiography. With Zita Dresner, she edited *Redressing the Balance: American Women's Literary Humor from the Colonial Period to the 1980s* (1988).

Walker currently serves as general editor for the period 1800–1914 for Twayne's United States Authors Series and is editing a new critical edition of Kate Chopin's *The Awakening* for St. Martin's Press.